Chicken Soup for the Soul®

Find Your Inner Strength

Chicken Soup for the Soul: Find Your Inner Strength
101 Empowering Stories of Resilience, Positive Thinking & Overcoming Challenges
Amy Newmark. Foreword by Fran Drescher.

The publisher gratefully acknowledges the many publishers and individuals who
granted Chicken Soup for the Soul permission to reprint the cited material.

Front cover and interior photo courtesy of iStockPhoto.com/GlobalP (© GlobalP).
Photo of Amy Newmark courtesy of Susan Morrow at SwickPix.

Cover and Interior Design & Layout by Brian Taylor, Pneuma Books, LLC

Distributed to the booktrade by Simon & Schuster. SAN: 200-2442

Publisher's Cataloging-in-Publication Data
(Prepared by The Donohue Group)

Chicken soup for the soul : find your inner strength : 101 empowering
stories of resilience, positive thinking & overcoming challenges /
[compiled by] Amy Newmark ; foreword by Fran Drescher.

pages ; cm

ISBN: 978-1-61159-939-8

1. Resilience (Personality trait)--Literary collections. 2. Resilience (Personality
trait)--Anecdotes. 3. Conduct of life--Literary collections. 4. Conduct of life--Anec-
dotes. 5. Anecdotes. I. Newmark, Amy. II. Drescher, Fran. III. Title: Find
your inner strength : 101 empowering stories of resilience, positive thinking &
overcoming challenges

BF698.35.R47 C45 2014
155.2/4   2014946342

PRINTED IN THE UNITED STATES OF AMERICA
on acid∞free paper

24 23 22 21 20 19 18 17 16 15 14   01 02 03 04 05 06 07 08 09 10 11

Chicken Soup for the Soul.

Find Your Inner Strength

101 Empowering Stories of Resilience, Positive Thinking & Overcoming Challenges

Amy Newmark
Foreword by Fran Drescher

Chicken Soup for the Soul Publishing, LLC
Cos Cob, CT

Changing lives one story at a time™
www.chickensoup.com

Contents

❶

~Overcoming Self-Destructive Behavior~

❷

~Fighting Health Challenges~

❸
~Powering Through Loss~

❹
~Moving Past Disabilities~

❺
~Accepting the New Normal~

❻

~Accepting What Makes You Different~

❼

~Learning to Reach Out~

8

~Rising to the Challenge~

9

~Pursuing Your Dreams~

10

~Taking Back Your Life~

Foreword

I suppose I was asked to write the foreword for this book because I've been pretty public about my personal encounters with adversity and how I've managed not just to survive, but also to blossom as a result.

Let's face it, bad things happen to good people. It's an unfortunate fact of life, but what we do when adversity strikes, how we grow through it, and what becomes of us as a result, is what makes the difference!

Most things, both good and bad, are opportunities for us to become more refined versions of ourselves. What I mean is, a better human being: more compassionate, more mindful, more present, more generous, and more loving. It's through the rough spots that we see what kind of stuff we're made of.

It's usually on some random Wednesday afternoon, that life decides to bite you on the ass. Quite suddenly and without warning, your world, as you knew it, changes forever.

It's extremely difficult to wrap your mind around what has happened to you. It's so very hard to grasp how irreversible and permanent it all is. And alas, to realize that there is no way out.

How long can I indulge this agony? How bitter am I allowed to be before I begin hurting myself even more than I've already been hurt?

From the depths of despair you must choose: remain mired in grief, anguish and self-pity, or pull yourself up, dust yourself off, and play the hand that you've been dealt. Play it as elegantly and courageously as you possibly can!

This is the crossroad where one eventually stands. Are you to continue on the path of the *living dead*, or will you embrace a *new normal*? I chose a *new normal*.

I am a cancer survivor. After two years and eight doctors, I was finally diagnosed with uterine cancer. At age forty-two, I was told I would need a radical hysterectomy. "What? Say that again. This is ME we're talking about!"

I, who never had children, now never would.

I can't tell you how angry and frustrated I was. I felt betrayed by the medical community as well as betrayed by my own body. Over and over I questioned, "Why me?" I'm the one who was everyone else's caregiver, not the one who needed care!

I actually thought of myself as some kind of superwoman, brought to earth to be the strongest, smartest, most over-achieving human. I felt responsible for my entire immediate world while demanding nothing short of perfection from myself.

So being diagnosed with cancer not only shook me to my core, it cracked open that protective veneer, the *false self*, I had identified with for most of my life.

For the first time ever, I became someone who was terribly frightened, extremely vulnerable and worst of all, out of control.

Cancer instantly leveled me to the ground. I suddenly found myself in a situation I couldn't sweep under the rug or go it alone.

I had to accept I wasn't a superwoman but just a woman that walked on the ground with the rest of the mortals.

After I hung up with the doctor, I had to muster up the courage to call my parents, knowing full well my news would cause them great pain.

I had always avoided being a burden to anyone, but especially my parents!

My mom was surprisingly strong, although I'm sure she had a primal scream after she hung up the phone. I allowed them to make it about me (I did have cancer after all) and accepted their offer to fly to LA and stay through my surgery and recovery.

It was in that moment I felt the profound shift from being needless to having needs. From being the caregiver to being cared for.

My old way of being was totally dysfunctional and I'm quite sure contributed to my getting cancer in the first place.

I mean a person can't just give, give, give, but never take. That's how you become emotionally bankrupt; and frankly, I had been running on fumes for a very long time.

Life lessons and silver linings continued to gently reveal themselves.

Another example was with my ex-husband Peter. At the time, we were not on speaking terms.

He was opposed to our divorce and felt so hurt and abandoned by me, he moved to New York as soon as we completed the final season of *The Nanny*. (This became an ongoing source of pain, guilt and sadness for me.)

But when our manager Elaine told him I had cancer, he instantly burst into tears and in that moment, all of his anger melted away and all that was left was his love. We remain the best of friends to this day.

Then it happened! I had an inspiration that would help me on the road towards a *new normal*. I decided to write a book so what happened to me, (misdiagnosis and mistreatment), wouldn't happen to other people.

It took me four drafts, longhand, before I struck a chord with my comedic voice. The process was very cathartic, but also helped me realize that, *side by side with grief lies joy*.

My boyfriend coined the title *Cancer Schmancer* and the book became a New York Times Best Seller. Thus began my *new normal*.

The book led me on the lecture circuit during which I began to develop a vision. It became clear there was a need to adjust our thinking, lifestyle and activism, when it comes to our health. Hence began the Cancer Schmancer Movement.

-Transform from patient into a *Medical Consumer*.

-*Knowledge is Power* and Stage 1, when cancer is most curable, is the cure!

-*Detox Your Home* because the home is the most toxic place we spend the most time in.

-Voters and elected officials need to fight for more awareness, education and chemical regulations.

Believe it or not, I helped make a law!

My efforts got me a mention in the Congressional Record and an appointment as Public Diplomacy Envoy for Health Issues at the U.S. State Department.

The global political, literary, and medical worlds opened up to me.

I realized that turning *pain into purpose* was healing and helped to make *sense out of the senseless*. I suggest it for anyone wishing to add a greater depth and resonance to their lives.

I'm now a far healthier woman than I ever was before the cancer, with a true connection to my feelings and vulnerabilities. I'm finally able not only to give but also to receive, and factor *my* needs into my decision-making process.

I've emerged out the other side an activist, philanthropist and an environmentalist.

Also, my growth has enabled me to be in a mature and loving relationship with a new and wonderful man, Shiva, the love of my life.

I'm not glad I had cancer and I wouldn't wish it on anyone, but I am better for it!

Sometimes the best gifts come in the *ugliest* packages.

~Fran Drescher

Introduction

Perhaps I am stronger than I think.
~Thomas Merton

All the Chicken Soup for the Soul editors are talking about it. We are awed by these stories, and I think this may be one of the most powerful collections we have published in our twenty-one year history. I am thrilled to introduce you to some of the most inspiring people you'll ever meet in these pages.

What struck me the most in these stories is the strength of the human spirit, whether our contributors are powering through health issues, disabilities, financial turmoil, the loss of a loved one, or other crises. They don't complain about their situations—they just get up off the floor and deal with them.

And of course that impressive resilience starts with our foreword writer, the actress, comedian, producer, and activist Fran Drescher, who takes us through her battle with cancer. Fran turned pain into purpose and made sense of the senseless by founding the Cancer Schmancer Movement, the non-profit organization she founded to fight cancer and promote healthy living in three ways: early detection, prevention, and advocacy. Fran is quite a role model for all of us, and we thank her for being part of this important book that is designed to help you find your own inner strength, survive, and thrive, as she has.

I was really affected as I selected and edited these stories. It was hard not to internalize the struggles of the contributors and to feel weighed down by their problems, but on the other hand I couldn't help but feel uplifted by their fortitude, their good humor, and their lack of self-pity. These brave contributors, who have weathered so much and come out strong on the other side, are such an inspiration to us all. And they sure put our own problems in perspective!

Most of our contributors were surprised to find that they had so much inner strength. It was just waiting inside them for the day it would be needed. If you are going through a battle of your own right now, you will undoubtedly realize that you CAN handle it after you read a few of these stories, from ordinary people just like us who found themselves becoming extraordinary people because they needed to.

In Chapter 1, you'll read about people overcoming self-destructive behavior, such as Leigh Steinberg, the super sports agent who was the inspiration for the character Tom Cruise played in *Jerry Maguire*. Leigh shares his story about overcoming his alcoholism and rebuilding his career, and most importantly, his relationships with the people he cares about.

Rissa Watkins will inspire you in Chapter 2, which is about fighting health challenges, with her story about treating her acute lymphoblastic leukemia while making sure that her six-year-old son was okay. She made him feel like a hero for everything that he did for her.

In Chapter 3 you'll read many inspiring stories about powering through the loss of a loved one. We may not all get cancer, but we all face the inevitable loss of a loved one, and these stories will help you figure out how to handle it yourself. Cheryl Hart's story about how her father finally told her that he loved her on the day of her mother's funeral brought tears to my eyes, and is a great example of how we can rebuild relationships even in the face of despair.

You'll meet some truly inspiring people in Chapter 4, which is about living with disabilities, including Lorraine Cannistra, wheelchair-bound due to cerebral palsy, but living independently. She pushed herself fifteen miles in her wheelchair on a bike trail in order to raise the money for her service dog's ACL surgery. And in Chapter 5, which is about accepting your new normal, you'll meet many brave people living with chronic disabilities or illnesses, including Jill Davis, who manages her bipolar disorder and has a full, happy life and a devoted husband.

You'll also read about Carol Goodman Heizer in Chapter 5, who discusses how she dealt with the early months of widowhood. Guess what Carol doesn't tell you in her story? Shortly after her husband died, so did her son, quite unexpectedly. And then she got breast cancer too. But Carol, like many of our contributors, doesn't share a whole laundry list of problems with us. She just wants to pass on her tips and advice to the widows coming up behind her. It reminds me of Fran Drescher. Did she mention in her foreword that besides divorce and cancer, she had previously been the victim of a brutal assault and rape? Nope. Fran focuses on the positive and on how she can help other people.

In Chapter 6, you'll read stories from people who have learned to accept their differences, whether they are on the autism spectrum, unusually short or heavy, or encumbered by a lifelong illness. Jo Eager talks about how her little son was helped by a visit from another little boy with diabetes shortly after his diagnosis. Having another kid explain the injections to him was a big help.

Learning how to reach out and accept help from others is a big theme in Chapter 7, where you'll meet Alaina Smith, who realized that she needed to use her friends for support after she was unexpectedly fired from her job. I also loved the fact that she used a Chicken Soup for the Soul book's story submission deadline as her own deadline for making gratitude part of her daily routine. You'll also meet Nick Fager in Chapter 7. He gives us an inside look at how a contestant on *Survivor* routinely used fair practices and faith to stay calm and centered even as he was repeatedly voted off the island.

I was struck by the maturity of teenager McKenzie Vaught, who just started college. While her single, drug-addicted mother was in prison for dealing drugs, McKenzie managed to raise herself and not only did she make it through high school, but she also took Advanced Placement courses and worked part-time. She tells her story in Chapter 8, where you will read about numerous inspiring people successfully rising to the challenges in their lives.

Shannon Francklin's story in Chapter 9, about pursuing your dreams, will make you want to look her up on the Internet, which is exactly what I did. And there you'll see Shannon, a quadriplegic, and her husband, a paraplegic, both wheelchair athletes, with their adorable little daughter, who Shannon carried herself when there was no other way to have the child they both wanted so much.

Chapter 10 is called "Taking Back Your Life" and it is about people overcoming divorce, disease, and disasters, and then getting on with their lives anyway. I was tickled by Sandra Sladkey's story about evacuating her home in the face of a San Diego wildfire. She optimistically cleaned the house from top to bottom before she left, knowing full well that it might go up in flames. I know I would do that too! When her house burned to the ground, she found something amazing while she was poking around in the ashes — her hand-painted Nativity set, intact except that the figures were now pure white, the heat of the fire having removed all the paint. Sandra knew her family would be okay at that point.

It seems we are all stronger than we think... when we have to be. These stories give me hope that I will be able to face my own challenges some day, hopefully as well as these contributors did. They are all brave, courageous people who I admire. They are role models for all of us.

~Amy Newmark

Chapter
1

Find Your Inner Strength

Overcoming Self-Destructive Behavior

Spiral

All that is necessary for the triumph of evil is that good men do nothing.
~Edmund Burke

I was lying on the bed of my deceased father in our family home drinking vodka. There I was, sixty-one years old, with three kids, and my only thought for the future was how to find more vodka. I had closed my apartment and business, run through a theoretically unspendable amount of money, and alienated family and friends. I had spiraled down over the last three years in the face of a series of personal reversals. No hope. I felt like Gulliver, lying on the beach, tethered down with ropes, surrounded by Lilliputians sticking forks in me, powerless. Powerless. Wanting to escape from unsolvable problems. More vodka.

Finally, an epiphany, a moment of clarity. My father had taught me two core values: 1) Treasure relationships, especially family and 2) Have a positive impact on the world, helping people who can't help themselves. And he taught me perspective—I wasn't a starving peasant in Darfur, didn't have my last name in Nazi Germany, didn't have cancer or a crippling disability—what excuse did I have not to try? This was my only life and I could not waste it wallowing in self-destruction.

This wasn't me. Since 1975, I'd represented more than 300 professional athletes—NFL, NBA, MLB, golf, Olympians. I represented the number one NFL draft pick a record setting eight times. I'd dedicated myself to athlete representation and strived to be an agent of change, not just a sports agent. So much so that my career served as the inspiration behind the main character in the movie *Jerry Maguire*. But now, I was out of control. I realized I had to get my life back on track.

I went to Sober Living, joined a unique fellowship and dedicated myself to a twelve-step program. After a few months, the craving for alcohol left, but that was the easier part. I had to wade through enormous amounts of financial and emotional wreckage. A Mount Everest of amends and debt. I felt like Sisyphus rolling the massive ball up the hill, only to have it roll back on top of me. Or the boy at the dyke, plugging hole after hole. A Damocles Sword of debt and frayed relationships hung over my head. Would I ever be able be able to pay people back? Would my son ever talk to me again? Would I ever have a relationship with a woman again and a family? One step at a time.

I had never been particularly religious, but I was able to connect with a higher power to guide me through. I started to remember who I was. I remembered how I had built a practice in sports based on values like self-respect, nurturing family and caring community. I remembered that I had guided hundreds of athletes to established charitable and community programs at the high school, collegiate and professional level that raised almost a billion dollars for charities and stimulated positive imitative behavior. And I knew that this was why I was brought back from the brink—to speak and write and make a difference once again in the world.

To push the concept of a Sporting Green Alliance, which aggregates sustainable technologies in wind, solar, recycling, resurfacing, and water to integrate into stadia, arenas and practice fields at the high school, collegiate and professional level that will drop carbon emissions and energy costs. It will also transform those venues into educational platforms so that millions of fans can see a waterless urinal or solar panel and think about how to incorporate these practices into their own homes and businesses—sports in the forefront of combating climate change. My mission is to use sports to raise concussion awareness, fight against domestic violence, bullying, racism, and make it a better world.

If I stay linked to my higher power, maintain sobriety and fulfill my role as a caring parent, anything else is a blessing.

~Leigh Steinberg

Holier Than Thou

In order to change we must be sick and tired of being sick and tired.
~Author Unknown

As a teenager, I had a self-righteous, almost sanctimonious attitude regarding substance abuse. I probably seemed judgmental and intolerant of anyone who indulged in drugs, and almost certainly annoyed people with my smug self-control.

But then in my early twenties I had a bad fall that resulted in severe back pain. When it didn't diminish, I was forced to seek medical help. My family doctor ordered X-rays, diagnosed a bulging disc and prescribed pain medication. Having never taken anything stronger than the occasional aspirin, I wasn't prepared for the warm sensation of well-being that seeped through my body. I instantly recognized it for that "buzz" people raved about when they got high. I felt like I was floating, as if all my problems were suddenly insignificant.

Before even a week passed, however, the happy haze lifted and the pain returned. I called my doctor and he told me to double the dosage, instructing me to stop by his office for a renewal. I did, and after a quick examination, he told me it could take up to six months to heal. Then he cautioned me to take my medication sparingly and only when the pain was intolerable. Armed with a generous new prescription that included refills, and a follow-up appointment in three months, I left.

I continued to take two tablets every six hours for the next two weeks. Soon, I needed something after four hours. Afraid to take them closer together, I began to take three at a time, five hours apart, snarling at my husband when he worriedly suggested I slow down.

"You have no idea what I'm going through, so leave me alone!" I yelled defensively, not wanting to admit he was right. After that, I dosed myself when he wasn't looking.

Before I knew it, my second bottle was empty. When I tried to renew it, the pharmacist gently reminded me that I was taking a strong addictive narcotic. He filled my order, but warned me that I had to wait at least a month before he could give me more.

The next day, I made an appointment with another doctor at a nearby clinic after work. I agreed to more X-rays knowing they'd show the disc was still inflamed. I got another script, which I filled at a different drugstore. Computer databases weren't established then, so no questions were asked.

It wasn't long before my life became a terrifying spiral of frustration, deceit and desperation. I seemed to pop pills constantly. Every waking moment was spent in either a cloud of stoned bliss, or anxious hours coaxing doctor after doctor to give me more tablets. I endured numerous tests, subjected my body to countless X-rays and lied about the degree of my pain. When my husband tried to talk to me about my intake, I tuned him out. Even he didn't know the extent of my abuse. I denied that I had a problem—to him, myself, and anyone else that questioned my need to overmedicate.

I was convinced that I wasn't an addict. Addicts used needles and lived in filthy squalor. They didn't work, and most were ruthless thieves that stole from their own families to get high. I had a job, a husband, and paid my rent on time. Anything I took was legally prescribed. I wasn't one of them, I assured myself pompously!

I learned to keep careful notes of every drugstore and doctor I frequented, carefully rotating my visits so as not to arouse suspicion. No matter how clever I thought I was, though, I couldn't fool everyone. Many physicians refused to give me anything or disdainfully handed me a prescription for three or four pills just to get rid of me, warning me not to come back. Undeterred, I would match the ink color and add a zero to the amount, forging renewals on the bottom.

My tolerance level continued to rise. My back healed, making my quest for a fresh supply of narcotics more difficult. I became completely desensitized to any physical discomfort. I'd find bruises on my body and be mystified as to how they got there. I burned myself on the stove and was unaware until a blister appeared. The tension at home escalated, but I didn't care. I only cared about my next high. My husband pleaded with me to get help, always reaffirmed that he loved me, and remained ever loyal, yet I still continued to feed my growing habit.

One weekend, while he was out bowling with his friends, I was relaxing at home. I had just filled a fresh prescription, so I was calm and happy. I decided to spoil myself with a long, luxurious bath.

I set a candle on the edge of the tub. When I went to light it, the match sparked. To my horror, I watched my entire arm go up in flames. The flash of light disappeared a second later without leaving a mark.

I stared at the unblemished limb in shock. I could only assume that the chemicals from all the pills had begun seeping through my pores, and that caused the reaction I'd just seen.

I slumped to the floor, shaking. A tear slid down my cheek and onto my lip. I licked it and realized it had no taste.

"It should be salty," I whispered out loud. "Tears are supposed to be salty."

I stood up and stared at myself in the bathroom mirror. My hair was dirty and lifeless. I hadn't styled it in months. My pupils were dilated, my skin puffy, bloated and gray. I saw a dying woman looking back at me. It was my moment of reckoning.

"You're an addict!" I told my reflection, and with that admission, relief overwhelmed me.

I walked through my home with a robotic, yet determined purpose. I pulled pills from every one of my multiple hiding places. Grabbing the bottle I had just bought, I strode to the bathroom. I poured everything into the toilet without hesitation and flushed. I didn't dare wait to dispose of everything in a more environmentally safe manner because I knew I would weaken.

Several months later, I was out shopping. After a painful, self-imposed "cold turkey" withdrawal, I was once again healthy and sober. My marriage was back on track, and I was treating my husband, who'd stood by me through it all, with the love, gratitude and respect he deserved.

I stepped up to the pharmacist's counter to pay for the skin cream I'd bought. I reached into my old winter coat that I'd dragged out of my closet that morning, and my hand closed around a cylindrical plastic tube. I pulled it out to find a vial of pills I'd forgotten I had. I stared at them, hypnotized. I could almost taste them.

"Ma'am?" the druggist prompted me out of my daze, and I smiled at him.

"Could you please dispose of these?" I asked him, handing him the bottle. "They've expired."

I paid for my purchase and left. As I walked out, tears flowed freely, but I smiled, welcoming their warm, salty taste.

~Marya Morin

Am I Crazy?

Above all else: go out with a sense of humor. It is needed armor.
Joy in one's heart and some laughter on one's lips is a sign that
the person down deep has a pretty good grasp of life.
~Hugh Sidey

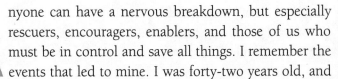nyone can have a nervous breakdown, but especially rescuers, encouragers, enablers, and those of us who must be in control and save all things. I remember the events that led to mine. I was forty-two years old, and my husband was serving in the U.S. Navy on a ship we jokingly referred to as the USS NEVERSAIL. As assistant ombudsman, I was the one to call if you had a problem. My list of burdens felt endless, and I was hurtling toward a total emotional crash.

I started giving away my favorite possessions. Everything I did had a finality to it that screamed, "I'M STILL IN CONTROL!" But I wasn't. I started dropping my classes at school, and I talked about death a lot. At the time, I had no relationship with God, except an internal screaming of "Please help me!"

One day, after spending an hour on the phone with a woman who had called to enumerate all her troubles, I began to slip to the end of my rope. Everyone was persecuting her, and nothing was ever her fault. Could I please tell her what to do? I tried to advise her, and she hung up on me, right after she screamed into the phone, "STAY OUT OF MY LIFE!"

The day continued to spiral downward. I worried about my husband

and his dysfunctional ship. Younger wives depended on me to give them strength and advice. One after another called me all day. I encouraged here. I advised there. I was an equal opportunity rescuer. Everyone got rescued — except me. I felt alone, hounded, and exhausted.

Then the phone rang. This time I had to bring jumper cables to a young woman who left me standing in a restaurant parking lot. It was nearly midnight, and my homework was still not done. The world seemed to be going crazy around me, but I was the one who lost it. In a daze, I simply did what I always did. Help. Save. Encourage.

I don't remember much after that. Life seemed as though it was happening at the wrong end of a telescope, distant and vague. I don't remember driving home. I remember sitting in the driveway with the car running, wishing I were breathing carbon monoxide. But I couldn't hurt myself. It just wasn't in me to take that awful step.

I turned off the car, and went into the house. My two beautiful, young daughters sat on the couch. I said some awful things that they both heard. It pains me still to think how much it must have hurt them. Their concern was only for me. Jenny called a therapist friend, who gave me the only advice that she could legally give, but only after I insisted.

"If it were me, Jaye, I would admit myself to the psychiatric ward." I knew she was right, and she called a wonderful psychiatrist, who immediately accepted me as his patient. He made arrangements with the civilian hospital, but I had to make arrangements through the Navy hospital and get a waiver.

Jenny, her young face filled with fear and concern, dialed the phone and handed it to me. It was a Sunday night. A young lieutenant with no medical experience was the weekend duty officer. What a blessing he was. The first thing I did was sob. Then I stumbled through my story. He was so kind.

"No problem, Mrs. Lewis. I'll handle everything. I'll wake people up if I have to. Don't worry. We'll take care of you, and my wife and I will pray for you." He took my information, and I thanked him through shaking sobs. In retrospect, I realized he was the one who notified the

Red Cross, who notified my husband's ship. I was ready to go to the hospital. Now all I had to do was find a ride.

Jenny, at fifteen, did not have her full license yet, so she couldn't drive me. Several ladies in our Navy Wives Support Group were called. They gathered at my house and had an endless circle of dialog as to who could drive me to the hospital. Each had a reason why she couldn't. It's only much later that I realized they might have been afraid of me. I felt abandoned by my friends.

In the end, the ladies chose an alcoholic Navy wife to drive me to the hospital, which was an hour away. Although kind and well-meaning, this woman began every day with thirty ounces of cola, of which she poured out half, and filled the rest of the cup with rum, whiskey, or vodka, whichever was available. She gargled with so much mouthwash between drinks that if you lit a match she would catch on fire. Thankfully she didn't smoke.

And this was who my trusted friends chose to drive me to the hospital.

Somewhere in my mind, beyond the pain, a sense of the ludicrous began to take shape. I could almost feel a chuckle bubbling somewhere deep within.

So the women packed my clothes and a few personal items into the car of the totally smashed woman. I wanted to grab the stuffed puppy dog that my husband had given me. But then I thought if they saw me with a stuffed dog, they'd think I was crazy! Hello, reality check! I was going to a psychiatric ward with an alcoholic! Of course I was crazy. Again that distant chuckle. I left the dog at home and climbed into the car. "Please, God, don't let her kill me," I prayed.

The woman was reassuring, kind, and all over the road. First we started down the wrong side of the interstate. Then, with a hysterical suggestion from me, she crossed the median and weaved her way to the right side of the highway. Then she headed for the outside lane, completely passing over to the shoulder, almost plummeting into a ditch. Whoa! Quickly she turned the wheel to the left, and we were headed toward the median. Then she reverted back. Back and forth we went, as my life passed before my eyes.

I didn't know whether to pray that the police would stop us, or pray that they wouldn't notice us. I began to imagine the conversation, as they pulled us over.

"Offisher," her voice would slur, "I'm sssssshoffering thish woman to the pssshychiatric hoshpital."

"Well, I'm sorry ma'am. I have to give you a ticket, and you'll have to change drivers. Ma'am," he would say, looking at me, "do you have your license with you?"

"Well, yes, officer, I do, but I can't drive."

"You don't know how to drive?"

"No, sir. I know how to drive; I just can't drive."

"Well, why not?" he would ask, irritated by now.

"Well," I would explain, "you see, I'm on my way to the psychiatric ward. Trust me. You don't want me to drive."

Thankfully, angels surrounded that car, and we arrived at the psychiatric hospital unscathed. I couldn't have been happier than to hear the huge, steel door clang shut behind me. By this time, I was just glad to be alive. I began to laugh as the kind nurse led me to my room. In some crazy way, I knew that all this could only happen to me, in quite this way. Laughter brought hope, and hope began my healing. And low as I was, I was certain that with time, excellent care, and the grace of God, I would become well again.

~Jaye Lewis

Don't Be Like Me

We acquire the strength we have overcome.
~Ralph Waldo Emerson

This last Christmas I celebrated five years of sobriety. I haven't had a drop of alcohol in five years, but I am still an alcoholic because I know that I have no control when it comes to the bottle. I will always be an alcoholic because of the way I used it to medicate my pain. Tears spill onto the keyboard as I write these words and read them out loud to myself. But there is a freedom that comes from shining the light on something so ugly.

I used to say that I would never ever be a drinker. I wasn't one of "those" people. I had too much self-control. My Christian upbringing would keep me on the straight and narrow. I didn't touch the stuff until after I was twenty-one, unlike most of my friends who had dabbled in it much sooner. I was a waitress when I tried it the first time and it was no big deal. It did not take control over my life right away. I was able to forego drinking for years with no problem at all. I got married and started a family without giving alcohol a thought.

Alcohol did not touch my lips again until a friend's wedding. I was under a tremendous amount of stress. My son Andrew had just been diagnosed with autism two months earlier, and we were in the midst of trying to figure out how to help him. I was at a loss. He was beating me up daily. Literally. Therapies were not working. They seemed to make him angrier. I would come home from sessions with bruises and scratch marks on my arms, and bloodied lips from him head-butting me as I tried to keep him from throwing himself on the ground and getting hurt. I felt so weak. So when I was offered a glass of wine during the rehearsal dinner, I gladly took it. I had no idea what that one action would start.

Now let me make one thing clear. I do not think that people who enjoy having a drink or two are alcoholics. There is absolutely nothing wrong with that. If you drink because you love trying different wines, or you order drinks when you go out to dinner, or you like a cold beer with your nachos — that is not what I am talking about. I have friends who are part of wine clubs, or will have a drink with dinner nightly. No problem. The problem doesn't come in the type of drink, or the amount even. It comes in the "why." I drank as a coping mechanism. I drank because I was in so much pain, and I didn't know how to deal with it.

My reliance on alcohol came slowly. A glass of wine here and there. But it manifested quickly into a problem that I was not willing to face. I would look forward in desperation to the end of the day when I could have that shot of vodka... or three. I didn't drink because I liked the taste. I liked the warm burn down my throat. The tingly feeling in my fingers. The fact that the pain and grief would slowly disappear and I wouldn't have to think about what I was dealing with on a daily basis. And I stupidly justified it by telling myself that I was a more relaxed wife and mother with a drink or two in me. That was the biggest lie ever. My drinking went from one or two drinks at the end of the day, after Andrew was asleep, to a shot here and there after 4 p.m. when I knew I was home for the rest of the day. The bottle moved from the kitchen, in plain sight, to the closet in our room. I didn't want my husband to know how much I was drinking, and that was the easiest way to hide it.

My time of self-medicating with alcohol only lasted about a year, but by the end of it I was completely out of control. It culminated in drinking too much on Christmas Eve and coming to the ER with my husband at my side and a doctor asking me stern questions about how much alcohol I had drunk. I denied having more than a couple of drinks of course. My wonderful husband was so worried about me and had no idea how deep my addiction had gone. He thought I had perhaps accidentally doubled up on my antidepressant or something of the sort. He was completely blindsided, and to this day I feel so sorry for what I put him through that night.

I continued to deny the reality of the situation when we got home that night. We went to sleep. I woke up with a terrible hangover and was sick all day. Bryan waited until I was feeling better before talking to me about what was going on. He also presented me with evidence of why he had taken me to the ER—a fleece sleeper my son had worn the night before. It had my vomit all over it from throwing up on him as I tried to rock him to sleep. That was rock bottom. That was also the first day of my new life.

Immediately after the New Year, I went to my first Celebrate Recovery meeting. It is a Christian 12-step program. Bryan was adamant about my going and I had no room to argue with him. I was very nervous. Luckily, so many people were there that I slipped in pretty much unnoticed. But it didn't last long. They talked about the intense step classes starting a couple of weeks later, and I knew that I needed to commit to attend every single Wednesday of the nine-and-a-half-month course. The class started with thirty-three ladies. By the time graduation came and the twelve steps were completed, only eleven ladies were left.

Recovery is a terribly hard road. The not drinking is only part of the struggle. Facing the reasons behind the addiction are even more difficult. The first three months of sobriety were the most unbearable. The physical need for alcohol disappeared pretty quickly, but the mental addiction had a death grip on my self-control. Every single time I went to the store to get groceries, I had to call my sponsor, or my husband. Someone needed to talk me through the store so that I wouldn't go down the liquor aisle and lose all of my willpower. Vodka was my coping mechanism, and I hadn't figured out a new one yet. I needed to ask for help from others to get past those desperate moments. It was hard for me to ask for help. Getting clean was a humbling experience indeed.

I remember the moment that the desire to drink went away, for at least a short time. It was about three to four months into the program. We were at Step 4. By that time, more than half of the women in my group had dropped out. We were at the point where most people who are going to quit, do. Step 4 calls for us to take a moral inventory. It is the hardest step by far, and critical in the healing process. I had filled out the chapter for the week, and it was time to go around the circle and share our answers. We were to talk about guilt. About the "what ifs" we say to ourselves. It was my turn, and what came out of my mouth surprised even me. It wasn't what I had written.

"I feel like it is my fault my son has autism. What if I hadn't had to get that root canal when I was pregnant? What if I hadn't eaten so much tuna? I was supposed to protect him and I didn't. What if I caused my son to regress into autism?"

In that moment, I felt a thousand pounds lighter. It was the first moment since Christmas that I did not want a drink. I had admitted out loud what had been eating away at my soul for years. And it felt good. I still struggle with those thoughts, especially with having two kids on the spectrum now. But they don't control me anymore. I can push those thoughts away by giving myself grace instead of reaching for the bottle.

Why am I writing this to a bunch of strangers? Because I don't want you to be like me. Don't be full of pride. Don't try to be so strong that you won't ask for help when you need it. Asking for help is not a sign of weakness (I am still learning this). Accept help when it is offered, even if you didn't ask.

Don't be like me. Realize that no one is perfect and everyone has their weaknesses. You don't have to be Super Mom, Super Dad, Super Spouse, or Super Person. You are doing yourself a disservice by putting that much pressure on yourself.

Don't be like me. You can't control everything that happens around you. You do the best you can, and then you have to let go and realize that life will take the turns it will.

And this last one is especially for parents of special needs kids. Some deal with it well, some do not. Make sure you get time to yourself, or with friends, or with your spouse to refill your emotional tank.

Our job is tough. It is life-long. If you don't take care of yourself, you leave yourself open to unhealthy ways of managing stress. You deserve breaks. Your children will survive without you for a few hours. Your health is as important as meeting their needs. You can't help them if you don't help yourself.

Don't ignore that voice in your head telling you that you are reaching your breaking point.

Don't make the same mistakes I made.

Don't be like me.

~Wendy Letterman Hoard

Finding My True Friends

We have to learn to be our own best friends because
we fall too easily into the trap of being our own worst enemies.
~Roderick Thorp

"One more pushup, one more crunch. One less snack, one skipped lunch." I sat on the floor locked in my room, typing away furiously at my computer to distract myself from my growling stomach. Writing poems was highly therapeutic to me, and it also helped me to brainstorm simple ways to shed even more body fat. Already at sixteen percent body fat, I was entirely committed to reaching zero. My malnourished brain could no longer think rationally; I could not see how emaciated I had already become.

My hunger-inspired poem was a perfect representation of how I slipped into the darkness of anorexia. As a freshman in college, I was painfully lonely. With my best friends at different colleges, I was determined to make new best friends at school. But my acquaintances just weren't evolving into "BFFs" as quickly as I wanted them to. To add to my frustration, it seemed like everyone else had already found their cohort of best friends. The perceived rejection took an immense toll on my well-being. I felt unworthy of friendship and began to hate myself.

"Ugh, I'm so fat," I thought as I entered the dining hall. "And fat people certainly don't need to eat." Succumbing to the negative thoughts in my head, I decided to cut my lunch in half. No big deal, I reasoned. But to my surprise, my increased self-control sparked a huge adrenaline rush. It was a sickly-sweet pleasure that distracted me from my intense loneliness. Feeling lonely every single day was unbearable. So I began finding sneaky ways to feel that instant high again. If that meant cutting my meals in half or skipping them altogether, so be it.

Losing weight became a game to me, and each day provided a brand new challenge to see how little I could eat. My hunger would be so extreme that even a bowl of plain lettuce tasted like a delicious, heavenly meal.

Weeks passed, and my weight plummeted. My peers grew increasingly concerned. As my track teammate and I were walking back to our dorm rooms, she softly inquired, "Zoe, is everything okay? You've lost a lot of weight." I fought back a proud smile. It was exhilarating to know that people were noticing my weight loss. Finally, I was getting the attention I so desperately craved.

"Yeah, everything's completely fine," I told her, avoiding eye contact. I feared that my sad eyes were open doorways exposing my inner demons. One glance and she would have understood the profound pain I was in. She gave me a concerned look, making it evident that she didn't believe a word of my lie.

Rumors started flying around about me, and I loved every single minute of it. The attention was addicting, and the more of it I received, the less I ate. Anorexia had me in its death grip.

Six months passed, and by then I had lost twenty-five pounds. "Please eat this," my teammate begged as she handed me a PowerBar.

"I'm not hungry," I lied. I glared at her. She just didn't get it. Snacks were strictly forbidden. They were a sign of weakness and poor self-control. How could she not see how unreasonable she was being?

But deep down I knew I was the one being unreasonable. We were on the bus traveling back from a track meet and I had conveniently forgotten to replenish myself after my grueling race. I was so ravenous that I thought I would pass out at any moment. Here I was, severely underweight and too hungry to function, and all I could think about was getting back to my room to do more pushups.

For the first time in six months, I admitted to myself that I was in trouble. I needed help.

●●●

"Alright, let's all check in," said Mindy, the group leader. Four of us sat in a circle in folding chairs. I had been searching for an eating disorder support group and found one that held weekly meetings in the basement of a church.

"Checking in" meant saying your name and how you were doing with eating. Oh, and you had to share your feelings. I despised that part. "I'm feeling fat," I'd declare, hoping to avoid sharing anything too personal about my life.

But over time, I grew to be great friends with the girls in the group. It was unbelievable to me that they could know the worst parts about me and still love me unconditionally. As I gained their trust, I began to share more and more about myself. Saying things aloud to them helped me to clearly see just how distorted my thoughts had become.

The group kept me honest. But most importantly, they challenged me to get better.

"That's your eating disorder telling you that you're fat," Mindy explained at one of our meetings. "You need to tell anorexia to shut up." Her blunt comments made me realize that I had become a prisoner in my own mind. Anorexia was stubborn; she took up far too much of my energy to allow me be friends with anyone else. I vowed to get better; I had suffered for too long and no longer wanted to feel this way.

It was now or never. Anorexia needed to go. So one night after my meeting I sketched a tombstone in my journal. "Today, I need to say goodbye to anorexia," I wrote. "For a while, she was my very best friend. May she rest in peace."

Through countless hours of therapy and my incredible support group, I slowly recovered. As I began to remove anorexia from my life, I was finally able to make room for people who loved me.

Getting better was a turbulent journey filled with setbacks. But my support system grew so strong that it became impossible to be discouraged. They would help me find my way back to the road to recovery every single time.

The defining moment in which I knew I had "made it" was when I was at a restaurant with one of my best friends. As we were eating, she looked at me and smiled. "You know, Zoe, you've changed so much throughout college," she said. "You are truly becoming beautiful on both the inside and outside."

She could not have possibly known how much her comment meant to me. It was at that moment I knew I never needed to starve myself again. Anorexia was never a friend to me; she was just an evil disease lurking inside my mind. Letting go of her was the hardest thing I've ever done. But once I did, I could finally love myself, and ultimately find my true friends.

~Zoe Knightly

His Way, Not Mine

God's will is not an itinerary, but an attitude.
~Andrew Dhuse

can vividly recall standing just outside the Chronicle building countless times early in the morning, trying to clear my head enough to focus on my duties as editor of the small weekly newspaper. And I remember praying—begging, really—that God would deliver me.

My co-workers would begin arriving soon, so it was time to plaster a fake smile on my face and crack a few jokes. But in my mind's eye, I was in a deep cylindrical pit, the walls hard and smooth as granite. It was pitch black and empty, like my life had become. And there was no way out.

I prayed, but I knew God wasn't listening. And I couldn't blame him; He knew as well as I that I was thinking about my next drink even as I promised to stop if he would come to my rescue.

I had no idea then, but He was listening. And waiting.

I was fifty, married, a father and a grandfather. A successful journalist. I was also a hopeless closet drunk, albeit a high-functioning closet drunk who spent nearly every waking hour drinking, planning to drink or disposing of the evidence of my addiction. It's an exhausting and pitiful existence. I lied constantly and worked tirelessly in an effort to live a normal life and at the same time secretly feed this insatiable, abnormal habit that never really satisfied me.

It's the sort of insanity that prompted me to get out of bed every morning and take that first drink. Usually a bout of puking followed, then I'd attempt another drink, and another, until I could keep down enough of that poison to ease the shakes.

In spite of my efforts to rotate from one store to another, nearly all of the clerks knew what I wanted as soon as I walked in the door. I wasn't fooling anyone. I hated myself, because while I was never an abusive drunk, I knew deep down I'd rather spend an hour with a six-pack than with any member of my family.

The only thing more important at the time was my job. I was proud of my writing. I knew that as long as I could write, I could hang on to one last shred of self-worth.

But fear of losing everything, of getting called out for my drinking, of my liver exploding, was choking out any hope for peace of mind. A few more drinks and I wouldn't care. Well, at least not for a few hours.

"Dear God, don't you see me? Can't you hear me?" I'd pray. "I'm going to die! Don't you care?"

Nothing. But in my isolation, I continued to pray. I'm not sure why. After all, I knew alcohol would always answer my prayer to escape. It gave me what I wanted when I wanted it.

Until another weekend binge left me feeling sick. I literally couldn't get drunk, and as I forced myself to walk into the office early that Monday morning in December, just before the paper's biggest issue of the year, I found myself unable to concentrate on anything. I was sick deep inside.

I finally gave up and walked out the door, confused, hurting, without hope. Completely broken, because I had just walked away from the one thing I thought made me worth something.

I wanted to die. I prayed, waiting for an answer I knew wouldn't come.

I finally made the decision to get some help, no matter how frightening the prospect. My wife and I made a couple of calls and everything fell into place for me to admit myself into a residential treatment program.

I walked through the doors, alone and scared to death. What I didn't know was that, in fact, I wasn't alone.

I went through detox and several rigorous days of rehab meetings, therapy and group sessions before finding myself wanting to pray again as I sat on my bed.

"Dear God," was all I could get out before an overwhelming feeling came over me. My face was flushed and the tears began to flow uncontrollably. For a few moments, I knew what it was like to feel God's presence inside every fiber of my being. It was incredibly intense, like electricity shooting through my veins.

I went to sleep that night without fear for the first time in years. And with the personal realization that God works His will according to what we need, not what we want.

Looking back, it was so clear how perfect His plan was for me. He was listening all along. It just never occurred to me that He might expect me to start cleaning up my own mess before taking over the reins. Had He simply "delivered" me, I probably would have gone on my merry way without trying to lean on Him, and without realizing how much I need His presence in my life every day. The truth is, I'd probably be drinking again today if He had answered my prayer the way I wanted Him to answer it.

These days—several months later—I still pray outside the Chronicle building, alone, but today I offer sober words of gratitude, knowing that He's listening, just as He was more than a year ago when I was drowning in a cesspool of my own self-loathing, fear and selfishness.

I'll never look at prayer the same way again. Just when I was ready to die rather than continue living in my own personal hell, He gave me another shot at life.

His way, not mine.

~Tom Montgomery

Learning to Thrive

Life is not merely to be alive, but to be well.
~Marcus Valerius Martial

"No, Haylee! Stay awake!" my roommate and best friend Izzy screamed at me. "Promise me you won't fall asleep!"

I groaned at my friend, wishing she would be quiet and drive a little less like we were in a Grand Theft Auto game. My body sunk into the passenger seat like a dead weight. Izzy didn't know what to do. Her words were slurred to me, but I knew she was sobbing.

Next thing I knew, she was calling my stepmom. "Haylee took a bunch of pills," she said through sobs. "Um, I don't know. I think a lot." She hung up the phone, pushed harder on the gas and cried to me, "Your dad is going to take you to the hospital."

I was now slouched over the center console. Everything was getting dark. I could see Izzy's panicked face. I could make out the tears streaming down her cheeks. She fearfully glanced down at me and sobbed, "Why would you do this to me, Haylee? Why?"

The last thing I remember from that car ride was my drowsy response, "Because maybe Jameson had it right." And then I blacked out.

The doctor said I was lucky. In my head, I was anything but. My vitals were somehow strong. My heart rate returned to normal. My stomach burned and ached as I slowly came back to reality. But I was angry that I had survived. I was angry that I was now being held captive in a hospital hallway lined with crying and groaning patients. With my dad at my side and my stepmom dabbing at her tearful eyes, my doctor asked the most important question, "Did you intentionally try to overdose, Ms. Graham?"

I shook my head no, and said that I'd just had a headache.

My dad looked over at me. "Tell him the truth. Tell him what you told Izzy."

I rolled my eyes, feeling like everyone was being overdramatic. "That my friend had it right."

"Her friend killed himself a month ago," my dad explained in a venomous tone, as though he resented Jameson for planting the idea in my head.

The doctor nodded slowly, now understanding. His eyes burned into me. "You thought he was right about suicide, so you tried it yourself."

And something about his words—perhaps it was the truth in it all—got through to me. I slumped over my knees, held my face in my hands, and sobbed so loudly that it silenced the nearby patients in their beds. Everyone watched me, slightly surprised by my sudden confession.

Then, between my hands, I cried, "And it wasn't the first time, either."

I soon was confined to my own hospital room. In four hours, I would go to the nearest psychiatric hospital to be committed for three days.

What had I done? I hadn't thought about how my death would affect other people.

For hours, I lay there silently, alone and afraid, like a child sent to her room to think over what she had done wrong. A kind nurse named Randy tended to my every need. For an hour, he even let me spill my heart out. I told him how unstable my life had been for the past ten years. I told him how my mom used to date men who were either drug addicts or expressed anger with their fists. She and I had struggled in extreme poverty, where scrounging for pennies just to have food became the norm and a good day was when we had lukewarm water for bathing.

Then, I confessed that by age fifteen I had already tried killing myself twice. Randy listened intently as I explained that for four years, self-injury was my stability and my razor blade gave me a different kind of pain I craved. As soon as I graduated high school, I battled alcoholism, promiscuity, and for months was addicted to cocaine and crystal meth. Then my dear childhood friend pressed a gun to his temple and took his own life. That was the last straw and was when I decided to end it all with the eleven pills that I swallowed with a bottle of NyQuil.

By the time I was done, I was out of breath from my sobs. Randy observed me quietly and after a few minutes, stated, "It sounds like you have had to learn how to survive. But that's not what life is about. Don't just survive anymore, thrive." He gently held my arm. "Forget the past, forget the bad things that have happened, and learn to thrive. Promise me you'll try and do that."

With tears running down my cheeks, I grabbed Randy's hand. "I promise."

For three years, writing was my outlet from the very dark world I lived in. By 2013, I was an official author with four completed full-length novels. So when I was admitted into the psychiatric hospital, I found my outlet and wrote a diary of my experiences. In just three very scary and revealing days, I learned more than some people learn in a lifetime. The nurses within those walls scolded me for what I had almost done, telling me to appreciate the life of grace I had. The friends I made there encouraged me and most of all, showed me how blessed I truly was.

So, on my third day, I left with the motivation to create a life worth living. I had many apologies to make, bad habits to break, and several relationships to rebuild, but I restored myself, stopped using drugs, and grew into a better person. One year later, I'm still an author, selling my four novels online while also managing a music-based nonprofit and a charitable hat company giving back to hospital patients. I live in a stable home, am surrounded with wonderful friends, and I have finally tasted the happiness I've always searched for. I no longer survive. Now I live a beautiful life not just for me, but also for the friends who encouraged me during my darkest hours at that hospital. I fulfilled my promise, started over, and finally learned to thrive.

~Haylee Graham

Looking Forward, Looking Back

Nobody can go back and start a new beginning,
but anyone can start today and make a new ending.
~Maria Robinson

Blood dripped from my knees, elbow and face as I limped home whimpering in pain that day. I'd taken a dive and had fallen face down trying to rescue my team at a game of base invasion. I was about eight and to expect sympathy for my injuries was a delusion. In fact, as soon as Mother saw the state I was in, she grabbed me by my hair and shook me like a rag doll. That was just the introduction to the beatings that followed. "How many times do I have to tell you not to run," she hollered.

Violence was something I was used to as a child. I was raised in a family that saw nothing wrong in physically assaulting kids to put them in line. Child battering was a tried and true system. It was passed on from generation to generation. As far as my family was concerned, no one had been seriously harmed by it. The fact that no one turned out to be a criminal or a junkie in our clan was testimony to its effectiveness. So why stop a disciplinary method that proved to work? Great-grandma beat Grandma and Grandma beat Mother. In our case, since my father died when I was two, Grandma and Auntie gave Mother a hand in raising my sisters and me; that meant two more pairs of hands to beat us.

It was no secret. I remember Grandma always bragged about how well behaved her six children were. And it was because they weren't spared the rod.

In my generation, there were many ways by which beatings were delivered: by hand, with the handle of a broom, a slipper or a wooden rod. As to what infractions justified a beating, there were no clear-cut rules. Aside from running, I was bashed with a wooden rod for walking barefoot in the house. I also earned it for doing terrible things such as answering back (oh yes, that was on top of the list) or throwing mud on the neighbor's porch. At times I was bashed for doing something wrong. At other times I was bashed for being at the wrong place at the wrong time. Depending on the mood of my punisher (Mother, Grandma or Auntie), I received a blow to any part of my body with any of the above-mentioned instruments—no matter where or with whom I was.

I endured so many beatings in my childhood, my mother wondered if I developed immunity to pain like certain bacteria developed resistance to antibiotics. Eventually, it wasn't the physical punishment that hurt me the most.

When I was eleven, Mother left to work and never came back except for biennial visits. That shattered my heart beyond repair. I kept her picture under my pillow and cried every night for at least a month. The wound remained open long after the tears dried.

Left to the mercy of Grandma and Auntie, the beatings continued. But it was Auntie's scathing tongue that wrecked my self-confidence the most. Auntie loved to pick on my appearance for her personal entertainment. She called me names and didn't miss a chance to make snide remarks. She'd say, "I bet you think you look very pretty wearing those earrings, don't you?" Or "I can just imagine how you'd look dancing—like watching a corpse haul itself out of its grave and make an eager attempt to wiggle before finally crumbling into pieces." A resounding witch-like laugh often following her comments to give them an extra bite.

And she knew exactly how to pack a punch. My education meant the world to me. It was my exit route from misery and poverty. At school, I felt confident about what I could achieve. But Auntie didn't even give me that. She wrung that last drop of hope that kept me going with a constant reminder—"Do you really think you have any chance of going to college? Uh-uh, not with the kind of money your mother sends."

During those times when everything in life seemed bleak, I took strength in believing that good things would happen to me in the future. I believed that every time a person was wronged, God made sure to make it up to that person one way or another. I clung to that belief like it was my lifesaver in an open sea with no boat in sight.

Many a night, I lay in bed wide awake, staring at the silhouette of a santol tree through our flimsy curtain. Amidst the darkness, the shadows cast on the walls and the whirring of the oscillating electric fan, I ruminated about my grievances: those that I wasn't allowed to voice to those who treated me unfairly. It was during one of these moments that I realized that Mother, Grandma, Auntie and I all had one thing in common—we were all victims of the same upbringing. Would I be just like them when I had my own children? I vowed to do everything in my power not to. I promised to break the tradition of mistreatment that ran in our family. "My children won't go through this," I swore.

Since nothing in the present looked rosy, I looked forward to the future: when I would no longer be poor, no longer be mistreated and no longer be helpless. After I filled my mind with positive thoughts about what would happen, I woke up in the morning ready to face another day.

The day came when the blessing I was waiting for came true. At thirteen, I took a national competitive exam that earned me a scholarship to one of the most prestigious high schools in my country. The scholarship provided for my board and lodging—my ticket out of the house. As for college, it was true that my mother couldn't afford to send me. It turned out that she didn't need to spend a dime. I qualified for a scholarship that enabled me to earn a bachelor's degree from one of the best universities in the nation. After graduation, I landed a sought-after job that opened me to a world of opportunities.

Many years later, mother confided in me how she regretted beating us when we were kids. "If only I knew then what I know now," she said. I often wondered how my life would have turned out if I had a better childhood. But that doesn't really matter much, does it? What matters more is that I survived despite of my childhood and I'm stronger because of it.

Now that I have a child of my own, I struggle to keep the vow I made as a child. Despite my best efforts to be a loving parent, I erupt sometimes and act like all those women who raised me.

Come to think of it, it's ironic how life pans out. As a child I found inner strength by looking forward to the future. Now as an adult, I've learned that the only way I can overcome my struggle is by looking back. It's only by healing the wounds I sustained as a child that can I become a happier person and a better parent to my child.

~Jacqueline Lauri

Frightening Memory

Dreams are renewable. No matter what our age or condition, there are still untapped possibilities within us and new beauty waiting to be born.
~Helen Keller

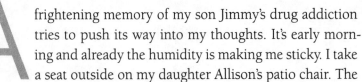frightening memory of my son Jimmy's drug addiction tries to push its way into my thoughts. It's early morning and already the humidity is making me sticky. I take a seat outside on my daughter Allison's patio chair. The shade from her apartment building and a slight breeze give me some relief. Blooming pink flowers sway in the flowerbed while Allison's dog, Rocky, lies at my feet.

Few cars pass on the street in front me in this congested area—early morning hours do not fit into the schedule of most people on a Saturday. It's been fun visiting the city, to stay at my daughter's apartment until we get electricity back at our home. The storm last night left many people in the dark. We are lucky Allison still has power and a cool place for us to sleep. But to live in this city every day is not for me; I'll be glad to get back to my little country town.

An hour passes and the line of traffic at the stoplight grows longer. A few people walk by on the sidewalk. I wonder what they're thinking. Are they making plans for the day? Worried about finances? Pushing frightening memories away like I am?

But I can't push the memory away any longer; it comes into my thoughts like a hurricane crashing through a window. I mentally relive the day when we kicked Jimmy out of this apartment. He was living here with Allison. What a horrible experience it was to force our son out into the streets, to live homeless with the other drug addicts. That day he had gone out to get drugs with money stolen from Allison. When he returned, it was on this patio where he stood asking us to let him in, or at least give him the gun in his room. His father held a crowbar ready to fight.

As an addict, Jimmy had stolen from all of us too many times; it was time to take a stand. His dad gripped the crowbar tightly with one hand, bouncing it up and down in the other as he said to Jimmy, "You can wait right here if you like; you are not coming in. I've called the police and we will see if they give you the gun, if someone on probation is even allowed to have a gun."

Jimmy had been in jail, rehab, and homeless. Now he was about to be homeless again. I did not know when or how this would ever end. All I could think about was Jimmy lying dead from a drug overdose if we kicked him out. Tough love is horrible for everyone in the family, but there was a greater risk of him dying if we didn't do this. Jimmy left the premises with his girlfriend, also addicted to drugs, before the police arrived. It was like tearing my heart into pieces, a slice of it disappearing with my son.

Then I heard sirens. Many police cars raced into the parking lot, blocking other cars from getting out, blocking the entire street. Policemen in bulletproof vests with guns aimed at the patio ran toward us, all of them screaming, "Where is the gun?" They entered the apartment quickly, searched Jimmy's room and found empty bags of illegal drugs with many syringes. His dad led them to our car, where he had hidden the gun in case a fight erupted. Police confiscated the gun because neither Jimmy nor his girlfriend was allowed to own one; it was a violation of their probation.

It's okay to think about these things today because now Jimmy is clean, sleeping peacefully in Allison's apartment, the illegal drugs out of his blood. Living homeless helped him to reach bottom. Jimmy turned his life around and now works in a job he has kept for four years. He is learning taekwondo and attending college to become an addiction counselor.

Last week I watched him in a white martial arts uniform performing for the entire class, Master Kim saying, "Jimmy is really good!" I sat with the other parents in the observation area of the classroom with tears in my eyes. Did they wonder what I was thinking? If they had asked, I would have said with a big smile and lots of pride, "That is my son!"

~Susan Randall

Writing My Recovery

Love is the great miracle cure. Loving ourselves works miracles in our lives.
~Louise L. Hay

For many years I struggled with a psychological disorder called body dysmorphic disorder, otherwise know as BDD. During this challenging time, I habitually rejected my appearance and body, thinking I was too ugly to be alive. I suffered from low self-esteem, depression, and suicidal thinking.

Nearly every time I looked at myself in a mirror, it was as though I was looking into a funhouse carnival mirror. However, to me it was more like a house of horror as I routinely battled against the appalling image. Sad to say, I spent countless hours trying to "fix" my so-called imperfection, only to end up failing—surrendering to extreme anxiety, social paranoia, and unbearable heartache.

I acted upon my suicidal impulses several times. Not only did this disorder affect my daily life, it also affected my relationship with my loved ones, my work, and life in general. It prevented me from going out and enjoying life to the fullest with others.

In the height of this battle against self, I came to a rousing awareness that the only way out of my situation was to write about the torment ruining my life. Thus, writing became my saving grace, a source of healing. Whenever I wrote I stopped thinking about my supposed ugliness or suicide. That, in turn, allowed healing, transformation, and a new life to blossom.

When I started writing about my battle with BDD, I found it

therapeutic and liberating as I dealt with wounds from my past and learned to love myself. A therapist once told me, "When you learn to love your self, in a healthy way, it is one of the greatest gifts you can give yourself and others." This upturn in spirit brought about a brighter future not only for me, but for my loved ones too.

Upon finishing my proposed book, with high expectations of helping others, I put the manuscript on my shelf for an entire year and a half. During this waiting period, I was inspired to keep writing, but for a different audience. I began to write Christian devotionals for women for a wonderful organization, Power to Change. My weekly devotionals were scheduled, published, and released to over 20,000 women throughout the world. Not only did I change the course of my life through writing, I also was blessed with the opportunity to become a Blog Mentor, a position that allowed me to minister to hurting people all around the world.

As time went on, I knew that it was time for me to publish the book I had put aside. Accordingly, I set out to publish *Arise My Daughter: A Journey from Darkness to Light*. I knew in my heart that it would be a valuable resource to those reading it — to those struggling with similar battles.

Today, I'm still writing. I believe writing saved me. It gave me a purpose. I am a transformed person, from the inside out, filled with desire to reach out to others through writing, blog mentoring, and leading women's small groups.

I thought I would never escape the pain from my past and the disorder that spread havoc all around me, but I'm so grateful that I was wrong. Once I tapped into writing, journaling, and reaching out to others, I found a new way of living. Through all this, I have learned that without loving who you are, it is nearly impossible to love others.

~Barbara Alpert

Full of Possibility

Once all struggle is grasped, miracles are possible.
~Mao Zedong

t is early morning on St. Patrick's Day and the rain falls in a fine gray mist against my kitchen window. The parade crowd has gathered in the street below and I strain my neck to catch a glimpse of the excitement. I shift awkwardly in the old wooden chair that has become my grave. My cigarette smoke dances under the cracked window as a chilly gust of wind blows off the Hudson River.

A small child pays the street vendor and runs away flying a brightly colored flag. My breath catches in brief delight at his moment of wonder, helping to distract me from my worry. My husband didn't come home last night and I really don't blame him. A woman throws her head back laughing as the band director whispers in her ear. Why don't I just take a short walk and be a part of the celebration?

My hand shakes slightly as the rum hits my lips. Breakfast. I'm wondering if this drink is enough to kill the pain in my soul. Who am I kidding? I'm a disconnected, useless woman. I haven't showered in three days. Below me on the street are the normal people with places to be and lives to live.

Anyway, I am safe in here. I am like a shadow against the window frame that no one notices. The marching band stirs outside and I walk away.

Another morning and I watch the sun rise again and the blood rushes to my head when I stand. When did I eat last? My heart races and I think I'm dying. I am so alone. I stumble across the room and a newspaper crunches under my foot. I pick it up and look at it stupidly. Something has to change for me. I have nothing. No husband. No money. No dignity.

I search the church directory for something to grab me and give me some hope. I only feel numb. Tears flow now, hot and fast on my drunken cheeks. I crumple the paper and throw it aside. My beautiful six-year-old son stirs in his sleep in the other room. When he wakes, I will try to look sane. If I don't get better soon, he will stop loving me.

I look around wildly. There is truly nothing left to do. I am desperate to be free of this constant, haunting ache. It occurs to me suddenly and inexplicably to pray. I move to my bedroom and light a candle, placing it on the floor. I kneel, face down, and feel a small flush of heat on my cheek. My nose is pressed crookedly into the carpet and my chest is wet with silent weeping.

I whisper, "God, if you are there and you are real, I need help. Help me. Please."

•••

I shuffle through the metal door. They are admitting me for detoxification. The clock is ticking too loudly. The other patients look dangerous. I feel a cold, slimy sweat pour over me and my belly is hollow.

They ask, "Do you know why you are here, Megan?"

I say, "I want to learn."

•••

I slip into the bubble bath and let steamy air fill my tired lungs. It's Easter and I'm looking forward to walking barefoot in the grass with my son. I am grateful to be doing something simple. It might be fun. I can't handle much. I am still raw and ashamed. Last night at the recovery meeting they said, "It will get different before it gets better." I know I belong, but I'm not thrilled about being labeled an alcoholic. It really doesn't matter. I am part of something bigger than me now. I'm beginning to understand I'm not a horrible human being. Yes I have lied, manipulated and allowed myself to be abused. But I am not that person today. Some might say I don't deserve to feel any peace. Yet, I do. I am not alone. The tiniest flicker of grace fills my heart. I sink deeper into the bath water.

• • •

Today, my car broke down again. I am overwhelmed with worry about how I will get to work or afford repairs. I need to stay in the moment and focus on what is working right now. I have a home, my family, a good job, people who care about me. I am sober, but barely sober. All this responsibility is too much for me. What am I going to do? I cannot find my balance. I am sick of my useless car. I work so hard and never get ahead. I am trying not to get pissed off at the powers that be. I do everything right and I still get punished! My bowels churn and I head for the bathroom.

I sit on the toilet and the tears come spilling out. They clean the dust off my attitude though. I hear the gentle voices of wise women in sobriety reminding me that my thoughts are heading in a dangerous direction. When I'm resentful, I can create the havoc that I fear. Long, slow breaths. Find something to appreciate. I begin with the intention, "I want to feel grateful. I want to feel peaceful."

Right then, I think of a man I was helping at work who spoke of a young woman who had to have her colon removed. And it occurs to me, "Good God, Megan, at least you have your colon!" Now, I am laughing at my own ridiculousness. I've survived worse than a broken car. I'm laughing and crying all at once and the tension disappears.

• • •

I'm at my old rehab today visiting a friend and giving back what I've been given. I can forgive myself when I serve others with tolerance and acceptance. Lately, I admit I've been a little lost simply living life. I appreciate work, softball practice, cooking dinner. Standing in the rehab lobby, I see where I have been. Yet, the memory of this place does not claim me. I am no longer frail and lost. I feel wide-eyed and ready. I am a complete circle, really. I've had many truths in my life, each one leading to the next. With a small smile, I go ahead and accept myself.

• • •

I am lying in bed sensing the soft light of early morning. My thoughts are like wispy fog and I am refreshed. The future is a mystery but knowledge isn't necessary to feel full of possibility. I am not unique but I am bold enough now to say I can forgive myself and I deserve joy.

I feel this joy to the extent that I can give it away to others. I think I'll share my story so someone else might know they, too, are on the verge of a gorgeous metamorphosis. Today, I believe in miracles because I am one.

~Megan McCann

Chapter 2

Find Your Inner Strength

Fighting Health Challenges

Hope Beats ALL

I have sometimes been wildly, despairingly, acutely miserable, but through it all I still know quite certainly that just to be alive is a grand thing.
~Agatha Christie

I woke on Christmas Day writhing in pain. The presents were forgotten as we rushed to the hospital. After numerous tests, I was admitted. My platelets were at 3,300; normal would be over 150,000.

A few days later I got the diagnosis. Leukemia. Acute lymphoblastic leukemia (ALL) with the Philadelphia chromosome, to be exact. ALL is a fast-acting leukemia. We had to move equally fast with my treatment. Before I could process how back and chest pain could turn into cancer, I was transferred to a hospital in another city that had a transplant ward.

I had never spent the night away from my six-year-old son. How could I tell him Mom would be staying in the hospital, possibly for months? Worse yet, how could I explain that if things didn't go well, Mom might never come home? How do you tell your child that? How do you tell yourself that?

Since it was flu season, my son wasn't allowed to visit me. My baby boy needed his dad, so I sent my husband home to comfort him. I stayed alone in the hospital watching reruns, despairing at the thought of not watching my son grow up. That was the one thing that devastated me most.

Reading and writing books had always been my escape, my comfort, but the medications made it impossible for me to focus enough to think straight. It was as if another part of me was being taken away. My health, my family, and now my ability to think—how much more would I lose?

With chemotherapy alone, I had a twenty percent survival rate. A bone marrow transplant raised my odds to thirty to fifty percent with a twenty percent chance of dying from the actual transplant. I thought those odds would be my biggest challenge, but I was wrong.

The hospital wouldn't consider the transplant unless my insurance covered it completely. At the same time, the news interviewed a man who had state assisted insurance and they denied his transplant. He died while I waited to hear back from my insurance company.

Even if I sold everything I owned: my house, my car, even the clothes off my back—I wouldn't have enough to pay for it. Luckily, we had picked the highest coverage plan available at my husband's work and my transplant was covered.

But first we would have to a find someone who could donate.

My sister was tested to see if she could be a donor, but wasn't a match. My brother had disappeared from our lives shortly after my mom passed away from ovarian cancer. We hadn't heard from him in over ten years. My niece tracked him down online and he flew from Washington to be tested and offered to move back to care for me, as I would need a twenty-four-hour caregiver after the transplant.

The cancer that threatened my life had brought my brother back home to us.

It was a bittersweet reunion when they said he wasn't a match either. I'd need an anonymous donor. People of mixed race, like me, have a difficult time finding a match. Many never do. I prepared myself to die.

Despondent one day, I asked my oncologist if there was any hope. He said, "There's always hope."

He proved to be right. They found a match.

Before I could get the transplant, I had to go through chemotherapy treatments, including injections of chemotherapy directly into my spine. I also had to have another bone marrow biopsy, which meant a very large needle jabbed into my bone to remove some of the marrow for testing. Did you know they can't numb bone? The pain was unbelievable. There were times I didn't think I could endure it, but I did.

To cope, I made vlogs, funny and sad, to post online throughout my treatment. Complete strangers commented that I inspired them.

The morning I woke and left most of my hair on the pillow, I wrote a haiku and posted it with a picture of me bald and smiling. I let my son draw on my head with markers so he wouldn't be scared.

Once I was in remission, thus increasing the chances of the transplant being successful, I received the marrow through a simple transfusion. The effects were debilitating. I was on a morphine drip for the pain and couldn't eat. Due to complications, I was in the hospital for forty-four days.

It was one of the hardest things I'd ever faced. Staying alive. But I fought. I got out of bed every day and exercised however I could. I visualized watching my son graduate from high school. If I could survive through sheer will alone, I would do it.

I was shocked at how much strength I'd lost. Just walking across a room was exhausting. One day, unexpectedly, my legs gave out. I couldn't get up, and I was blocking the door so no one could get in to help me. I had to crawl out of the way to get help.

I had a three-hour nosebleed right before getting a blood transfusion. My face felt funny, so I looked in the mirror. With the gauze up my nose, bruises all over my arms from low platelets, and swollen eyes, when the nurse asked what happened, I answered, "The first rule of Fight Club is..." and laughed.

It sounds horrible—it was horrible—but we dealt with it with laughter, prayer and many tears. I joked with my husband, when he had to help me shower, that he hadn't been in the shower with me that much since our honeymoon. I learned to brace myself to keep from falling. When I did fall, I called my son my hero for helping me up and watched him puff up with pride. I walked every day, a little longer each week, to build up my strength.

Shortly after my release, my father passed away unexpectedly. I was devastated. I hadn't been well enough to see him in months.

Sinking into a depression would've set my healing back, so instead I remembered our last Christmas Eve together before I was diagnosed, before he was gone. I was happy I was able to tell him, just days before he died, that the transplant was successful—there were no signs of cancer.

At Christmas, a year after the diagnosis that changed my life, I realized it was time to go from fighting for survival to living my life. While I could've despaired about my ordeals, I chose to count my blessings: the overwhelming support from friends and family, the return of an estranged brother, and the boundless generosity of a stranger donating marrow and life.

Now, three years later, we are saving to go to Disney World, without the wheelchair. Much to my son's delight, the whole family went camping at the Grand Canyon. I finished writing my second novel. I work with Be The Match to bring the gift of life to others. Christmas is no longer a bad memory. I have overcome the challenges I never thought I could. My life has been truly blessed.

~Rissa Watkins

What Cancer Did for Me

My cancer scare changed my life. I'm grateful for every new,
healthy day I have. It has helped me prioritize my life.
~Olivia Newton-John

At the age of thirty-five, I stood in the shower and felt something unusual. I double-checked. There was definitely a lump in my breast. Throughout a restless night, I continued to check, praying it was my imagination, an anomaly, anything but a real bump. At morning's light, it had not disappeared. As soon as my doctor's office opened, I called. Over the next few days, the doctors shuffled me from one test center to another.

When I heard the diagnosis, my world changed. With no family history and being only thirty-five, my doctors seemed as surprised as I was. I spent several days in a fog, feeling a range of emotions from panic to denial. When I finally accepted the diagnosis and my new reality, I decided to do for myself what others could not.

First, I had to face it. The onslaught of treatment required my complete mental, physical, and spiritual attention. I wanted to be well informed, so I went to a nearby medical library and dug through journals and books to research ductal carcinoma. I headed to the copier and got enough reading material to educate myself about the various options my team of doctors had suggested—surgery, chemotherapy and radiation.

The next morning, I organized the articles according to the doctor's three-step treatment plan. To avoid drowning in information overload, I focused only on surgery—the how and why. By the time I entered the operating room, I was prepared as well as I could be for someone losing a body part.

After several days, I had the most frightening moment — looking in the mirror at my scarred body. I removed the final wrapping. Although I looked like a patchwork quilt, I also felt like one, patched together by the love and support of my friends and family during the previous overwhelming weeks.

While healing, I tackled chemo and radiation information in bite-size pieces. I felt better prepared to work with my doctor to choose the best options to fight my disease. For me, this meant agreeing to chemo but going against my doctor's advice for radiation. It would have killed off a portion of my heart and lungs, and I wasn't willing to compromise my active lifestyle for the "chance" to extend my life.

The first time I went for chemotherapy, my jaw dropped. Not only did the strong smell of chemicals take my breath away, but the large room lined with lounge chairs also made me gasp. It wasn't as I'd imagined. Men and women weren't cloistered in private rooms or left in the dark to face the chemo demon. Instead, patients were lined up in rows like cattle hooked to milking machines. Uncomfortable with invading this personal time, I avoided eye contact with those hooked to chemical drips and instead focused on my nurse as she took me deeper into the room.

She offered me a lounge chair between two other patients who chatted casually, ignoring the drip of red and blue chemicals in their IVs. When I sat between them, I apologized for the interruption. Instead of being offended, they brought me into the conversation. They asked me to share my story and then shared theirs. It wasn't long before I realized my form of cancer was a cinch compared to theirs. How could I feel sorry for myself when others were dealing with worse?

An hour into their treatment, my new friends fell asleep. I soon learned it was a common side effect from some chemicals. I dug out my historical fiction and started reading. During future visits, my chemotherapy sessions became my escape. While the chemicals dripped, I traveled to other places and times. It made the hours spent attached to the IV seem less useless.

For the next six months, my routine became simple—move from the bed to the couch to the bathroom and then back again. On the days when I felt better I performed routine tasks and went to work.

The months of treatment wore me down. I learned to graciously accept offers of kindness. If someone wanted to bring dinner, I said, "Yes, thank you." An offer to help clean house? Absolutely. Grocery shopping? Oh, please. My friends and family were a godsend. Without them, it would have been easy to crawl into a dark corner and huddle there.

I knew my spiritual approach to the challenge of the Big C would be just as important as my physical healing. I read Bible verses about God's healing touch. I also imagined my own heroic Pac-Woman traveling in my blood stream, chomping down on carcinoma cells. She was fearless and relentless. From my little toe to the top of my head, I pictured my system being cleaned of bad cells. This thought process not only empowered me, it allowed me to focus on feelings and not just the overwhelming physical toll cancer had taken on my body.

Other patients had told me it would take at least a year for my body to regain the energy I'd once had and for my mind to clear. The day I woke feeling like my old self, I wasted no time. I opened myself to life—new people and places, more variety, and all with unconditional joy.

My normal has changed. Now, I don't hesitate to drive nine hours to see a reported rare bird or crawl through a snake-infested jungle in South America to enjoy a rare orchid. When asked to taste a foreign dish of odd-looking parts, I think why not? Trying goat innards is nothing compared to beating cancer.

Each person has a different road to travel when faced with a life-altering challenge. I would have preferred to not have the Big C in my life. But without it, I might have missed two things—opportunity and growth. Now, I tackle challenges and changes with more gusto and compassion. And, I'm grateful for each and every day no matter what it brings.

~Gail Molsbee Morris

Chicken Soup
for the Soul

Thanksgiving
for the Impossible

Mother love is the fuel that enables a normal human being to do the impossible.
~Marion C. Garretty

After an easy pregnancy, but difficult forceps delivery, our son was born. I was eager to be a mom and quite thankful for this little life in my arms. My husband, Mark, and I had planned on natural childbirth, including soft music and lights in the delivery room, warm water to bathe the baby after delivery, and immediate bonding with breastfeeding; but major problems disrupted our plans. Our son was presenting himself face up. In those days, a mother-to-be had to hope the infant would turn over on his own while she lay there connected to contraptions resembling TVs with bad reception. In all the chaos of the emergency, the lights went on, the basin of water was pushed aside, the music stopped, and my husband was kicked out of the room.

The doctor hastily administered a spinal injection, and our son was brought into the world. When he was finally placed in my arms, I noticed the scratches on his forehead. I recall thinking that he was a tough little guy, having survived the squeezing of those metal prongs. Two months passed as Mark and I relished the experience of parenting. Thanksgiving was fast approaching, and we looked forward to our first holiday with our son.

While breastfeeding my baby on November 20, I began to develop a headache. Within hours, I was in extreme pain and found it difficult to bend my neck. By the time Mark came home from work, I was in dire straits, with a 105-degree fever. Mark decided to take me to the ER. Friends agreed to care for our son, and reluctantly, I kissed his little face goodbye and promised him I'd be home soon.

On the way to the hospital, every bump in the road sent pain radiating throughout my back. Once in the emergency room, I explained to the doctor that I was lactating. I requested something for the pain, so I could return to my nursing baby. The doctor didn't answer. After examining me, he left the room to speak to Mark privately. In my delirium, I could pick out words like "contagious," "specialists," and "life-threatening." Mark's voice sounded anxious as he responded with questions. Returning to my side, the doctor announced that I would not be going home—that I must be admitted to isolation, as I had contracted spinal meningitis. "Menewhat?" I retorted, weakly. "How?"

"We don't know how, and we're not sure if it's bacterial or viral, so precautions are necessary," the doctor responded. "We'll administer antibiotics immediately."

Overcome with pain, my maternal instincts still wouldn't accept that I'd be separated from my baby. "Who is going to care for him and his daddy?" I pleaded. I needed to go home, but it was useless to argue as my fever was rising.

Visitors to my isolation room had to don gowns and masks. Friends called with encouragement, but I was so high on painkillers that I never remembered our conversations. Each time the drugs wore off, I requested a breast pump to keep my milk flowing for my return home to my baby. Mark had to work, so family members pitched in to help with our son. He was slowly getting accustomed to a bottle, but he cried a lot.

The spinal taps were extremely painful, but necessary for the doctors to track my progress. Once the doctors determined that the disease was viral, they discontinued the antibiotics and told me that my body would have to fight the illness on its own.

When Thanksgiving Day arrived, my family gathered at the home of my in-laws. As they shared turkey and all the trimmings, I lay in my hospital bed, feeling the meningitis eat away at my substance. As the disease attacked my brain's left side, muscles in my right leg began to spasm and atrophy. I prayed repeatedly for healing and hope. I yearned to hold my sweet baby boy.

Suddenly, I noticed something outside my hospital window. I focused more intently, and tears formed in my eyes. Outside the window were my husband, his sister, and his mom holding up my baby for me to see. My two-month-old son peered through the glass that separated us, and our eyes locked. I felt a renewed determination and faith. I was thankful as I smiled back at my child. I knew I would return home soon!

On the eleventh day of my hospital stay, another spinal tap was performed. My right leg had diminished to half its normal size, but to my doctor's surprise, I was seventy percent improved and could be released. So Mark took both of us home. I tried nursing my baby, but I was no longer lactating. Disappointed as I was, it remained a miracle that our son hadn't contracted meningitis from breastfeeding the day I got sick!

I'll never forget the nurse's words to me on my follow-up visit to the doctor. With pain in her voice, she told me of her husband who was paralyzed from the same disease. I was speechless, but gratitude filled my heart for God's mercy upon me. My doctor agreed that I was extremely fortunate, yet his prognosis was that I would never walk without a limp. I simply responded, "I have a little boy and I'm going to run with him. I WILL recover!" My faith increased daily as Mark and I began our own regime of physical therapy. I couldn't step out of the tub without falling, or hold my baby unless I was sitting down; but I kept hearing that old song, "Ooh child, things are gonna get easier, ooh child, things'll get brighter."

It took a year and a half to reach my goal. I regained full use of my right leg. Although the tests showed severe nerve damage to my thigh and outer calf, my leg returned to the size it was prior to my illness. The strength in my muscles increased. By my son's second birthday, I not only walked without a limp, but I ran. Soon, I was teaching an aerobics class and even won a dance contest!

With a heart filled with gratitude, I will always remember that Thanksgiving Day. The world told me I was done, but through the eyes of my child, God told me I had won. Today, no one would ever know that I fought such a difficult battle one November so long ago. There are no signs to show the world, except my own heartfelt words of thanksgiving for the impossible.

~Ginger Boda

Mom at Bedside, Appears Calm

We carry a nylon lunch bag everywhere we go, royal blue with purple trim, containing two plastic syringes, each preloaded with 5 mg of liquid Valium, plus packets of surgical lubricant and plastic gloves. At the first sign of blinking or twitching, we lay him on his left side, tug down the elastic waist of his pants, part his small buttocks, and insert the gooped-up tip. Within moments, the motion stops, as if an engine has been switched off. Then he falls into a deep sleep. When he relaxes, so do we.

He's five years old, the first time. Our babysitter takes him to a pizza place for lunch. He laughs mid-slice, blinks his eyes several times, slumps to the floor, and climbs back onto his chair. She hesitates—what was that?—and then calls 911. She pages me. I keep the message stored in my beeper, periodically daring myself to relive my first reading of it.

I meet them in the ER at the community hospital near our home, showily flashing my downtown hospital ID tag. Soon my husband rushes in, wearing the ID from his downtown hospital. All the tests are negative, they say. Bring him back if something else happens.

Something else happens. The next day, I skip work and keep him home from school. He sits happily in front of cartoons while I pace and polish, pace and fold. Maybe the babysitter overreacted, I reason.

Maybe he's just a goofy kid. The moment I stop watching him, he cries, "Look, Mommy! Look what my hand can do!"

Downtown. No mistaking it this time. Grand mal, big and bad, right on the gurney. Lumbar puncture. MRI. All negative. Before we go home, the neurologist asks if we have further questions. "Just one," I say. "What do we do if he does it again?" The neurologist seems surprised. His raised eyebrows silently ask, "Aren't you both doctors?" He hands us a pamphlet.

Dilantin. Chewable yellow triangles three times a day. Triangles to first grade and the beach and day camp and a sleepover. The other kid has cochlear implants. "Don't worry," his mother says, accepting my baggie of pills. "My kid comes with instructions, too." We become members of an exclusive club no one wants to join.

One day, almost exactly a year later, the school nurse calls. "It's been ten minutes and it's not stopping," she says. I'm home that day and I screech over in seconds, leaving one tire on the schoolyard curb. He's in the nurse's office, lying on the plastic divan reserved for kids with sore throats, bellyaches. Fakers. I know what this is called, this shaking that will not stop. I know how to treat this, in adults. But all I know now is how to hold him, jerking, foaming, soaked with urine.

In the ambulance, the foam turns bloody. I ask the ponytailed EMT whether he will die. She pretends not to hear, turns to adjust his oxygen. At the local ER, I bark instructions. "He has a neurologist downtown," I say. "He needs to be transferred." The ER attending, who has been bending over him with her lights and sticks, straightens. "I think," she says, not unkindly, "Mom needs to wait outside."

Tubed, taped, lined. Ready for transfer. There is one last thing. The ponytailed EMT hands me a specimen cup in which the source of the blood that had burst my heart open rattles. "Here, Mom," she says, smiling. "For the tooth fairy."

Back at home, forty pills a day, crushed, on spoons of Breyers cookies-and-cream ice cream. Still he blinks and shakes, shakes and drops. The weeks go by like a slow and sickening descent, landing on the carpeted floor of the playroom in our basement. We spend most of the day there because it's the only place in the house where he can't fall down the stairs. At night we tuck him tightly into Star Wars sheets but still find him on the floor in wet pajamas. If the Valium fails, we call 911. A fire truck arrives with the ambulance, and the firefighters, with their giant boots and helmets, crowd along with the EMTs into the small bedroom our boys share, delighting our younger son.

He is admitted. He is discharged. He is admitted and discharged again. Admitted. Discharged. Admitted. Discharged. dmitteddischargedadmitteddischargedadmitteddischargedadmitteddischarged. My husband, too tall for the fold-out-chair bed, takes the day shift. I pad in slippers through the hospital at night with the other parents. We buy one another coffee. We commiserate. I grow more at ease in this sleepless company than with anyone else—my family, my friends, my medical colleagues. I also cling to the nurses, Jen and Sarah and Kristen and "the other Jen," as we call her. One leaves my son's chart in his room, and I sneak a look. "Mom at bedside," a progress note reads. "Appears calm."

Finally, a break. The sixth or seventh MRI shows a subtle irregularity in the right temporal lobe, possibly a tiny tumor, a focus. We love the very word "focus," a raft of hope in a vague and endless sea of anxiety. Never have parents been so happy to learn their child might have a brain tumor.

The surgery works. The medications are discontinued. I don't ask to read the pathology report, the operative note. I am startled by my lack of medical curiosity. I wish to know nothing other than that my son no longer shakes. After the staples come out, we pile into the car and take a nine-hour drive—unthinkable during the previous months—to visit my in-laws. On the way home, my husband glances at the back seat through the rearview mirror and, returning his eyes to the road, says, "He's blinking again."

A second surgery. A third. This time, we're lucky. "The luckiest unlucky parents ever," I joke.

Years pass. We renovate our kitchen and find the lunch bag with two dried-up syringes of Valium in a cabinet about to be torn down. Our emaciated boy doubles in weight and then doubles again. He graduates from high school. He graduates from college. He moves away from home.

I do not know how much he remembers. He rarely speaks of those years, except to comment on whether a barber has done a good or not-so-good job of hiding the scars.

As for me, occasionally my terror will snap to life again, as if I've been holding it by a long and slack tether. It happens when I am walking through the peaceful, leafy streets of our town, pumping my arms, working my aging heart and muscles, quieting my busy mind. A siren sounds. An ambulance appears. Though I know from reading the log in our local paper that the emergency is rarely dire—a dog bite, an asthma attack—and I know that my son is nowhere near, I still stop to see which way the ambulance is heading.

People ask, "Is it easier or harder to have a sick child when both parents are doctors?" But this is the wrong question. There is no hard, no easy. Only fear and love, panic and relief, shaking and not shaking.

~Suzanne Koven, MD

From *The New England Journal of Medicine*, Suzanne Koven, M.D., Mom at Bedside, Appears Calm, Volume 370, Pages 104-105. Copright (c) 2014 Massachusetts Medical Society. Reprinted with permission from Massachusetts Medical Society.

16

Cross My Heart

Good health is a duty to yourself, to your contemporaries,
to your inheritors, to the progress of the world.
~Gwendolyn Brooks

ubstantial disease, substantial thickening, substantial, substantial. The word kept repeating itself in my head. All I could hear was the word "substantial." I sat in the hot car with the Arizona heat engulfing me and tears flowing down my face.

The day had begun with a routine checkup at the cardiologist. I went to receive the results of annual blood work and an ultrasound of my heart. After surgery to treat an arrhythmia eight years earlier, I had been heart-healthy and had no reason to think otherwise. That's why the test results shocked me.

"You have substantial heart disease that has begun this past year," the doctor stated matter-of-factly.

"What?" I stammered in shock, hearing only the word "substantial."

"Yes, the lower chamber of your heart has substantially thickened this past year."

"What do you mean? How did this happen?"

"Probably from high blood pressure," she said.

"But I don't have high blood pressure." Numb, I felt like I was stuck in a bad dream.

"Your blood pressure probably has been spiking with stress. Have you been under stress?"

"Yes." This had been the most stressful year of my life at the high school where I worked as a guidance counselor. One of my colleagues took an emergency leave of absence during the first week of the school year. No other counselor was hired, leaving me as the department chairman with two job descriptions to fill. The days had been long and the work unending. I survived only because a retired colleague stepped in to help. The stress at work added to the stress at home. I was exhausted and at the end of my rope.

"It's time to change your lifestyle," the doctor told me as my visit ended.

I barely got to the car before the tears started to flow. I called my husband and tried to talk between sobs. "The lower chamber of my heart has thickened; eventually it will lead to congestive heart failure if left untreated."

After a period of stunned silence, I heard, "We will figure this out together. I'll help you do whatever we need to do."

Luckily, we left on vacation the next week. Getting away helped me gain perspective. It took me several days to process the diagnosis. Playing on the beach together as a family reminded me that life is beautiful and worth the fight. My young adult daughters were as supportive as their dad. I knew I needed to make changes in my life. I wanted to be around for grandchildren and great-grandchildren. My husband and I had things to do and places to go! I trusted God had future plans for me. I knew the road ahead was not going to be easy. I promised my family and myself that I would be healthy, active, and alive for as long as possible.

With that promise in mind, I made an action plan. I gathered information from the Internet, from books, and from health magazines. I began to attack the problem from several different angles. My heart health was only one issue. The other big problem was pre-diabetes, or insulin resistance. There was no easy fix. I took a deep breath and jumped into healthier living.

First I focused on the physical issues. With my doctor's help I began blood pressure medication and a drug for pre-diabetes. I researched several supplements that were good for the heart and insulin resistance. I read about removing simple carbohydrates from my diet and changing my meals to include lean proteins, vegetables, and salad. Instead of snacking on muffins and bagels, I stuck to apples, berries, nuts, yogurt, protein bars, and protein shakes. I joined a gym that was located on my drive home. For the first time in my life, I exercised daily. Instead of thinking, "Am I going to the gym today?" I began to think, "What time am I going to the gym today?" At the gym, I walked on the treadmill. I planned my walk for a time when a TV show I liked was on. At first, I clung to the bar on the treadmill. But before long, I was swinging my arms and challenging myself to increase the speed and incline. After a few months, I could run for thirty-second intervals between periods of walking.

While I implemented a plan to recover my physical health, I also focused on improving my mental and emotional well-being. I spent time with colleagues and friends who were supportive and positive. Their words of encouragement were almost as satisfying as a dough-nut—and without the sugar! I read every health article and magazine I could find. I made an effort to slow down the pace of my life. I cut my hours at work and I took Fridays off each week. I worked hard Monday through Thursday, but slept longer Friday through Sunday. My body responded positively to more sleep three days a week. I spent time taking walks with my dog and watering the plants on the patio. As I took the time to slow down, tend to the flowers, and throw the dog's ball, my stress level dropped. I felt my body and mind recovering and healing. I pictured my new future, healthy and happy.

The last piece of my healing fell into place when I joined a support group of women who were working on their personal healing. With their support and the love of God, I began to understand how I arrived at this unhealthy place.

The healing in my life didn't happen overnight. The process took over a year and will be a life focus. When another ultrasound was ordered eighteen months later, it showed a healthy heart—a complete turnaround! I lost over forty pounds and no longer needed the blood pressure medicine. Heart health and balanced sugar are something I will fight for all of my days. This healthier lifestyle is not easy, but I know that following the plan is non-negotiable.

The day I received the results of the healthy ultrasound, I called my husband and kids. "My heart is normal. I'm well!"

"Wow! That is great news! We'll help you keep it going," they all promised.

With heart-filled gratitude, I responded, "I promise to do my part, too. Cross my heart."

~Gwyn Schneck

17

How I Survived

A mother's love for her child is like nothing else in the world.
It knows no law, no pity. It dares all things and crushes down
remorselessly all that stands in its path.
~Agatha Christie

When a teacher called with her concerns about my daughter's pallor and lack of energy, her comments failed to set off alarm bells. Like her two older siblings, Jill didn't always eat right or get enough rest. When she came home from school, I asked, "Have you been feeling okay? Your teacher thinks you need to see a doctor."

Jill let out an exaggerated sigh. "She's crazy. There's nothing wrong with me."

Although I sided with my daughter, I pushed fruits and vegetables her way and grounded her from late-night phone calls.

Her teacher contacted me a week later and asked if I'd followed up with a doctor's visit. There went my Mother of the Year Award. When she said Jill had been dozing off at her desk, I worried she'd fall asleep at the wheel.

After school, I quizzed Jill, but she slammed her book bag on the counter and yelled, "I'm NOT sick!"

Despite her protests, I called her primary physician. Suspecting mononucleosis, he ordered blood work. Results showed a low platelet count. He suggested we consult a hematologist. Although I feared the worst, I assured her it was probably nothing.

After searching the Internet for the probable causes of low platelets, Jill came to me, sobbing and said, "Mom, I have leukemia."

I hugged her tightly and suggested other possibilities that weren't life threatening. Tilting her chin so she could look me in the eyes, I said, "Sweetheart, I'd gladly trade you places if I could. Let's wait and see what the experts have to say."

The hematologist ordered a bone marrow biopsy along with X-rays to rule out an enlarged spleen. Directing her anger at me, Jill stomped out of the clinic and raced to the car. Apparently this was all my fault.

At her follow-up visit, the hematologist greeted us with good news. Jill's test results came back negative for leukemia and her spleen was normal as well. I felt a huge weight lift off my shoulders. But when the physician revealed my daughter had a blood disease—idiopathic thrombopenia purpura, ITP, I felt as though I'd been hit by a wrecking ball. The doctor prescribed steroids and said Jill would need her platelets monitored on a regular basis. It could be worse, I thought. We can deal with this. Too bad the doctor hadn't kept the part about prednisone causing weight gain and insomnia to herself.

On the way home, Jill freaked. "Mom, I'm not gonna take a drug that makes me fat."

Getting her to take her pills became a daily battle. Going to the clinic for blood work was even worse.

During my routine mammogram six weeks later, a suspicious cluster of calcified cells sent me for a biopsy that revealed advanced stage III breast cancer. While the news devastated my entire family, Jill took it the hardest.

Late one night, I heard her sobbing in her room. I walked in, sat down on her bed and asked, "What's wrong?"

"Mom, remember when you said you wished you could trade places with me?"

Hoping to convince her it wasn't her fault, I tried humor. "Honey, I also promised to shave my head if your hair fell out from chemo."

Her eyes opened wide at the thought of parting with her long, blond locks, but then she saw my smile. A bald forty-year-old was one thing—a teenager another story.

Already worried I might not survive a life-threatening illness, I spotted the paperwork for Jill's high school class ring on the kitchen counter. I sat down, put my chin in my hands and released a deluge of tears as I wondered if her future would include me. My children weren't babies like they were when I had my previous scare, but my teenagers still needed their mother. And I needed them.

Since I had the utmost confidence in my oncologist and his entire top-notch staff, I called his office to schedule an appointment for my daughter but was told he didn't accept patients under eighteen.

At my next visit, I decided to ask the doctor myself. "Would you be willing to treat my sixteen-year-old daughter who has ITP?"

Reluctantly, he asked, "Is she mature?"

Deciding honesty was the best policy, I confessed, "If you don't count that she rebelliously flushed her prednisone tablets down the toilet because she'd gained a little weight."

He chuckled, but agreed to see her.

On her first visit, when Jill sat down in my chair to have blood drawn, I felt a terrible sadness. As much as I dreaded the procedure, I'd have gladly pushed her aside and rolled up my sleeve. She reminded me needles didn't upset her like they did me. I didn't bother trying to explain. She'd understand some day when she was a mother herself.

Jill pouted about having her platelet count checked weekly. But when the oncologist said she'd need to continue taking steroids until her numbers reached an acceptable level, she cried out, "That's not fair!"

The two of us already knew life wasn't fair.

On the way home, she pinched her puffy cheeks and said, "Mom, I look horrible!"

I glanced over and teased, "Chipmunk!"

She volleyed, "Baldy!"

My turn. "Don't forget. You have an interview at JJ's Restaurant tomorrow." Unable to resist, I added, "With your steroid appetite, if you do get the job, you'll most likely be fired for eating up the profits."

"You're right, Mom. They should hire you instead so customers won't have to worry about finding hair in their food."

All's fair in love and pettiness. She threatened to stock up on my favorite candy bars the week after chemo when food remained off limits for me.

Family and friends constantly praised my wonderful attitude. What they couldn't possibly understand was how thankful I was that it was me undergoing chemotherapy and radiation, not my daughter.

Most teenagers bonded with their mothers on shopping trips. Jill and I bonded at the cancer center where we spent the better part of a year getting blood drawn almost weekly. By the time I'd completed chemotherapy and radiation, Jill's platelets teetered on normal. She needed her counts monitored periodically, and I had checkups occasionally as well, but our lives slowly returned to normal.

Almost two decades later, I'm still cancer-free, and Jill remains in remission. Blessed to have been there for my children's graduations, weddings and the births of my precious grandchildren — two belong to Jill — I gladly share my story with newly diagnosed relatives, friends, and acquaintances. I tell them not to focus on the sorry hand they've been dealt, but on loved ones who need them. That's what helped me survive a potentially devastating late-stage breast cancer diagnosis, and that's what will enable them to survive as well.

~Alice Muschany

Feeling Full

*Recovery is remembering who you are and using your strengths
to become all that you were meant to be.*
~Recovery Innovations

nxious, obsessive compulsive, and anorexic — had you asked me months ago, I would have told you I was all three. I don't know why then it came as such a shock when the doctor stated I wouldn't be leaving the hospital that morning.

I recognized that I had a problem. But when a medical professional looked at me and said, "You're an anorexic. Your heart, in fact your whole body, is going into failure. You could die," it all suddenly became very real. That diagnosis meant that I couldn't run from it anymore.

I had admitted to my parents that I was suffering from an eating disorder towards the end of tenth grade. What had started as a desire to improve my health rapidly snowballed into a drastically unhealthy change in habits and alarming weight loss. I limited my caloric intake to about 800 calories a day and exercised up to four hours a day. I was consumed with thoughts about my body and how to maintain the "perfect" and completely unattainable goal I had in my mind.

All of this left me with intense emotional distress, physical damage, and a 101-pound devastated body. I had withdrawn and disconnected from my social life. I felt completely hollow and starved of everything in life. I was dying, inside and out.

At the beginning of the summer, after having told the truth about my struggle, my parents immediately did all that they could to help. Sadly, the reality of the matter was that help would be months away. I was put on a waiting list for an eating disorders recovery program, so we were left to face my anorexia as best as we could on our own. Though I still failed to consume an appropriate amount, I did will myself to eat more. And although the constant thoughts of exercise prevented me from concentrating, I did cut my workouts in half. Summer was an uphill battle, but come the end of July, my saving grace was just around the corner.

Camp Kintail was a Presbyterian summer camp near Goderich, Ontario, right off Lake Huron, and also known as my home away from home. That summer was my fifth year at camp, and one of my most profound. Kintail had always been my sanctuary. It was the one place that I could truly be my open and honest self. Every summer, I was graced with beautiful people, scenery, and opportunities to grow as an individual. As a result, I learned that no matter what life threw at me, I could be sure that my time at Kintail could get me through it. That summer I was to spend a month in their leadership program, which ultimately saved my life.

It was my intent to reveal my issue once I got to camp. However, that proved more difficult than I had anticipated. While I had many friends at camp, I felt we'd grown apart. Though I tried, I couldn't bring myself to share my problem. Three days passed and I hadn't told a soul. Then one morning in the lodge, for no reason other than a gut feeling, I approached one of my fellow leaders in training. I knew little more than her name.

"Hayley, can I talk to you?"

Within minutes, tears were pouring down my face as I choked out the truth. To my surprise, she began crying too. She patiently listened to me as I expressed how I felt, but she already knew. When I finished, she looked me in the eyes and said, "One year ago, I was exactly where you are now." Hayley explained that she had overcome her eating disorder the prior summer and firmly believed camp had saved her life. I honestly believe in that very moment she saved mine.

For the rest of camp, Hayley was like my guardian angel. No matter how stressful things got or how difficult I became, she did everything in her power to keep me happy, safe, eating, and feeling supported.

Going home was the hard part, because it meant tests and evaluations, and then waiting until late October for my meeting for the recovery program. But on the third day of school, my stepmom told me that my evaluation had been bumped up. "They saw the result of your preliminary ECG, and they're concerned. They want to see you tomorrow."

With this urgent evaluation came the possibility of admittance into the hospital. It's funny how the world works, because that morning, Hayley (whom I hadn't talked to since camp) contacted me and asked how I was doing. I told her the truth, and she did the same with me. "This is when you have to get better. You're slowly committing suicide. Think about how much you have ahead of you." I honoured her words.

I went to my appointment that morning wearing my kilt and collared top, my hair done, my make-up on. I thought I would be going to school that afternoon. But there I was, sitting in that box of a room, the doctor's words still ringing in my ears. I would not go home for a month.

For quite some time, I blamed myself for this—for the inability to just eat a piece of cake or skip a run. People had reacted strongly upon discovering my illness: "I thought you were smarter than that" and "You've just got to eat." These responses only furthered my self-hatred, and I believed them. Until I started hearing the response from people uncovering the truth: "It's a disease."

It took a lot for me to finally understand that it is a disease. Lying in my hospital bed, devastated and sobbing, I recalled apologizing to my parents for all of the stress I had caused and that I couldn't just be better. They would have none of that. "Would you just tell a cancer patient to get better?" No, I suppose you wouldn't. Thinking that over, I finally accepted that I was sick, and not by my doing. However, getting better would be through my own doing.

My month in that hospital was hands down the hardest month of my life, but I got through it. And I still continue to recover from my disorder. Some days I feel unstoppable, and some days I feel stopped dead in my tracks. Each day, however, I continue to heal and recover, because I have an infinite will to do so.

"I eat. I'm still anorexic."

A friend recovering from her disorder once told me that. It's a statement that explains a lot and holds much truth. I eat, but I still struggle. I'm still ill, and I'm still a long way from being completely better, but that's okay.

It's okay because I have people like Hayley in my life, an incredibly supportive and understanding family, places like Kintail, and a strong drive to recover.

With all of that in mind, I know I'm finally on my way to feeling full again.

~Samantha Molinaro

Porcelain God

Warning: Humor may be hazardous to your illness.
~Ellie Katz

A lthough my grandmother lacked professional medical training, spending time with her resulted in a weekly diagnosis. She labeled unsavory behaviors an illness by simply adding the suffix "-itis."

"Why can't you just sit still in church?" she asked. "You must have fidgetitis."

The next weekend, while baking cookies, I suffered from impatientitis when I repeatedly opened the oven door. She claimed I had blatheritis when she tried to take a nap, and I had an interesting story to tell. With all of my afflictions, I swore I'd be dead by ten. Of course, the teenage years brought about dangerous complications such as flirtitis and disrepectitis, which required an immediate, life-saving treatment called grounding. This treatment possessed long-lasting, beneficial properties and cured me of many high school ailments.

My grandmother's earlier childhood diagnoses, coupled with adult bouts of bronchitis, laryngitis, and gastroenteritis, undercut my sense of panic when the doctor diagnosed me with interstitial cystitis or IC. It couldn't be that bad, I thought. It's just one of those "-itis" words.

Then I logged onto the Internet. Reading page after page of terrifying bladder symptoms and treatments, I developed Googleitis, which only heightened my anxiety.

My husband Michael asked, "What good is research going to do? You'll only worry more."

An admitted germaphobe, I faced an incurable illness that centered on, of all things, the use of a bathroom. I constantly darted to the restroom. The ladies room. The facilities. No matter the term, the environment in which the illness demanded I spend most of my time remained a dirty place, bathed in humiliation. I imagined hearing a flushing sound as IC sucked my life, as I once knew it, down the toilet.

I prayed the condition wouldn't be as bad as the medical journals portrayed. Maybe I wouldn't have to urinate every ten minutes. Besides, with a full-time job, a husband, two kids, and three dogs, I didn't have the energy to unzip my pants forty-five times a day, let alone get through the entire bathroom routine. I fought the urge to wear sweatpants. No, I'd continue to march to the bathroom looking stylish.

The illness whittled away at my self-esteem, and the constant pain affected my mood. Could I learn to ignore the searing pain and razor blade sensations in my bladder, which brought me to tears? I loathed the dietary restrictions even though they could help ease the unbearable pains. I called up a positive attitude. Coffee? Who needs it? Wine? Overrated. Give up soda? No problem.

Unfortunately, as with most people with chronic illnesses, I had to venture from the privacy and safety of my home every day. When using public restrooms, I closed my eyes and envisioned them sparkling with cleanliness. I noted the most sanitary restrooms en route to work, the kids' schools and other places I frequented, even charting new routes based upon their locations. Using various aliases, I filled out suggestion cards at gas stations and eating establishments, complimenting the cleanliness of their restroom facilities in order to reward positive behavior. I couldn't afford for them to become lackadaisical.

My husband knew my illness was serious when I named our toilet Raphael, something attractive and sexy, since we seemed to be having a love affair, albeit a one-sided relationship. But I loved Raphael all the same. He was mine. A porcelain god.

Amidst my suffering, an unexpected bonus surfaced: Michael stopped leaving the seat up for fear it would maim me in the middle of the night. Another perk—I uttered the I-need-to-use-the-bathroom excuse to score a little time away from the kids. I celebrated any benefits, regardless of how small, to offset the ugly reality.

I discovered potty talk made others nervous. When colleagues and acquaintances inquired about my health, at the mention of the word "bladder," they excused themselves and fled anywhere but the restroom for fear that I might follow them. On the flipside, if I wanted to avoid talking to someone, I merely said, "Whew, my bladder is on fire today. Don't you hate that?"

Dinner parties grew awkward with my third trip to the bathroom in quick succession. I felt like I should reassure my hostess, but the fear of drawing more attention to my problem kept me from saying, "It's not your cooking," or "No, I'm not peeking inside your medicine cabinet." After the fifth trip, I noticed some people refusing to shake my hand goodbye.

Obviously, staying home decreases my stress, but becoming reclusive won't make the problem vanish. It only provides more time to dwell on it. I've learned to ignore people's glances when rising for the third time during a movie to scurry to the restroom. Not their bladder, nor their pain, I tell myself as I knock their knees about like a human pinball. Sometimes I luck out and sit next to an older person or a pregnant woman, and they offer me a sympathy nod. I was once tempted to take food and beverage orders as a thank you for the moviegoers who quickly swiveled their legs to the side for me as I made a hasty exit. When I returned to my seat, my husband leaned in to catch me up on the plot, which sent another ripple of nasty glares our way from those less empathetic. There was a time when I'd turn around and leave the theater if an aisle seat wasn't available.

But I now accept that the illness doles out inconveniences to me and those around me and, to put it simply, I can't control what others think for the next forty-plus years. Besides, they should be thankful that I didn't choose to see a comedy since I've had issues whenever I laugh, with or without IC.

While IC is certainly no laughing matter, finding humor in the throes of adversity helps stave off some of the negativity. Yes, IC is agonizing.

Messy. Embarrassing. Inconvenient. Life-changing. It's something we're not supposed to talk about. But I don't hesitate when I say the word "bladder" any more than I would when I say the word "leg." I'm honest about my problem, so my friends understand my need to excuse myself in the middle of a conversation. My family shows patience during the used-to-be-ten-but-now-thirteen-hour drive to the Smoky Mountains for our annual vacation.

People with chronic illnesses know life's challenges, and each condition carries its own agenda, with or without the sufferer's approval. Since my diagnosis, I view the world differently: I'm more patient and compassionate. The man walking slowly and holding me up from my destination may have a circulatory problem. The woman having difficulty ordering at the fast food counter may have a processing delay or residual effects from a stroke. Who knows? Disabilities or illnesses don't announce themselves to others, and people who live with such struggles try their best to avoid inconveniencing those around them. But we have to live our lives nonetheless. With IC, I don't want sympathy. I merely ask that people step aside and let me dash to the bathroom. A porcelain god awaits me.

~Cathi LaMarche

A Healthy Dose of Humor

Every survival kit should include a sense of humor.
~Author Unknown

The saying, "Lead, follow or get out of the way," almost applied to me. Mine, however, was more like, "Get outta the way. I'll lead, you follow." I had two speeds: full speed ahead and sleep. I was always the picture of health. I was trim, in good shape, had all my teeth and hair, and never looked my age. My glass was always at least half full and "I can't" was never a part of my vocabulary. I had a beautiful wife, intelligent children, a nice home and a good income.

Then, one day I found a small lump on the right side of my neck. I thought it was a swollen gland. My ENT disagreed with that. He looked into my mouth and gasped! This is a reaction most of us would rather not see from our medical professionals.

"What is it?" I asked.

"Ya really wanna know?" he replied. Of course I wanted to know! "Looks like cancer on your right tonsil," he blurted out. "Let's get a piece of that and have it biopsied," he announced, as he tore off a chunk and blood rushed down my throat. At that point, I really wasn't as concerned about cancer as much as I was about choking to death or drowning in my own blood.

I didn't feel sick or look sick. I played golf and worked in my yard every week. I worked every day and didn't tire out. Maybe he was wrong! A few days later, he called me while I was having lunch.

Yep, it was cancer. But I didn't smoke, I ate healthy food, I exercised. I was unstoppable!

"Okay, so what do I do next?" I inquired. He told me I needed to see an oncologist.

I knew of one oncologist from church, so I called his office and made an appointment. I sat in his waiting room with my wife Debbie and my son Grant, admiring the paintings and sculpture that adorned the area. I remember thinking that treating cancer must be a lucrative business. When we were ushered back to one of the exam rooms, Dr. Kirby Smith came in, shook hands with all of us and sat down. He crossed his legs, placed his clipboard on his lap, and folded his arms. He sat there and talked to us like we were the only people he had to see the entire day.

We visited, talked, listened and got to know each other. He explained what I would be going through in detail, and made all three of us feel much better. The last thing he said to me was, "Nick, don't lose that sense of humor and that positive attitude. That's gonna help you get through this." Anytime I would feel the least bit down, I remembered two things: the hundreds of prayer warriors who were lifting me up daily and Dr. Smith's encouraging words.

I knew God wasn't through with me. I knew He was going to heal me, because He had other plans for me. I took radiation treatments every morning, five days a week for seven weeks. This took about thirty minutes of lying on my back with my head strapped down to a table so I couldn't move it. I wore what I referred to as my Batman cowling. It was white, nylon netting that had been molded to the exact shape of my head, my features and my shoulders. It had no back, but it had a flange with wing nuts all around it that the technicians would screw into the table. Something that looked sort of like a dental X-ray arm moved all around my head, spewing radiation and taking X-rays. As I lay there each morning, I prayed the entire time. It became part of my daily quiet time routine. I've been asked if I have any lasting side effects from all that radiation. Well, when I get up during the night to go to the bathroom, I don't have to turn on the light. What flows glows!

I also took chemotherapy treatments every Wednesday afternoon during that same seven-week period. These treatments took most of the afternoon, but I got to sit in a very comfortable leather recliner while covered with a soft blanket the entire time. Chemo does three things while it's flowing into your arm: it makes you sleep, it makes you cold and it makes you run to the bathroom frequently. This huge room full of recliners and cancer patients had only one bathroom. It was not unusual to see people lined up holding onto their IV stands. We were plugged into these things, so wherever we wandered, they went with us. With the backlog outside the restroom door, it was not unusual to see some of the men trying to open windows.

I was told I would eventually have to get a feeding tube. A feeding tube? Not me! There was nothing wrong with my appetite. Given enough radiation in your head and neck area, swallowing becomes impossible. I was also told that Dr. Cattau, who would surgically install the feeding tube, was President Reagan's gastroenterologist. I think that was supposed to make me feel more at ease. Just before they put me to sleep, I told Dr. Cattau that I had talked to Nancy Reagan about him the day before. Well, he bit and asked me what she said. I told him I would tell him if I woke up.

Actually, the feeding tube wasn't all that bad. It was about a quarter-inch in diameter and eighteen inches long. It protruded from the middle of my stomach and was wrapped up like a cowboy's lasso, and taped to my side with Velcro. I thought a ten-gallon cowboy hat should come with it. Instead it came with a giant syringe without a plunger. Six times a day, I unrolled the lasso, plugged the topless syringe into the end of the tube, and poured a can of Boost Plus into it. Having tasted that stuff once, I was grateful for the feeding tube. The funny thing is, when I would pour a glass of water in it, to flush it out, my mouth and throat would become moist.

There is light at the end of the tunnel. I was diagnosed in June of 2007, and I was declared cancer-free in October of that same year. This was a brief journey that changed my heart, strengthened my relationship with God and my family, and brought a better balance to what is really important and what is not in my life. I thank God every day for my good health and I try to "pay it forward" to other cancer patients. By the way, Dr. Cattau got me back. Before he yanked the feeding tube out of my stomach, he told me it wouldn't hurt!

~Nick Nixon

Unexpected Presents

Life is short, so live it. Love is rare, so grab it. Fear controls you, so face it.
Memories are precious, so cherish them. We only get one life, so live it!
~Author Unknown

When I woke from anesthesia after surgery to remove a seemingly benign ovarian cyst, I received some unexpected and unpleasant news. My doctor told me that I had cancer. The dreaded "C word!" And worse yet, ovarian cancer, also known as "the silent killer."

Questions and emotions overwhelmed me. Was I going to live? What was going to happen next? How would I tell my loved ones? Would I lose my hair?

From thereon out, it was a whirlwind. Everything happened so quickly. Chemotherapy began two weeks after my diagnosis. I learned that on days fourteen through seventeen of my chemotherapy treatments, my hair would start falling out in clumps. I was a newlywed of only six months. How would my husband feel about a pale, puffy-faced bald wife with scars, nausea and all the other dreaded potential side effects of my upcoming journey? How would I retain the strength, confidence and charisma that attracted him to me? Should I offer him a pass? After all, he certainly did not sign up for this.

I was terrified and felt powerless and alone. How could I regain my balance? Rather than watching my hair fall out day after day, I decided to take control. On the fourteenth day, I checked into a fabulous oceanfront hotel, outfitted with an assortment of wigs and champagne.

My beautiful daughter and my closest girlfriends met me there with scissors and Wahl Shaver in hand to have a Head Shaving Party. I always love a party and this certainly was an original theme.

Truthfully, I could not bear to see the shocked, fearful looks on their faces one by one when seeing me bald for the first time. Instead, I wanted to have them be a part of creating my "new look." We laughed and cried as each of them took turns cutting and shaving my head. We shared an intimacy that most people never share. It was one of the most profound, memorable days of my life. I stood before them more vulnerable and exposed than I had ever felt before. I stood on the balcony feeling the wind on my naked scalp while stealing a glance at my reflection in the window. To my surprise, it was liberating! Instead of feeling weak and insecure, I felt an inner beauty and unstoppable strength and courage! We all knew that this could happen to any of us.

I changed that day. I bared my head and my soul to them. I realized that none of us really knows what our future holds. All that is certain is now. So I mustn't spend my time fretting or wallowing in my circumstances. I must spend it celebrating the love, friendship, beauty and joy that surround me. I chose to live fully each day, with or without hair.

~Debbi Singer

Chapter 3

Find Your Inner Strength

Powering Through Loss

Daddy's Words

The pain passes, but the beauty remains.
~Pierre Auguste Renoir

My life changed the day of my nineteenth birthday. Daddy and I were leaving for the funeral home. As I opened the front door, its familiar creak made me cringe. Before Mom went to the hospital for the last time, she had asked me to oil the squeaky hinges because the noise often woke her. I hadn't gotten around to it.

It didn't matter anymore.

"Wait," Daddy whispered. "Come sit with me a minute." Reluctantly, I followed his lead and sat with him on the foyer stairs. His legs trembled. So did his hands. And the warmth of his body beside mine threatened to melt my numb reserve. I couldn't be still. I had to move. To do something—anything—to keep from thinking. From feeling. From facing the fact that Mom was gone.

I'd spent the previous day scurrying. Preparing meals nobody ate, braiding and re-braiding my little sister's hair, and cleaning the already spotless house. Staying busy seemed to hold back the heaviness of my loss and prevented it from shattering me. The only time I spent with Daddy in that whirling twenty-four hours was choosing Mom's final dress.

Being near Daddy was painful. The hollowness of his steel-blue eyes and the sagginess in his broad shoulders confronted me with reality, and reality was just too painful to face. I remained stoic and stiff. I witnessed Daddy enter the brutal, tortured, grieving world and didn't want to join him there. I had to be strong.

Glancing toward the front door, I secretly longed to leave him. To get as far away as I could. But I knew that wasn't possible. He needed me.

Daddy, normally a strong military man, needed me. What a strange thought. Sitting so close to him felt awkward too. I know that sounds bizarre, but we never really... did that. Especially since Mom's condition took a turn for the worse. Our times together were usually distant, spent doing daily tasks, caring for my sister, and making sure Mom was comfortable. Now we sat together in a dark, heavy silence.

The door, slightly ajar, allowed the morning dampness to seep in, carrying with it the floral scent of the red rosebush in the yard. My stomach turned. Even the air reeked of a funeral.

Daddy reached over and clasped both of my hands in his. I stared at the door and wondered if he heard the pounding in my chest. "You know I love you, don't you?" His voice was shaky, and the banging in my ears nearly drowned him out.

A mass of emotion swelled in my throat and choked out any thought of speaking. My chest pounded louder — faster.

He tightened his grip, then released and stood.

My hands, still warm from his, reached out. Wait! Don't go, I wanted to say, but only delivered a soft moan. The dam I'd spent months building collapsed, and the pent-up emotions spilled out.

Daddy pulled me up, pressed me to his chest, and we sobbed.

"You've never told me that before, Daddy."

He placed his palms upon my wet cheeks and kissed my forehead.

"You've never told me that..." I repeated, "...but I've always known it."

I tried to blink away the blurring tears, but the flow was unrelenting. The imprisoned fears and guarded emotions had finally been granted freedom. Though I still felt the pain of losing Mom, her battle with cancer was over and the tender embrace of Daddy's love had begun the healing.

I clung tightly to my father, and to the words I'd waited all my life to hear. The moment provided a salve to my brokenness.

"I love you too, Daddy." When I said the word too, a small smile crept over my face. I realized I'd never added that word before.

Undefeated by the pain that invaded our lives, I wiped my tears and faced the tasks before us head-on. By facing reality, an odd sense of relief came over me.

Daddy loved me. And life, although forever changed, would go on. It was one of the most difficult days of my life, yet it overflowed with wonderful words of love.

At the funeral home, many people stated, "There are no words to ease your pain." They were wrong. Daddy's words already had.

~Cheryl Hart

23

A Mother's Promise to Her Son

Not everything that is faced can be changed,
but nothing can be changed until it is faced.
~James Baldwin

t was 6 a.m. and I had just tightened the laces on my running shoes when I found my twenty-year-old son Ian dead in his bedroom. My cries for help were heard two blocks away.

The night before the funeral, I couldn't sleep. I feared that when the sun rose I would not be able to bury my son. Everyone wanted to know how Ian died. We said we were waiting for the toxicology report. But we knew. His doctor told us to say Ian died of an aneurysm or a heart attack. But that was a lie.

Ian was a good kid—a promising college student with everything to live for. He was bright, athletic, popular, and handsome. He made an unhealthy decision to use drugs, but I was not ashamed of him. I would not bury him with a lie. Then I had a vision about speaking out. I woke my husband and said, "Larry I want to speak out. If this is happening to us, it's happening to other families." Larry immediately agreed. So the next morning we buried our beloved son Ian and spoke the truth about the cause of his death.

They say the truth will set you free, and I believe it. Once I made the decision to be honest about Ian's addiction, I became the strong one at the funeral. I held many young girls in long black dresses in my arms, and comforted the sobbing boys, now looking more like men. Their grief left me even more determined to devote myself to ending the silence surrounding addiction.

There was so much to learn. I received scholarships to attend courses on addiction and researched drug abuse on the Internet. Once I felt ready, I had to decide where to begin. Armed with a wealth of information, I approached Dewey Amos, principal of Norwalk High School, Ian's school. As we sat with a box of tissues, talking about Ian, Dewey and I decided I would tell Ian's story to his students. I gave my first presentation at Norwalk High School and I continue to share Ian's story across the country to students, parents, educators, law enforcement, and at state and national conferences.

The night Ian died, Sunny, our family Beagle, climbed four flights of stairs from Ian's bed to mine and tried to wake me, but his message was undelivered. Ian had told me something before we went to bed and I was having my first deep sleep in a long time: "Mom, I want to see the doctor in the morning. I need to take care of my problem. I need help." But then Ian went back downstairs and used the drugs one more time.

Years later, I was sitting on my deck with Sunny and my friend. I looked at Sunny and said, "If Sunny could talk, he would have a lot to say." That pivotal moment is when I decided to write a book from Sunny's perspective about Ian's story and reach children and parents in a very different way.

Sunny was Ian's best friend and the pulse of our family. I wanted *Sunny's Story* to be a compelling drug prevention book detailing the bittersweet life of our dog, who needlessly lost his best friend to drugs. Our family pet and narrator, Sunny, was the keen observer of the damage done by drug use to his young master, Ian. He tells a heartwarming, but tragic story, beginning with meeting Ian at an animal shelter and ending in a futile attempt to save Ian's life.

Since its release, *Sunny's Story* has been read at dinner tables across the country, in schools, as part of our drug prevention programs, and as a stand-alone book for children of all ages, parents, teachers and professionals in the substance abuse field.

Sometimes it is still hard to believe my son has died. He was only twenty years old. Although, I don't have all the answers, I believe I have a mission to fulfill. Someone said I have a lot of work to do before my long and healthy life ends. And at the end of my life, I will have accomplished what I know I have been put on the earth to do.

I made a promise to Ian the day he died to do everything in my power to prevent this tragedy from happening to another family. I established The Courage to Speak Foundation, Inc., a nonprofit organization dedicated to "saving young lives by empowering youth to be drug-free and encouraging parents to communicate effectively with their children about drugs." With teams of prevention professionals, we developed The Courage to Speak drug prevention programs for elementary, middle and high schools, and a course for parents to keep their children safe from drugs.

I never thought this would happen in our family, but it did. Addiction crosses all age ranges, economic and ethnic backgrounds and races, and I will never stop speaking out until I see changes in our world.

~Ginger Katz

24

The Boy I Loved and Lost

*When you're a nurse you know that every day you will
touch a life or a life will touch yours.*
~Author Unknown

"Y ou'll make a great nurse someday," Helmut said as I helped him out of his sweat-drenched hospital gown and washed his back. His words were meant to be encouraging but they tugged at my heart. How could I hope to be a great nurse when I couldn't even save the one person I loved most in this world from the cancer that had been slowly destroying his twenty-one-year-old body? Helmut was in the end stage of osteosarcoma, an aggressive bone cancer that, in 1971, resulted in death for more than 95 percent of its victims.

I was eighteen years old and because of his illness and my desire to care for him, I had changed my college major from English to nursing. In the twenty-two months we'd been together, Helmut and I had talked about his cancer but had never spoken about the fact that, barring a miraculous cure, he was going to die from it. Now it was obvious to both of us that his death was imminent. He was emaciated, too weak to walk or bathe himself, required oxygen to breathe and had constant pain in his bones. Physically, he looked more like a concentration camp inmate than the strong, healthy construction worker he'd been when we'd started dating, but to me he was still as handsome as ever.

I poured lotion into my hands and began massaging his back, wishing I knew the "right" way to give a back rub. Lacking clinical training and skills, I made random motions with my hands, trying to transmit the love I felt for him through my fingers and concentrating on my desire to take away his pain.

He sighed and said, "You have a great touch, so gentle and soothing that it brings me more comfort than the pain pills. That's how I know any patient you care for will be blessed to have you for their nurse."

He paused then, and his voice cracked as he struggled to say what was in his heart but had never given voice to before this moment of uncharacteristic verbal tenderness. "I never thought that you'd stay with me through all this and be there for me the way that you have been. It means so much to have you by my side. I love you and want to thank you from the bottom of my heart for all you've done for me."

Hearing the words I'd longed for was bittersweet because I knew they were his final goodbye. He simply couldn't die before uttering them. Fighting back tears, I whispered the words I said every time we were together: "I love you. There's no place else I'd rather be than with you."

I knew the reason he'd doubted my commitment to stay was the fact that his first love had left him a week after he told her he had cancer. But there had never been any doubt in my own mind that I was in this for the long haul.

I was still by his side when he slipped into a coma the next day and took his last few breaths.

For a few months after he died I felt like my whole world had collapsed. I became depressed, angry and mired in self-pity. I wallowed in grief and even considered suicide to put an end to my own misery. One particularly bad day, while lashing out at God for allowing suffering in good, gentle, loving people like my Helmut, I realized I had two choices. I could either add to the misery in the world by remaining depressed or I could alleviate the pain and suffering of others by finishing college and becoming the kind of nurse that Helmut predicted I'd be. I chose the latter course and pursued my nursing studies with passion, silently dedicating my future nursing career and professional life to the fine young man I had adored.

In nursing school, several instructors commented that I had a "gift" for alleviating pain and for nursing. None of them knew that gift came from my love for Helmut and from the prophetic words he'd spoken to me. In becoming a nurse, I'd found my life purpose and it helped me move out of the intense grief I felt and get beyond my own wants and needs.

Having a life purpose also gave me a sense of direction and helped bring joy back into my life. During my senior year of college I met my husband, Fred. He too had found his life purpose in the midst of misery. Fred had served two tours in Vietnam and lost army buddies in the war. During his second tour he made the decision that if he survived he would go to college and become a teacher, because the thing that brought him brief moments of joy during the war was spending time with the young children who had sometimes followed him around in Vietnam.

Fred earned his teaching degree the same year I earned my nursing degree and we got married that summer.

That was thirty-nine years ago, and though we've had a lot of challenges to overcome during those years, our love and commitment for each other have given us a solid foundation to build on and great happiness in our lives.

A Soren Kierkegaard quotation beautifully sums up what I learned from the two great loves of my life: "When one has fully entered the realm of love, the world—no matter how imperfect—becomes rich and beautiful; it consists solely of opportunities for love."

~Gail Sobotkin

25

Bit by Bit

Life is a flame that is always burning itself out,
but it catches fire again every time a child is born.
~George Bernard Shaw

"Bad news, it's a tumor." These words, spoken to me matter of factly by an ER doctor, changed my life forever. I knew I would never find joy in life again.

My five-year-old son was dying. There was nothing that could be done to save him. The tumor in his brain was inoperable. A doctor looked me in the eye and said, "Your son will die."

I begged my surgeon husband to find some place, some hospital that could perform a miracle and save him. His silence night after night as he researched and read e-mail responses gave me the answer I dreaded. There was no hope.

Joey was a vibrant child. I knew that from the moment he was placed in my arms for the first time, his wide eyes already taking everything in. He was energetic and joyous and laughed often. He had a child's passion for life. He had three younger brothers who worshipped him as he was so good and kind to them. He was the thinker of ideas, the player of games, and the doer of good things.

But there were the headaches that would stop him short, intense pain and vomiting interrupting his five-year-old play. Never in a million years would I have imagined that a beast was taking over in his brain.

After his diagnosis, he was still curious and happy, but different.

His razor-sharp memory was gone — the tumor had stolen it. His interest in new games and toys waned — the radiation treatments took care of that. His slim, energetic body that could run and jump and leap was replaced by a bloated, sore, uncomfortable shell — the steroids saw to that.

For fourteen months I watched as my sweet little boy became unrecognizable to me. Day by day, he faded away and there wasn't anything I could do about it. I wanted to cling to what was left of him; but that meant neglecting the rest of my family. They needed me too.

I had to let go of him in pieces — his energy, his infectious laugh, his wonderful ideas. We took him out of kindergarten and eventually stopped the chemotherapy. Soon, he was merely a fragment of what he had been.

And during one summer night, I lay with him all night long and held him as his breathing slowed until it ceased altogether. My sweet little firstborn child was gone.

The rest of the summer found me falling asleep on the couch with the television on. I didn't want the silence and darkness to remind me of the pain and sadness of losing my son. When I did crawl into bed, I didn't want to leave it. I would sleep late, listening to my three other sons taking care of themselves downstairs.

Cancer had robbed them too. It had robbed them of their brother, friend, and idol. Joey was the fun-maker, and without him, I had no desire to do anything that would make me remotely happy. The long, lazy summer days of setting out on adventures with my sons were gone. Everywhere we went, everything we did, reminded me of Joey.

That fall, life was moving forward. The boys were back in school and, out of necessity, I had to keep busy. But I was still depressed, aching for my son, and not taking care of myself.

And then, I was pregnant again. But I didn't want another baby.

I had turned forty the month before Joey died. The month after he died, I gave away all of our baby things. Part of my depression and misery was accepting the fact that I would only have three children — not four like I had always wanted.

Because of my age, because of three previous miscarriages, because of Joey's cancer, because one of his brothers was born with a birth defect, I was terrified to have the baby. I was sure something would be wrong with it, and I knew I wasn't strong enough to handle that. All of my strength had been spent on the cancer.

I prayed for a miscarriage. I prayed to God that He would take the baby away and give it a better home. But ultrasound after ultrasound revealed a strong heartbeat, a perfect baby with no defects. Only, it was another boy, and I didn't want another boy. I didn't want a replacement son. I wanted the one I had lost.

I never looked at the ultrasounds. I didn't want to get attached to this baby. I didn't want to love someone that much again because I knew it would be too painful. But the day of his birth came, and he was perfect.

And he, like Joey, had his eyes open wide as he was placed in my waiting arms.

As he grew, I noticed so many similarities to his brother. "Look," I would say to my family. "Look at how he curls his toes around his toys like Joey did."

Or I would say, "Look at the baby. Look at how he is bouncing forward on his bottom. Joey used to do that."

In the dark and quiet of his room, as I was rocking and nursing him, I would look down at him and whisper, "Joey?" I was certain that my son had been sent back to me. I needed to believe that.

As time went on and Baby Evan grew older, he became happy and vibrant, curious and verbal—all traits Joey had as well. But I noticed him developing his own little personality too. He was becoming a little person apart from who I thought he should be. Bit by bit, I accepted that.

And over time I let go of the notion that he was supposed to be Joey sent back to me as some kind of Karmic compensation. I accepted the fact that he was simply a gift meant to heal me and teach me how to love again. He was meant to bring back the joy in our every day.

It has been almost four years since Joey died. Not a day goes by that I don't think about him and feel a sick sadness in the pit of my stomach. But now I look around me and I find joy in the memories we have of Joey. When my older boys hug and help Evan, I see what they learned from Joey. When they beg me to tell stories about when they were younger, they laugh the hardest at the parts about Joey. And Evan joins in the laughter too. Even though he will never know his oldest brother, he will hear the stories and see the pictures and make memories of his own.

Bit by bit, with the help of each other and our memories of Joey, we are all healing.

~Kathy Glow

26

The Gift

Even hundredfold grief is divisible by love.
~Terri Guillemets

My son was dead. Danny was alive one moment and then in one horribly cruel, unforgiving second, he was killed by a drunk driver. My life was changed forever.

My daughter Elizabeth, also in the wreck, was hospitalized with a fractured vertebra. She and I would spend a long time drifting in the void known as grief.

With Danny's funeral fresh on our souls, I brought my daughter home. Elizabeth was shattered mentally and physically. I struggled to console my daughter. She struggled with the pain of her loss and guilt of the survivor. She could no longer function and repeatedly skipped school. She couldn't sleep and barely ate. Her depression was too extreme for either of us to manage.

I found the best treatment center in our state for grief-based depression. I didn't want to lose Elizabeth too.

One evening on the way home from my weekly visit with Elizabeth I noticed four horses in a field. On impulse, I stopped at the farmhouse next to the field. An older couple came out of the house. As I stepped from the car I asked, "Do you have a horse for sale?"

The man said, "Well, we hadn't thought of selling any of them."

"Please, I really need to buy a horse."

The woman's face softened. She beckoned toward the house. "Won't you come in?"

I followed them inside. Most of our conversation is a blur. I remember telling them again that I needed to buy a horse... then suddenly I was telling them about the accident that killed my son and maimed my daughter. I remember crying and the woman, who introduced herself as Barb, told me she'd heard of the accident.

Then Barb told her husband Delbert to walk me out to the field. I prayed as we walked into the pasture. My daughter loved horses as I did. If Elizabeth and I shared the care for a horse, it could help the two of us heal together.

Delbert called, "Skipper!"

A gelding stuck his head around the corner of the barn but didn't move.

"Call Shadey," Barb suggested.

Delbert did and a mare came out of the barn. She trotted to us, the gelding following.

The moment I saw the mare I knew I wanted her. The gelding nuzzled my arm and I stroked his face. He was beautiful. When the mare started shoving her nose into my other arm I stroked her too.

"Will you sell me the mare?" I asked.

Delbert chuckled and shook his head. "Barb would never part with Shadey. She raised her from a foal. She's her child."

He glanced at his wife who was standing on the other side of the fence.

I stroked both horses as we stood talking. When I stopped touching the mare, she shoved her head against me. I was falling more in love with both horses. I knew I should save myself the trouble of hearing "no" again by leaving.

Barb turned and walked into the house. A few minutes later she returned and stood beside the pasture fence.

She said, "I'll sell you both horses."

Delbert's mouth dropped open as my heart skipped a beat. Delbert said, "I never thought she'd ever part with that mare!"

We walked to the house and I wrote a check for the amount Barb asked.

Elizabeth and I began the mending process living one day at a time, sometimes minute by minute. We took care of the horses together, feeding and grooming them and babied them through their first horseshoes and saddles. We healed as we shared the love and work that went into raising horses. The sadness that surrounded my daughter began to disappear.

I knew the pain of losing my son would never go away, but as I devoted time to caring for my daughter and encouraged her involvement with the horses I slowly learned to laugh again.

The time came for our mare to be bred. I located a breeder, called him and we made arrangements for Shadey to go to his ranch. She would stay a month.

I made many trips to Phil's ranch to visit Shadey. I wanted her to know we hadn't forgotten her. On my second visit I met Phil's mother. Thelma was a gentle woman, thoughtful and kind. She invited me in for coffee. I accepted, grateful to have another woman to talk to.

After she'd poured my coffee she asked, "Did you know that Barb, the woman who you bought Shadey from, was my sister?"

Surprised, I said, "No. How is she?"

Thelma lowered her eyes. For a moment she said nothing. Then her cool blue eyes stared into mine as she said, "She died."

"Oh Thelma, I'm so sorry."

She shook her head and reached over to touch my hand. "It's all right. It was unexpected but she went peacefully."

The older woman sighed. "I want to tell you something I think you should know. Barb knew she was dying. She didn't tell any of us, not even her husband, but her doctor told us that she'd known for months before she went."

I didn't know why Thelma was telling me this. It was such a private thing.

She took a deep breath. "Barb would never have parted with Shadey. That mare was like her child. But when we discovered she knew she was dying we also knew why she sold the mare to you. Delbert told us how you kept touching Shadey, the way you looked at her, and the way the mare stayed beside you. Shadey never went to other people. My sister saw something in you that told her she could trust you.

"She knew you would love Shadey as much as she did. She needed to be sure that Shadey would be cared for by someone who would love her. Knowing my sister as I did, I know she wanted to ease the pain of your loss with the only thing she could: the mare that was like her own child. Barb died six months after she sold Shadey to you."

I wiped tears from my cheek as Thelma touched my shoulder.

"I'm glad you have my sister's mare. I've seen you with her and I know what Barb saw when she decided to sell her to you. She saw love and kindness and gentleness."

When I left Thelma's house that day, I left with a gentle peace in my heart for the woman who, through her unselfish love and compassion, had given me the greatest gift—the trust to give me that which she loved, a gift that started the healing my daughter and I had needed.

~Jo Davis

27

The First Birthday

The manner of giving is worth more than the gift.
~Pierre Corneille

M y courageous and selfless mother, at age seventy-nine, died from breast cancer. Her name was Betty. She asked for one thing only—that she make it to her eightieth birthday. She believed that if she made it to eighty, she could consider her life long and well lived. We focused on that birthday.

When Mom lay dying in July, she was still eight months away from her March birthday. The staff in hospice had kindly offered to throw her a party, but I declined. She was so sick, how could I invite people? And, if I am honest, I didn't think I could bear anything else on my shoulders, especially planning a party, even a small one. Selfish perhaps, but I just couldn't do it. The week my mother entered hospice, we also moved my father to the nearby VA hospital due to his Alzheimer's disease. My heart was breaking. Then mom died. It was like losing both my parents at the same time.

I somehow managed through the holidays. But Mom's upcoming eightieth birthday was weighing on me. The first birthday after Mom's death. What should I do for it? How should it be acknowledged? How would I make this a celebration when my heart was still so sad?

I thought about what my mother would have liked for her birthday. She loved being with her children, grandchildren and great-grandchildren and, in the last few years, not having to cook. That was a start. I would host a dinner with my family and grandchildren at our home. We would sing "Happy Birthday" and have a birthday cake decorated with sugary frosting and bright-colored roses, the colors of spring. She always felt that her birthday announced the arrival of spring, even if it was snowing.

Something was still missing, however, and I couldn't place it. I didn't want the occasion to be gloomy. No, Mom wouldn't have liked that. I didn't know what to do.

That is, until the day before her birthday dinner.

That morning I hung a quilted wall hanging in the dining room that Mom had sewn. My mother called it "The Birthday Quilt." It was white with multi-colored Sunbonnet Sues and exploding fireworks. Perfect.

Next, I realized you couldn't have a birthday celebration without presents. But I couldn't give my mother a birthday present. How would that work? Then it came to me.

Before Mom passed away and Dad went into the nursing home, she had instructed me to distribute all their belongings to family members who wanted items and then donate or sell the rest. That wish was carried out for the most part, but I still had jewelry and several boxes of items that hadn't been distributed for any number of reasons.

Hanging on to those items solved my First Birthday dilemma.

I spent the afternoon going through boxes. I thought about which family members would be at the birthday dinner. They included my husband, son and daughter-in-law, daughter and son-in-law, and four grandchildren—ages eighteen months to six years old, three girls and one boy (the oldest). I went through those boxes with an eye toward any item that might fit as a gift from my mother to that dinner guest. I shed many tears but they were tears of love and remembrance. I also used some of Mom's stationery to write each person a note about the item, how or why my mother had it, and why I connected it to that family member. Then I wrapped the "gifts" in colorful birthday wrap and tied them with fancy curling ribbons. I attached the cards. After singing "Happy Birthday," and after the great-grandchildren blew out the candles, I said, "You can't have a birthday without presents!"

My son looked at his sister and said, "I didn't bring a present, did you?" She had not. It made me chuckle to see their concern. But I said, "No. These are presents from your grandmother."

My daughter received a white gold necklace with an aquamarine stone (my mother's birthstone). I told my daughter it was because the stone reminded me of her eyes, which her grandmother had always loved.

My daughter-in-law received a necklace of silver charms from a designer my mother liked a lot. The style was well suited for my daughter-in-law.

My son received a set of pilsner glasses, as he likes beer. I told him in his note that his grandmother was very fond of having a cold beer on a really hot day and that when he used those glasses he should think of her.

My ice-cream-loving son-in-law received my mother's ice cream scoop. I wrote to him that my mother and father were known to occasionally eat ice cream instead of dinner.

I explained to my grandson that it was hard to find something for a boy in his great-grandma's things but I hoped he liked what I found. He snuggled right up to me. I told him that I didn't know why Grandma Betty had the little toy deer in her belongings, but I thought it should go to him because he was interested in hunting. He also received a masculine-looking sterling silver ring. I told him how it had been created, and that it was made from silver that could be found in the earth. He's a very curious boy and likes to know all about things. He kept it on his finger the rest of the evening.

My oldest granddaughter received a silver bracelet made of connecting porpoises from a trip Grandma Betty had taken to the ocean. Because this little granddaughter had enjoyed her own visit to the ocean, I knew she would like this bracelet.

To the next granddaughter, I gave a blue star sapphire pendant. I told her it was one of Grandma Betty's favorite stones and that if it was held up to the light just right, she could see a white star on it.

The youngest granddaughter received my mother's silver baby

cup from the early 1930s. It had been lovingly used and had the dents to prove it.

In every note I told the recipients how much their grandmother or great-grandmother had loved them.

Even though it has been a while since that First Birthday, I have heard different things about the gifts. My granddaughter, now four years old, told me about the necklace she has with the white star on it from Grandma Betty. I heard my son is looking forward to summer parties when he is going to bring out the pilsner glasses, and my son-in-law used the ice cream scoop the night after the party.

But I think the best comment I have heard was the day after the party when my daughter said, "Mom, it was just right."

If you are struggling with how to get through that First Birthday consider having a party with gifts from your loved one. You might find that "it's just right."

~Betsy Alderman Lewis

28

Joy Conquers Fear

We cannot banish dangers, but we can banish fears.
We must not demean life by standing in awe of death.
~David Sarnoff

t has been a little more than ten years now since the automobile accident that claimed my younger daughter's life. She was vibrant, intelligent, involved and beautiful. She met each morning with a smile on her face. I never even had to wake her on a school morning.

There were none of those "dragging the teen out of the bed" scenarios with Amanda. She was organized, efficient, and dedicated. She had represented her high school at Girl's State, at the Governor's Ball, and in Washington, D.C. at various conferences. She had a beautiful voice. But the one thing people always mention about Amanda was her smile. She was always smiling.

A rain-slicked highway on a summer afternoon ended all of her promise, all of her potential, all of her talent, all of her smiles. She was only nineteen. My immediate reaction to the news of her death was one sentence: "My life is ruined." I cannot begin to recount the following minutes and hours. It is the singularly most painful time of my life, of our lives—my husband's, my older daughter's, and many of Amanda's loved ones.

Yet I remember, almost immediately, feeling another emotion nearly as strong as grief—guilt. I was a failure as a mother. I had failed to keep my daughter safe. While I was not driving the car or involved directly in Amanda's accident, the guilt overwhelmed me almost immediately. It was my job to keep the children safe.

I had been a stay-at-home mom most of the time when my girls were babies and toddlers. My husband went to work every day. It was his job to earn the money to pay the bills. It was my job to take care of the children. When I returned to full-time work, I worked at my daughters' school. I drove them to school. I was home with them in the afternoons. I supervised their activities and arranged their play dates.

I was the one who wouldn't allow either of my girls to cross the busy four-lane highway to hang out after school with their friends at a local hot dog stand/gas station. I wouldn't allow them to drink underage, even though many of their friends did. It was my job to protect them, and I had tried so hard. But I had failed.

The problem with guilt is the other emotions that accompany it. Along with the sheer grief of losing my precious daughter, I was also overcome by fear. It was like waiting for the other shoe to drop. What else would happen? I was afraid that my husband would have another heart attack, since he had experienced one just months before Amanda's accident. I was petrified something horrible was going to happen to my surviving daughter. My husband and I both stood at the door and sobbed when she left several days after the funeral and returned to her home in Myrtle Beach. It was such a long drive, and she was so grief-stricken. I was afraid to let her behind the wheel of a car; however, she had obligations. She needed to return to her home. But I was nearly overcome with fear.

I read countless books about grief. I understood completely the accounts of women who lost their children and went to bed for weeks. I envied them. I wanted to be in a numb state, even in a coma, where I wouldn't feel this pain.

Never has just opening my eyes in the morning been such an excruciating experience, because each day was another day without Amanda. Going to bed at night was just as painful. If I dreamed about her accident and her death, I would wake up sobbing. If I dreamed that she was still alive and we were happy, I would wake up sobbing. I dreaded sleep; it was not a solace or a time of rest.

I remember telling a friend that I would never feel truly happy again, because all of my joys would be overshadowed by the thought, "If only Amanda were here to see this." It also seemed to me that, as her mother, I would be doing her memory a disservice if I went a day without mourning her. What would people think if I were laughing and joking? Would they think I had forgotten about her? For the first four years after her death, I visited her grave nearly every single day.

But I was reminded by more than one friend that Amanda's life had been filled with joy. What type of memorial to her would it be for me, her mother, to carry this shroud of grief and pain around for the rest of my life? Her memory would be better served by my seeking joy and happiness than by wrapping myself in a cocoon of fear and anger.

So, today I choose joy. I seek beauty in nature. A beautiful sunset brings a sense of peace. The changing colors of the autumn leaves are a source of wonder. The ocean waves and their ebbs and flow connect me to the rhythms of the Maker himself. I have joined the choir again, something I had given up for many years. Music has always been a special passion of mine.

I find joy in the smiles and laughter that my little grandson brings to my world. I will not allow the fear I once had to control me. I still feel a need to protect him, but I will not permit my fear to smother or cripple him. And I am looking forward to another grandchild, a little girl, joining our family soon. I plan to snuggle, hug, rock, sing to and love her, just as I have her brother.

I am embracing joy. I will always mourn the loss of Amanda. There will be moments that hit me out of the blue, a stray song or random picture that will bring me to my knees in tears. But I will rise. And I will allow joy into my heart and into my life, for joy conquers fear.

~Kim Seeley

Paper Cards

Faith is the vision of the heart; it sees God in the dark as well as in the day.
~Author Unknown

A few years ago, I went to the grocery store to find a card for my dad's birthday. Sure, there were funny ones. Serious ones. Cards from the cat. Cards from the dog. But none of them was right. Shaking my head, I dropped them back in the rack. Even if I did find a good one, what would it say? Dad, I hope the cancer goes away and we have another year to celebrate?

They don't make that card.

Beside me, a teenage girl grabbed her card and smiled, carefree. I fought back tears. I wanted to know why the doctors wouldn't run more tests or why they wouldn't try chemo. And how did they know the brain tumor was inoperable? The teenager bounced down the aisle, leaving me to choose alone.

Part of me knew I would lose my dad one day, but I never expected it to come so early. Not when he was only fifty-three years old. He was supposed to live to see my husband and me have children, to see our new house morph into an old one, and to walk my sister down the aisle.

I left the store empty handed.

A few weeks later, Dad was moved to the hospice. There were moments when he would awaken and let loose one of his infamous corny lines as the nurse came in. Other times, he couldn't keep his eyes open. But always, his arm was chained to the IV, a constant drip to control the pain, a constant drip to give me a few more moments with the dad I loved so much. As I sat by his bed one day, holding his hand, I realized I had no control over the outcome, no way to fix what was broken, no matter how much I wanted to. I prayed, but God didn't answer me.

At least not in the way I thought he would.

Dad died that year, two and half months after his birthday.

A week after his funeral, I had to go back to work with the pain still fresh in my heart. I was a seventh grade history teacher. On the inside, I didn't want to be at school talking about cattle drives or the Texas Revolution, pretending to smile and be happy when I still felt disconnected and alone, hopeless at times.

When I reached my classroom, I pulled out my keys and found the door was already unlocked. I opened it, feeling strangely uncertain. Inside, a Welcome Back banner spanned the whiteboard. Stacks of brightly colored construction paper cards covered my desk. Two of the culprits were still inside.

"Mrs. Harp," Gina said with a smile. "We missed you."

Lizzie stood by my desk. "We're so sorry about your dad." She held out a paper card signed by several students, each name with a little note expressing sympathy. For a moment, I knew warmth again.

Every class period, more students hugged me and told me they were praying for me and my family. I was touched by their young hearts full of compassion. I read every one of their handwritten cards, notes and poems. By the end of the day, my fingers were stained with blue and red marker, but that didn't matter.

They cared.

They were there for me.

Searching for Dad's last card had seemed so important at the time—a gesture of love and an expression of how I felt. But as I held those construction-paper cards, some folded crooked with bent corners, others with a simple sorry scrawled across the inside, I realized it didn't matter what the card said or that I never found one. It was simply being with my dad during his last days, holding his hand, telling him I loved him.

God did answer my prayers that day.

He surrounded me with friends of all ages to hold me up. He gave me an amazing family to encourage me and walk beside me. And He gave me a husband who held my hand through all of the worst moments, when I wanted to give up.

That year, I lost Dad, but something inside me changed—my faith grew.

Before, I thought faith meant everything would somehow turn out okay if you believed. Now I know faith means believing even when you are a wreck. Faith means leaning on Him in those dark times, when everything is out of your control.

Even when bad things happen.

~Rachelle Harp

Until Death Do Us Part

Serenity is not freedom from the storm, but peace amid the storm.
~Author Unknown

"Al and I, Al and I, Al and I," kept repeating in my head. I didn't know who I was without him. This was not how it was supposed to be. He had turned thirty-nine the week before. I had teased him about the big four-oh coming up. I was already thinking about the party we would have.

Our sons, David and Gerad needed him. They were only nine and six years old. I needed him.

"Until death do us part." Now what? When I said those words at our wedding fourteen years ago, I assumed we would grow old together. Then suddenly, I was a single mother, a sole provider, and a widow.

I was at work when I got the call. They had taken Al to the hospital from his job. When I arrived at the hospital Al was awake and talking. I was worried when the doctor said they needed to get him into the trauma unit right away, but I never imagined that it would be the last time I saw him alive. He had been hospitalized with a blood clot the year before. They knew what the problem was—fix it and he would be fine. But then the doctor sat beside me in the waiting room and said, "We are going to try everything we can, but I don't know if he is going to make it."

I couldn't believe what I was hearing. It wasn't long before the doctor returned. I knew before he said anything. We later learned that Al had a hereditary blood clotting disorder.

Had it not been for the boys, I might have curled up in a corner and stayed there indefinitely. Instead, I was at the arena the day after the funeral to watch David play hockey. Life had to go on even though I was dying inside.

It was one day at a time. Sometimes that was too overwhelming. I had to convince myself that I could get through the next five minutes, or through a meeting, or through just one hockey game.

I realized the boys would need physical, concrete connections. We made a memory box for each of them with things of their dad's, pictures they made and things they wrote. We painted rocks and placed them at the cemetery. We ate lemon cake on Al's birthday.

There was a moment when I realized I could live the rest of my life with bitterness and resentment or I could cherish the memories and make the best of my life. I made the choice each morning to make it through the day the best I could.

I started a gratitude journal. Each night I wrote five things that I was grateful for that day. Some days it was a challenge to think of five things, but it got easier. It helped me focus on the positives.

The boys attended a group called Expressive Arts for Grieving Children. An art therapist and music therapist worked with groups of children dealing with similar losses. I knew it was important for them to know other children were going through the same things as them. Yet when a counselor suggested a bereavement group to me, I said, "I will try it." But what I was thinking was, "A group is not for me. I will go, but I am not going to talk. I will be able to say I tried it, but I won't go back."

Apparently, misery does love company. I was comforted to know others were dealing with similar loss and grief. I was surprised at how much I shared at the first session. When I shared how angry my son was and that he "hated me and wished I had died instead of his dad because then everything would be fine," I was sure the counselor was deaf or had lost her mind.

She said, "Isn't that great!"

It sure didn't feel great. But when she explained how unusual it was that a child would be able to express that so early in the process of grieving and to the surviving parent, it started to make sense. I started to believe that maybe we were going to be all right, maybe we would make it through this and maybe I was doing something right.

That was definitely a turning point for my son and me. I was able to let him know that he could say whatever he wanted, but I was going to keep on loving him. I explained to him, "It feels like we have fallen into a dark hole. Now we need to climb out. We may slip, but we need to keep climbing. We will get to the light again. Sometimes you may need me to pull you up and sometimes you might give me the boost I need. Together we will keep climbing."

Together we kept climbing. We slipped and we pulled each other up. Sometimes I glimpsed the light and sometimes I only saw dark, but I kept climbing closer to the light.

A few years later, when my son's counselor talked to me about sitting with him every night until he fell asleep, I explained that he needed that. But when the counselor looked at me and asked, "Does he?" I knew that I was the one who had come to need it. What had started as support and security for my son had become my security and comfort. It was then that I promised myself I would not hold my boys back because of my needs. This was a tough but important lesson to learn.

For several years, I dreaded Christmas. I went through the motions with a smile on my face, determined to make it special for the boys. Then one year as I was shopping I realized I was singing along to the Christmas music and smiled, without effort.

I am fifty-three years old. Three years ago, I took a risk and made a career change, then moved to a new city. I am pursuing my passions of writing and photography. I am content. My boys are successful young adults. David is pursuing his passion as a chef; Gerad is finishing school and next summer will marry his best friend. They are constant reminders of the man Al was and of the great love we shared.

It has been seventeen years since Al passed away. For me the only thing worse than living through this loss would have been never having Al in my life. I am grateful for what was and hopeful for the future. Since Al's death, there have been many blessings and many challenges in my life. I am grateful for both. Through the challenges, as the emotions come in waves and threaten to knock me off my feet, I know without a doubt that not only will I survive, I will thrive.

~Rose Couse

Bonus Check

If we shall take the good we find, asking no questions,
we shall have heaping measures.
~Ralph Waldo Emerson

can't feel my fingers or toes!" I said, hurrying to the safety of Rusty, the old white minivan my family had lovingly nicknamed. The night was chilly, with freezing rain. My son's soccer game had just finished. I longed to warm up with a hot cup of tea at home. Quickly, my sister Cheryl and I rounded up my three children, three of their friends, the dog, blankets, chairs, and soccer balls. We had barely left the parking lot when I heard: "I'm starving Mom. What's for dinner?"

"Who wants spaghetti?" I yelled over my shoulder while navigating through traffic.

"I do!" came the shouts in unison. I glanced sideways at my sister in the passenger seat to see she was smiling with two thumbs up.

Once home, I jumped into action, putting the teapot and pot of water for spaghetti on the stove to boil. We often had spaghetti dinners, so I could mindlessly do the whole routine for a quick meal. While setting the table I stopped to count aloud to my sister as I figured how many plates we needed: "Five plates for our family, three for friends, two for extra friends that stopped by unexpectedly, plus one for you."

My sister interrupted my counting: "No. You will need four plates for your family."

"What?"

"There are four of you now in your family."

I held my sister's gaze for a few seconds as the noise and commotion around me vanished into a dark swirling whirl that made me suddenly feel dizzy. Her words spoken gently hit me like a brick.

"Yes. There are four of us," I whispered back, as tears fell.

It had been almost two weeks since my husband Ben lost his battle with a liver disease. It was still so surreal that he was gone. Sweet memories flashed of him playfully impersonating the *I Love Lucy* show when he walked in the front door after work: "Lucy, I'm home!"

"Ricky, is that you?" I would yell back with a smile. This would be the signal for our children when they were younger, and they'd squeal, "Daddy!" and race to him for hugs.

Although I realized my sister's words were necessary, I did not want to hear or face them. My pain was still an open wound. I had just lost my best friend, and my world had been torn apart.

In the months that followed I kept my family together the best I could, and kept our household running smoothly to make it feel as normal as possible. My children continued in the same sports they had before their dad died. The consistency of their daily routines helped them stay stable, and gave them something to think about besides the sadness they felt. It was important for them to see that life would continue in a positive way.

It was interesting how each of my three children grieved and reacted so differently on the morning they heard their father died. Thankfully, pastors from our church, youth group leaders, and friends gathered in our family room early on a Sunday morning for support when we told them their daddy was gone. The waves of sadness were unbearable to feel and see.

My younger son Jordan, twelve, sought comfort from friends. A steady stream of friends came in and out of our house all day. It was heartwarming to hear and see them playing guitar, singing, crying with Jordan, and sitting quietly together.

My older son Benjamin, thirteen, was scheduled to play in a soccer game that afternoon. I thought for sure he would not go or feel like playing, but he wanted to play a game for his dad. It was important to him. So he left with a family friend who took him to his soccer game.

My daughter Amanda, who had just turned sixteen, snuggled next to me on the couch with a blanket and did not leave my side all day. We held each other as waves of sadness would come and go for both of us. We sought comfort from each other, as neither of us knew what to do or feel. The hours of that day ran together into the next days, weeks, and months.

Keeping my family together, paying bills, driving to sports practices, and working left me exhausted. I survived the days by going through our routine. By the time I went to bed at night I was beyond tired, but still greeted by the huge pile of clean laundry dumped on my bed. Pushing the laundry to one side I would often fall on my bed and cry myself to sleep. "How could this be happening?" I would cry out to God. "Lord, please bring Ben back. I can't do this alone."

One night felt particularly hectic after working, grocery shopping, taking kids to and from soccer, football, baseball, cheerleading practice, dinner and a band concert, and more dirty laundry waiting for me. I desperately needed something to give me hope and encouragement. I once again pushed the mound of laundry to the side of my bed and crawled under the covers exhausted, but too sad to sleep. Lying in the dark, tears streamed down my cheeks as I desperately tried to put what was happening to my family in perspective. "Dear Lord," I prayed, reaching for help. "Please give me something to get me through this difficult time. I cannot keep up this pace and I've lost my strength."

Then I had an epiphany. I contemplated what was important for me to accomplish at that moment and came up with the following:

Do you have clean dishes?

Yes I do.

Do you have clean underwear?

Yes I do.

Then everything else is a bonus!

So simple, yet so powerful to release my guilt! I needed to celebrate my successes and not focus on what I had not accomplished.

Several years have passed since that day and I have shared my fun expression with many who needed encouragement to renew their strength. It still makes me smile when I feel overwhelmed by a long to-do list. Then the quiet gentle voice reminds me:

Do you have clean dishes?

Check.

Do you have clean underwear?

Check.

Then everything else is a bonus!

~Patricia Ann Gallegos

Chapter 4

Find Your Inner Strength

Moving Past Disabilities

32

Pushing for Love

I think dogs are the most amazing creatures; they give unconditional love.
For me they are the role model for being alive.
~Gilda Radner

Here is a secret that everyone knows: I don't like to ask for help. Of course, my cerebral palsy means that I need assistance getting dressed and have to be driven everywhere, but that is precisely my point. Since I require so much physical help in my life, I don't like to ask for anything beyond that. I am fiercely independent about the things that I feel I should take care of on my own.

One night a few years ago, after my caregiver helped me to bed, I was enjoying my favorite part of my routine, snuggling with my yellow Lab service dog, Marshall. When I first got him, I knew that he could be trained to pick up things off the floor when I dropped them and to pull me in my wheelchair. What I didn't know was that he would grab hold of my heart and not let go. When the rest of the world made me feel "less than," Marshall made me feel like "enough." As he drenched my face in doggie slobber that night, the sadness of the day melted away. As usual, he jumped off the bed after a few minutes, but his surprised yelp and the pain in his eyes told me something was dreadfully wrong.

A few days later a trip to our vet confirmed my worst fears. "He has a torn ACL in one of his hind legs." Dr. Tom said. "It can only be fixed surgically."

My heart plummeted.

"Is he in pain?" I held my breath. I knew Dr. Tom would be honest, but I had to brace myself for the answer.

"Yes."

The room started spinning as I absorbed the news. My stomach lurched. I vaguely remember talking about details and Dr. Tom's soothing voice trying to soften the blow. I had one huge question: "How much would the surgery cost?"

"About $2500."

It might as well have been a million. I couldn't swing it. Social Security disability payments were my livelihood. I usually didn't have extra money to go to a movie, let alone pay for an expensive operation. The specialty vet clinic where Marshall would have the surgery did not accept payment plans.

I was beside myself with fear. Would Marshall be in this pain forever? Would I fail him this way? How could I deal with that?

Stronger than the sadness that threatened to overpower me, however, was my need to help Marshall get well. Each day I searched for a way to provide this surgery and each night I repeated a prayer for peace and answers. Most often, I fell into a fitful sleep. I couldn't let Marshall down. It was time to start thinking outside the box.

A beautiful nature and bike trail ran close to the apartment complex where we lived. On most of the days of our eight years together, Marshall and I used it. I loved the trees, the fresh air and being outside. Marshall loved to sniff and romp in the grass on the trail's edge. We both loved the peaceful solitude. Over the years, many of the "regulars" recognized us. Everyone loved Marshall.

Then one day it dawned on me. Could I ask these people to contribute to the cost of his surgery? The thought of asking outright made my skin crawl at first, but what about organizing a fundraiser? If I could push my wheelchair a certain number of laps and get pledges for every one that I completed, might I raise enough money for Marshall to have his surgery?

Our regular route was a mile and a half long. My goal was to push my wheelchair ten laps, a total of fifteen miles. Next, feeling very bold and a little desperate, I set a date. Then I made fundraising flyers and sent them to everyone that I could think of. I posted them around my apartment complex and all over the bike trail. My neighbors were concerned for Marshall and the pledges started coming in.

With renewed hope, I started to train. My dog had given me more than I could imagine. I had to do the same for him.

But I wasn't sure I could do it. This was ten times my normal distance. At first, I got winded after a couple of miles. The ache in my back and shoulders eased the pain in my heart. My love for Marshall kept me going. Instead of listening to my body, I focused on the voice in my head. One more lap. You can do this. Don't stop. Keep going. Marshall needs you. Keeping that voice louder than the pain became as important as the exercise.

Four miles. Okay. Breathe. Up and down the incline of the parking lot driveway to work on strength and endurance. Seven miles. My body won't make it. Keep at it. Did I set the goal too high? Marshall is in pain. Keep pushing forward. Arms back. Push. Again. Nine miles. You can do this. How much do you love Marshall? Twelve miles...

After six weeks of daily training, I still didn't know if I could pull it off. But I was determined to give it my all, the way that Marshall always gave to me. Watching him suffer so much was killing me. On the designated day, I started without ceremony at 6:30 a.m. The first few laps were long and lonely. Success seemed doubtful. But slowly the donors and neighbors came to watch. Some even cheered as I passed them. With every mile, more people came. There was hope after all.

Donations came from people in my apartment complex, even from a few of the maintenance men. A little girl gave me three pennies from her piggy bank so that I could "fix the doggie." And because of an article in the college newspaper, I even received a collective donation from the admissions office.

A neighbor in our apartment complex was about to go to boot camp. He made a donation and then brought me several huge bottles of Gatorade. After lap six, he gave a second donation, saying he didn't need money where he was going. He thought that Marshall needed surgery more.

The kindness from these people kept me going lap after lap. I could never have made it without their support. After twelve and a half hours, I finished all fifteen miles. By the end, the miracle had happened. Marshall's marathon had raised enough money not only to get Marshall's surgery but also to pay his vet bills for the rest of his life.

Weeks later, we were back on the bike trail, enjoying Marshall's recovery, saying hello and thanking many of the people who had helped make it possible.

I still don't like to ask for help, but amazing things happen when love makes you push.

~Lorraine Cannistra

33

A New Smile

Sometimes your joy is the source of your smile,
but sometimes your smile can be the source of your joy.
~Thich Nhất Hạnh

I t was a miracle I had survived the past eight months. I had finally made it to my third trimester after a pregnancy fraught with complications. It felt like I spent more time with my doctor than my husband, and I had an entire baby book filled with sonograms chronicling every few days of my tiny boy's development in utero. For the first time in months I could breathe; we were going to be okay. Needless to say, I was not expecting to wake up the next morning and have my life forever altered.

I woke up feeling off. While putting on lipstick I noticed that I couldn't quite press my lips together. I called to my husband and asked him if anything looked strange about my face. He paused a moment and, being the smart husband that he is, responded that I looked beautiful as always.

Within hours it was obvious that all was not well—half my face was paralyzed. I couldn't blink, smile or move the right side of my face. My hearing was off, the world was spinning, and there was a searing pain behind my ear. The pain was so intense it left me unable to function, and I ended up in the hospital.

After a quick diagnosis of Bell's palsy, the OB/GYN, neurologist, pediatrician and various nurses each made a point of telling me to "give it a few weeks" and everything would be back to normal. So I waited, and waited, and waited some more until it became quite obvious that I was not recovering and this was my "new normal."

Searching for answers, my husband and I visited a neurologist from a world-renowned teaching hospital. The doctor very quickly concluded that I had been misdiagnosed and actually had a very rare condition called Ramsay Hunt Syndrome. Although it didn't change the outcome, it did help me understand the symptoms, as well as the fact that I was one of the unlucky ones who would not likely recover. The right side of my face would be permanently paralyzed and I would never be able to blink my eye or smile again. I was stunned that I was going to have to spend the rest of my life looking like this. It was hard to believe I was only thirty-two years old—I felt like I had aged decades in a mere eight months.

I would like to say I just took a deep breath, accepted my situation and moved on with my life. But few things in life are really that simple. For a while I just ignored reality. I chose to look in the mirror as little as possible. I stopped making eye contact with people. I looked down when I was walking. The vertigo and sensory issues made large crowds almost impossible, so the physical issues from my illness made limiting social interaction easy.

I felt very alone. No one I knew had ever experienced facial paralysis. People told me they really didn't even notice, but I always saw the cringe a split second before they masked it with a smile and pretended everything was fine. Bless those sweet children who, in their honesty, often asked, "Lady, what is wrong with your face?"

Over time I grew tired—tired of having to tape my eye shut at night because I couldn't blink; tired of my face aching all the time; tired of headaches; tired of not being able to drink out of a water bottle because my mouth couldn't close around it; tired of people pretending nothing was different about me; tired of not being able to smile and express happiness; and tired of being limited.

Months passed, and I realized that the inability to express joy and happiness had sunk deep. It had passed from my outward expression to my soul. I had lost my smile. Not just the smile on the outside, but my smile on the inside. It is amazing how losing this one thing affected every part of who I was, and I grieved deeply for it.

There was no great sign from heaven, no life-altering moment when I realized I couldn't continue on like this. Little by little, it was a growing sense that I had to make a change. I did not like who I had become and how this illness had begun to define me. In my pain and exhaustion, I had allowed it to take over my life.

I started by doing small things I used to enjoy. I read a book, took a walk, and got a pedicure. I began talking to people again, attending functions, and going on dates with my husband. I decided to find simple ways to help others instead of always being the one who needed help. As I made these small changes, I noticed I felt better.

As I began to move forward with my life, I learned I was an ideal candidate for what is known as "smile surgery." This intricate micro-surgery took a muscle from my thigh and connected it in my cheek to give me the ability to smile again. In the hands of an incredible surgeon, I decided I was ready to have my smile back. The surgery took over eight hours, and several months to fully recover. Finally, three months after the surgery, I saw something truly amazing—for the first time in nearly three years I could smile!

While recovering, I realized I was searching for deeper meaning to this whole experience. How could I use what I had been through to help others, so I could feel some sense of good came from this? At first, it was just showing empathy in a new way. I had a perspective on pain that few have experienced. As I became more open about what I had gone through, I realized I had experience with misdiagnosis. My story was able to encourage others to seek second opinions and find answers. Most of all I could offer hope for those suffering with facial paralysis. So few know of the amazing options available to them.

It has taken years and the help of many wonderful, talented people to be where I am at today. Some days, it is still a struggle to not let this illness defeat me. It is difficult to find the energy to be me and stay positive, but I am grateful every day that I can smile. My old smile came effortlessly; my new smile has been achieved through tremendous pain and effort. Each time I smile I am reminded that I have something to give.

~Katie Bangert

34

Three Pounds Five Ounces

Being a mother is learning about strengths you didn't know you had,
and dealing with fears you didn't know existed.
~Linda Wooten

Thirty years ago, I found myself on board a Flight For Life plane as it rose into the evening sky. In a Denver hospital, 500 miles from home, my daughter was delivered by C-section. The doctor cradled her in his hands and brought her to me. I looked at the tiny new soul, covered with silken body hair, still in the fetal position. I cried with relief that she was alive.

"Hello little one," I said. "I'm your mother; your name is Meghann."

Two months premature, in critical condition, Meg was transferred to Children's Hospital Neonatal ICU. My blood pressure was out of control and though it was imperative during delivery that I stay awake, sedation was now necessary to save my life. I said a silent prayer: "Please let me live, to hold Meg in my arms."

As the medication took effect, and the noises of the operating room began to fade, the last thing I heard was the nurse telling the doctor, "Weight: three pound five ounces."

Five days later I visited Meg. She lay in an open incubator, naked, her body swollen and discolored. A tube had been taped to her face, forcing oxygen into her immature lungs. The smallest of needles were inserted into her transparent skin, on her head, arms and feet.

I gasped for breath and said, "Oh my God." Then I fainted.

The next day, I held Meg's hand, which was the size of my thumbnail. I couldn't hold her close to my heart so she'd remember the sound of a familiar beat, instead I kissed her and spoke her name. "Meg. Mama loves you." Meg opened her eyes at the sound of my voice.

While in NICU, Meg had a brain hemorrhage and corrective surgery to close a heart valve. Against the odds, she came home after three months, weighing five pounds.

In her baby book, I faithfully wrote down her first milestones with anticipation of the next. Then I grew fearful when they were not on schedule.

As Meg turned five months old, I enrolled her in a preemie program to observe her development. After several months I became concerned when she couldn't sit up or hold a rattle. I was advised that her slow progress was more than likely due to being premature. One day after a physical therapy session, Meg's therapist gave me a book to read and told me I should talk to the pediatrician. My heart raced as I finished the first chapter. A week later, meeting with the doctor, I handed him the book. "Why didn't you tell me something was seriously wrong with Meg?"

He looked at me and said, "You've been through so much already, I wanted you to bond with her."

I stared back at him in disbelief. "My God, did you think I would have loved her less?"

He touched my hand and said, "Not at all. I'll make the necessary assessments."

After evaluations at the children's hospital in Denver, Meg was diagnosed with cerebral palsy, at eighteen months.

I was the mother of a child with a disability. I felt alone and angry. What had I done wrong? Why did this happen? I mourned the loss of my dream child and then I faced the reality of my life ahead. I sought out other parents with children who had special needs. Together we forged friendships, and became advocates to improve the quality of life for our children.

In Meg's baby book, I continued to record her milestones each year. Along with her first smile and laugh, I kept a record of her first leg braces, wheelchair and communication device. Next to her list of baby shots, I wrote down her double hip surgery and spinal fusion.

Since Meg's wheelchair had its limitations, we made creative alternatives to do fun things at home and in school. A car seat was made into a backpack for hiking. A little red wagon was built with railings to race down the street in the summer. In the winter, our dog Lilly pulled her in a sled. Meg rode horses with a harness and roller-skated on her belly in the school gym. She painted with an adaptive easel and played the tambourine in the school band. At both her junior and senior proms, Meg danced in her power wheelchair with her classmates.

I not only became Meg's voice for inclusion and independence, but also her advocate.

Now thirty, Meg makes her home with me. She's an incredible young lady, her smile is constant, her laughter contagious. She is patient, forgiving, and loves unconditionally.

I shine in her shadow.

~Debbie McNaughton

35

Seeing the Real Me

Nothing splendid has ever been achieved except by those who dared believe that something inside of them was superior to circumstance.

~Bruce Barton

During the first part of my life, I was a victim of circumstance. I was born, one of three blind or legally blind children, to a blind mother and to an angry, alcoholic father. I became a shy, withdrawn, and frightened young girl who pretended to be invisible as the stress of my home life became unbearable. My father was abusive and although my mother was loving and kind, she was not strong enough to protect her young children from this angry alcoholic who held us prisoner.

To escape this fearful environment, I would run away to my grandparents' home where I would stay for the warmth and safety. When we attended church, I recall a man standing in the pulpit, yelling, screaming, and banging his fists. This frightened me even more and I withdrew further. I learned that God was a strong, punishing God and we had better be good, or else.

My grandparents loved me very much and became overprotective. I allowed them to do everything for me—they tied my shoes, dressed me—and I became dependent on them. Fearful to tell anyone of the anger and physical abuse at the hands of my father, I became non-verbal. When I went to school I was diagnosed as "uneducatably retarded" and sent to a mental facility. I felt like a true misfit.

Luckily, I had a kind and loving caregiver who saw something special in me. One day while she brushed my hair, I started talking to her. She soon realized my brain was not the problem, but my limited vision. She fought and successfully lobbied on my behalf to have me placed in a special classroom for the visually impaired called the "sight-saving class." I started to feel more comfortable, and with time, fit into the program. I realized that I could read the letters if they were big and black. I liked learning, and liked the positive attention I received when I did good work.

I began to let go of some of my fears. I struggled socially, but learned to reject fear and to challenge myself. At first when I was bullied and teased I ran away because that's what I had always done. Then, with some encouragement, I began to reject the bullying and teasing. I faced the bullies with determination and courage, and did not run away. Finally, they stopped teasing me and left me alone.

Then they came to tell me that I would be going to a regular high school in the fall! What? Were they crazy? Me, attend a regular high school with "normal students"? All of the old fears returned and I became a shy, frightened, and withdrawn child again. But with support and encouragement, I did attend high school that fall.

The first year was horrible. I was teased and bullied about my limited vision. I felt ugly. The pushing, bumping into me, and the name-calling all became too much and I ran away.

A special uncle invited me to visit and stay with him on the family farm. There, I found a whole new freedom. I could fall down and get back up, all by myself. Isn't this what life is all about? I had the freedom to play and laugh. I hid in the hayloft and began to discover the true me. Also, I had the love and encouragement to try everything. Among other things, I found a whole new Lynn emerging.

As I learned to get around the farm using my other senses, I grew more independent. I was opening up and blossoming into a beautiful young woman. I started to believe in myself. In high school, I worked hard at my studies and other students wanted to be my friend. I finally felt normal and accepted as part of the group. At first I thought I had to be a people-pleaser for others to like me. But that was not true. Eventually, I started making good friendships, dating, and found that people liked me for me!

When I graduated from high school, I went on to York University in Toronto, Ontario and participated in the social work program. I worked part-time at Sunnybrook Hospital as an admittance clerk, moved out of the dorm, and shared an apartment with my cousin Diane. One day we went shopping together. I bravely started to look at a few racks of clothes by myself. As I ran my hands over a few blouses I turned and wanted to go on to the next rack of clothes. All of a sudden someone walked right in front of me. I excused myself and moved to the left. Again the person stepped right in front of me. Giggling a bit, I excused myself again and moved to the right. Again the person moved right in front of me. Someone teasing me. As I raised my hand to give the person a little push to get out of the way, I realized I was arguing with a reflection of myself in a full-length mirror. How embarrassing! My cousin Diane was laughing hysterically! Instead of running away and hiding, I also laughed and learned it is okay to do dumb things and laugh about them. Humour is a wonderful part of life.

Eventually I got married and became a wife, mother, grandmother, and a very successful businesswoman in my community. And, like a beautiful butterfly, I emerged as the bold, sassy and independent woman that I am today. I am an entrepreneur with my own business, and I am a professional speaker, author, teacher, and mentor/coach. I believe my mission is to share my story and learning experiences so that other people can overcome their fears and obstacles to achieve their dreams and goals. Life is worth living and you need to take charge of your own destiny. Dreams do come true!

I did not allow my circumstances to stop me. I did not allow my disability to block me. Nor, did I allow fear to prevent me from succeeding and becoming the person I am today. Neither should you! "Don't allow anyone or anything to keep you down."

~Lynn Fitzsimmons

36

The Artist Within

All art requires courage.
~Anne Tucker

n April of 2013, I was ready to give art up forever. My lifelong blinding disease, retinitis pigmentosa, had struck again. It
had already robbed me of my social work position, my driver's
license, and most of my sight, leaving me legally blind with
vision of 20/400. Now it was taking my ability to create art too. I
could no longer see details well enough to do my celebrity portraits
with a Sharpie.

"I can't tell who that is," my family and friends would say of my
sketches. "Who is that?"

It was time to call it quits. I'd enjoyed my sketching while it lasted.
There was no such thing as a legally blind portraitist. I drew from reference photos, and they had to match up, or at least be recognizable.

"Oh well," I remarked on Facebook. "It was good while it lasted."
In an almost cynical way I added, "Now I'm trying to find a way of
painting that doesn't involve vision. I guess that would mean painting
with my fingers."

I didn't really mean it. I had heard of blind sculptors. But blind
artists who worked in visual art? Out of the question.

But a Facebook friend named Sonja took the idea to heart: "Let
your inspiration and your inner self guide you when you paint with
your fingers, Tammy. Intuitive painting is the purest kind of painting
there is."

I got up from my computer and walked around my living room, thinking. Could I finger paint?

I had had four years of high school art, and two or three more years of college art, plus all of those years of drawing. Impossible. I wasn't a painter; I was a sketcher. I had only one painting — "Yellow Flower" — and I'd used a brush.

But Sonja's words grew in my heart like tiny mustard seeds, until they compelled me to grab my white cane and walk down the street to a school supply store, where I bought a few bottles of acrylic and a pad of art paper.

This was new territory. My heart quickened with both hope and dread as I hurried back home. What if I couldn't do it? What if this really was the end of art for me? What if people laughed?

But what if I COULD do it? What if Sonja was right and I just needed to give this new method a try.

Once I got the paint home and set it all out in the kitchen, I realized I didn't have an easel, so I used my kitchen counter. I didn't care. I would have used the floor.

Then once I had the paint poured into little colored circles on a paper plate, I stood there and realized I had no idea what to paint.

I'd always used a reference photo before to draw my celebrity portraits.

Now I couldn't see photos well enough to use them. I couldn't see the details of a flower well enough to copy it. I lived a block away from the beautiful Ohio River and couldn't see it well enough to do a landscape of it.

Creating art from my own imagination — something original — was entirely new and different for me. What would I paint?

A little frustrated, I wondered why I had even bothered. And then I thought about what Sonja had said, what she really meant, and realized that I could not rely on sight, because it wasn't good enough. I had to rely on intuition, imagination, and memory.

I had to let go of my old way of thinking about art and my old way of doing art — which was vision-based.

My new way had to be intuitive, or it couldn't be done.

It took me about an hour of just standing there re-wiring my thoughts to this new way of thinking. And then only a few minutes to decide what I would paint from my imagination—all the memories of the rural scenery I'd grown up with in Kentucky. Barns, hills, shacks, trees, creeks, houses, farms, flowers—nature all around me that I could barely see with my eyes now, but was brilliantly vivid in my mind's eye.

I felt tears well up and a lump come to my throat as I patted my fingertips into my paint circles and touched them to my first piece of art paper.

I didn't know how it would turn out. I felt like a child standing there with paint on my fingers. But I pushed myself to do it, swirling my fingers to make the mental images I felt rather than saw.

Once finished, I couldn't really see how my first finger painting turned out. I'd have to show it to someone to find out how good or bad it was.

The next day I invited one of my best friends over for lunch. She was an artist too, and after she looked at my first finger paintings said, "I'm not sure. Keep trying."

Another mustard seed.

After she left, I walked around my apartment again with a growing hope and realization: I could do art again, just in a different way.

It wouldn't be perfect, it wouldn't be a copy of a photo, and it wouldn't be a celebrity. It would be me.

I could do this.

My new style of art has opened up opportunities. A few of my paintings have been included in local art exhibits, and I've sold a few.

But more important than the personal satisfaction of becoming a professional artist are the opportunities to help others. I taught finger painting to a group of children in a community outreach program called Camp Discovery, and I was invited by local art teachers to discuss ways to teach art to blind or visually impaired students.

Not only am I showing the world that the blind and visually impaired can create art, I am showing myself.

~Tammy Ruggles

37

Losses, Laments, and Laffy Taffy

The only disability in life is a bad attitude.
~Scott Hamilton

 week before Christmas, I received a package from an old college friend. "Can I open it?" my daughter, Leah, asked.

"Go ahead," I said, sliding a tray of cookies into the oven.

She tore open the bubble mailer and tipped the contents — a handful of candies and a small wrapped packet — onto the kitchen table. She looked confused. "Why'd she send you Laffy Taffy?"

I chuckled. "I'd forgotten about that! We used to eat it while we studied. There are jokes printed on the wrappers." The plump, square, fruit-flavored candies had sold for ten cents apiece in the college store. Banana had been my favorite.

Leah ate a piece, reading the jokes aloud as she chewed. Her sister Chloe ate one too.

"Aren't you going to have one?" Chloe asked.

"I want to, but it would be murder on my fillings." I grimaced. "I'd rather not have to visit the dentist this close to Christmas."

So the girls devoured the rest of the taffy as I read the note taped to the packet: "Just a little something from me that smells good. Love,

Lisa." Inside were two car air fresheners infused with essential oils. Sandalwood and lavender.

"Ohhhh, they smell so good," the girls gushed. "Can you smell them?"

Although they were a mere inch from my nose, I couldn't. In fact, I hadn't been able to smell for ten years. Suddenly, I began to laugh. Here I'd received two thoughtful gifts, and I couldn't properly enjoy either of them!

My friend wasn't at fault. Last time we'd talked face to face, both my teeth and my sense of smell had been intact. Since then, however, I'd developed an autoimmune condition called Sjögren's syndrome that affected my body's moisture-producing glands. A damaged sniffer and frequent dental visits were among the side effects of the disease.

These losses had been hard to accept. Even though I meticulously cared for my teeth, I faced having to replace all of them, all at once, with crowns—an expensive and painful procedure. Not being able to smell meant I couldn't taste certain flavors, enjoy formerly favorite fragrances, or detect when I'd left something in the oven for too long. That's why, even though I'd initially laughed at the irony of the gifts I'd received, a few hours later I felt depressed.

Look at what I had lost! It was so unfair. Why did I have to get this stupid disease?

My mind was halfway down that familiar road of sorrow when another, unexpected thought brought me up short: Was thinking this way going to lead to my happiness?

Over the previous year, I'd spent a lot of time working on my negative thought patterns. As I sat there, I remembered the advice of my therapist: "The instant you hear a negative thought in your head, turn it around!"

Okay, I decided, rather grumpily. What could I say about my situation that was positive?

Well... I couldn't smell good smells, but I couldn't smell bad ones either, such as garbage, mold, or dirty diapers. That was positive.

Another positive: If I had to lose one of my senses, I was glad it was my sense of smell instead of hearing or sight. Those would be a lot harder to live without.

And another: I might need a mouthful of crowns, but at least we had the money to pay for them. It had required refinancing the house, but still, the money was there, and my husband hadn't complained one bit.

Once started, I kept going, remembering all the blessings that existed in spite of—and sometimes because of—my struggles: My faith had grown. I had a better sense of humor. I'd learned about natural health. And strangely, but wonderfully, I was becoming more positive!

The truth is, back in the days when I consumed Laffy Taffy by the handful, I'd been a fairly negative person. The imperfections of life often got me down, and when bad things happened, I fell apart. Back then, I enjoyed lovely teeth and a working sense of smell, but I lacked one very important thing: the knowledge that dwelling on what I had lost, or on what I didn't have, or on what I didn't like about my life wouldn't help me. It was okay to grieve for those things, but I had to let them go if I were to be happy.

And I wanted to be happy.

So that day, after turning my mental car around, I made a note to write a thank you to my friend, tossed the air fresheners in the Goodwill pile and gathered up the empty taffy wrappers.

But before throwing them away, I sat down to read the wrappers and enjoy one last joke.

~Sara Matson

38

Chicken Soup
for the Soul

Friends in the Mirrors

Life is like a mirror; we get the best results when we smile at it.
~Author Unknown

"Leo, there's someone in the house." Dad got out of his padded lawn chair on the screened-in back porch to go check the house. Feeding the birds, rabbits, and squirrels was put on hold again.

He returned a few minutes later having found no one, but it was worth it to put Mom at ease.

When my mother was diagnosed with dementia, while my siblings saw it as a nightmare they could not deal with, I saw caring for Mom as an opportunity. It was a chance to find humor, which we did often, but most of all, I found a depth of love for Mom and learned a lot. There were challenges, but the difference between giving up on her and cherishing time with her hinged on allowing her to just be who she was.

Mom's belief that there were people in the house could have been the paranoia that can come with dementia, or it could have been Mom no longer recognizing herself in the mirror. Mom sometimes did not recognize herself. I helped her learn to talk to "those people" in the mirror and become friends with them. Soon, every time Mom saw a mirror she made a new friend.

In physical therapy, there was a mirror that patients used for visual feedback on the exercises. When Mom saw the mirror, she stopped and had a conversation. She smiled and laughed as she talked to her new friend.

Every time she went to physical therapy, she stopped to visit with her friend.

"Hi. It's good to see you again."

Short pause as she waited for a response.

"That's funny," Mom would reply to her friend.

Tim, the physical therapist, would encourage Mom to move on.

"I need to go. Come see me sometime."

Mom had many friends in mirrors. At home, her friend in the hall mirror was named Mary. Mary was her confidant. When Mom was upset or frustrated she often talked to Mary, and then she felt better. I encouraged her to talk to Mary when she was upset. It always seemed to help. Mary was a good listener.

Then there was Tom. Tom was in the mirror in Mom's bedroom. Tom was nice, but more of a casual conversation. Although one day when we were going to run errands Mom said Tom wanted to go, so the mirror had a place on the back seat of the car safely strapped in the seatbelt. Tom could be a good friend to have around, but he had a side that was a bit ornery.

One day I was in the living room, and I heard Mom in her room. She was very angry with Tom. When I went to investigate, she said, "Look at what he did," pointing to a bowl of chocolate marshmallow ice cream sitting on the floor. "I gave him that ice cream, and he threw it on the floor."

I didn't dare laugh, knowing how angry she was at Tom. Instead I picked up the bowl of ice cream, handed it to Mom and said, "Why don't you go ahead and eat it? Tom doesn't need any if he is just going to drop it on the floor."

We retreated to the living room, leaving Tom alone to think about his behavior.

Mirrors also helped to relieve anxiety. Mom could be in an anxious fit, see a new friend in a mirror, and everything would change.

During a lengthy wait in a doctor's examining room, Mom was becoming restless and fidgety. I simply placed a chair near the door and sat in it. There was no reason to do anything other than let her have the freedom to walk around and fidget.

All of a sudden she saw someone in the corner. Her eyes lit up. She went to the mirror and leaned towards her new friend. "Come on," she said, motioning with her hand towards the door. "Let's you and I get out of here."

Although Mom no longer recognized herself in the mirror, mirrors were important to keep her company. They were wonderful friends—as long as they did not throw ice cream on the floor.

Watching the progression of dementia was not easy, but it was not without opportunities to laugh and enjoy. I had to abandon my expectations of what she "should" be—of what she was in the past—and instead love and appreciate who she had become.

Since Mom's death, my memories of caring for her are even more special. I gained so much from my time with her during her last four and a half years of life on earth.

It didn't matter if Mom put her shirt on over her nightgown and wore them to the grocery store. It didn't matter if she ate oatmeal with her hands when she had difficulty using utensils.

Stuff did not matter.

Mom and her friends in the mirrors did.

~Carol Luttjohann

Cheerful Change

Cheerfulness is what greases the axles of the world.
Don't go through life creaking.
~H.W. Byles

While participating in my church's Hearts of Love nursing home outreach, I spent precious time with a wheelchair-bound woman named Louise. From the moment I saw her, I couldn't help but notice her cheerful countenance. It was inviting, friendly, and captivating. When she spotted my bright blue outreach shirt, she wheeled herself toward my side and introduced herself. "Hi, my name is Louise. Why are you all here? Is something special taking place that I'm unaware of?"

"It's so nice to meet you, Louise. My name is Barbara," I replied. "Our outreach group will be visiting here on a weekly basis. We look forward to spending time with you and the rest of the residents." Since she was unable to go outdoors on her own, I suggested, "Louise, would you like me to take you outside for some fresh air before lunch?"

"I would love that. Anytime someone can take me outdoors, I'm all for it," she said, clinging to my hand.

We found a lovely, cool spot under a shaded tree. As we chatted, Louise shared all she had gone through the past few years. I was caught off guard by what she endured in such a short time span. "A few years ago I lost my husband of fifty-four years. After his passing, I became ill, fell down, and lost the use of my legs. Not being able to live independently, I sold my home and car in order to move into here."

"That's a lot for one person to go through in such a short time period," I said. "I admire how well you have adjusted."

"Yes, it was a big transition. Especially when I lost the ability to walk. You see, I was a vibrant, daily walker. I faithfully walked two miles in the morning and two miles in the evening. I loved the life that I lived, but in the course of a few years, that all changed. What got me through it was my faith in God and encouragement from my family and friends," she explained.

Louise glanced at her watch. "It's getting close to lunch hour. Could you please bring me back inside so I can have lunch and then get ready for work?"

"Work! What type of work?" I asked, amazed, once again, by this ninety-one-year-old woman.

As I wheeled her back to her floor, she explained. "I knew I had to keep busy. It wouldn't be good for me to stay in my room all day long. I'd become too depressed thinking about all the different things I had lost. As soon as I settled in, I asked if I could do some volunteer work for the facility. While waiting for their reply, every night I prayed, asking God to grant me a position. Sure enough, a few days later, they gave me a position. I welcome and direct all the visitors entering the facility. I love it! It's the highlight of my day."

As months passed, Louise and I bonded. We spent hours outside the facility getting to know each other. On some occasions, when Louise was too ill to go out or the weather was rainy, we spent time in her room instead. Then one day, this amazing woman caught me off guard again. "Barbara, my granddaughter is getting married next month," she told me. "I so much would love to attend the wedding, but it's out of state. I'm not strong enough to fly and I don't want to be a burden on my family during the wedding. However, my family and the facility have arranged for me to watch the wedding 'live' in my room by webcam. Would you like to come and watch it with me?"

"It's such an honor to be invited," I said. "I would love to watch your granddaughter's wedding with you. It will be as though we are right there with them."

When the big day arrived, I stopped at the grocery store to pick up a small cake, paper plates, and plastic forks. I wanted Louise not only to watch her granddaughter's wedding live, but also to enjoy the celebration by having cake afterwards. Without a doubt, it was a splendid afternoon as I watched Louise's eyes tear up while witnessing her granddaughter walk down the aisle. The "icing on the cake" occurred when Louise's family came over to the webcam, one by one, to express their love to her. Yes, she could not attend the actual wedding, but with a flexible spirit, she still participated in it.

Although Louise lost much, the one thing that didn't change was her lovely, cheerful demeanor. I believe that her positive attitude paved the way for her to accept the changes life threw her way. In return, it allowed her to still smile and stand strong from the inside out, regardless of her inability to walk, cook, clean, shop, drive, travel, etc.—life's daily pleasures that many take for granted or perhaps even grumble about.

Here I thought I was going to serve and minister to those in need, but in fact Louise ministered to me. She taught me a valuable lesson. Life is full of transition and unforeseeable changes—some good, some bad, some inevitable, and some heartbreaking. However, with faith, family, friends, and a good attitude, we can make it through the various challenges of life.

As my one-year commitment to the Hearts of Love outreach neared its end, I faced a positive, yet challenging change that put me to a test. Having to let go of what I enjoyed doing, reaching out to the aging population, in order to become a women's small group leader was a tough decision. I had the choice to handle the change with an unsupportive attitude or an adaptable, positive one. Choosing the latter, as Louise often did, proved to be the healthiest choice in embracing the change taking place in my life and letting go of the familiar.

~Barbara Alpert

Insight Without Sight

The best way to predict your future is to create it.
~Author unknown

At fifteen, I couldn't wait to get my first job. Then I'd have extra cash to go out with my friends. The occasional Saturday night babysitting job wasn't reliable. To me, a regular paycheck seemed like a step toward adulthood. My enthusiasm didn't waver, but the routine act of going for working papers almost crushed my spirit. My parents had dropped me off at the clinic where applicants took their physicals for working papers. Although I also longed for a learner's permit, night blindness prevented me from driving. Since my vision was clearer during the day, I easily walked inside by myself. I wanted this adventure to be mine, and mine alone.

For a brief moment, I felt grown-up. Then the doctor began the examination.

He looked into my eyes with a bright light. "There appears to be something wrong with your retinas. I suggest your parents take you to an eye specialist," he said.

Suddenly, I wished they were there with me holding my hand. He paused for a long moment. He cleared his throat before continuing in an ominous tone. "I suspect you have a retinal disease. If you do, you'll never work a day in your life."

I swallowed hard. I blinked as tears pricked my eyes. The doctor had an unusually tough bedside manner, even for the 1960s. Doctors take an oath "to do no harm." Yet, they must know that words can cut like a knife. Where was the door? I hated this mean man and his cruel verdict for my future—a future that was just budding. I wondered whether to believe the man wearing the white coat with the MD after his name. It was a glimpse at how the public, even a doctor, regarded people with disabilities. Couldn't a blind person work and have a productive life?

For a week, I barricaded myself in my room. My parents may have viewed this as moody behavior in a normal teenager's life. I wanted to confide in them. Yet, I couldn't give voice to such a scary thought. Besides, I was determined to prove the doctor wrong.

My parents did take me to specialists. Several eye doctors peered into my eyes, with conflicting diagnoses. Some of them thought my vision would never get worse. All the doctors predicted that my vision would never improve. Many years later, after much time and money spent seeking an accurate diagnosis, it was determined that I had retinitis pigmentosa, a disease that slowly robs a person of sight.

Night blindness made me afraid. Sunsets were beautiful, but they signaled a switch being turned off in my vision. Still, during daylight, I could walk without assistance. I could read, but not for hours. My eyes began to tear and words slipped off the page when I read more than a few pages.

As the years passed, these symptoms were more troublesome and frequent. Unfortunately, during my school years, audiobooks were not available to legally blind students like me. Mom offered to read to me so my homework would not suffer. Books remained a huge part of my life. No matter how tired my eyes became, I never gave up reading. I knew the names of writers as well as I knew the most popular music stars. Their words were a powerful tool. I wanted to imitate them. Writing brought me some emotional release each time I wrote about my own feelings.

Over the years, I did find employment. Salad girl at a cafeteria was my first job. Though it was entry-level, I learned the important skill of looking customers in the eye. My self-esteem soared as they praised my friendly manner to my boss. Next, during college, I sold sandwiches at a campus café. After getting my degree, I was hired by an insurance agency. The job brought a regular paycheck but no satisfaction. My sight, though, continued to deteriorate. As I descended into the permanent fog of blindness, the idea of a professional job never left my thoughts.

My mid-life crisis differed from my sighted friends. I trained with a guide dog, got a talking computer and learned Braille. And I continued to write. Then, an important phone call from an editor changed my life. An article I penned appeared in a local newspaper. The newspaper, to my delight, continued to print my work. Next, a book series published several of my essays. The writing bug bit me, and I lit up with each acceptance. On the page, readers never knew of my blindness unless I chose to reveal it. For me, finding my voice through freelance writing gave me the pride and satisfaction I sought so many years ago. Now, I have numerous essays and articles in print. The highlight of my writing career is a children's book. It features my beloved guide dog and our adventures together.

Should I be thanking that misguided doctor? By falsely predicting that I could never do productive work, he fueled my motivation to succeed. He set the bar too low and focused on what I wouldn't be able to do. Instead, I proved what I can do.

~Carol Fleischman

Chapter
5

Find Your Inner Strength

Accepting the New Normal

A Lifelong Challenge

It takes courage to grow up and become who you really are.
~E.E. Cummings

t took nearly thirty years for me to accept that I'd spent most of my life operating under a delusion. As a first grader, I told my classmates my biological parents were coming to take me away from an unhappy home. Down the road when that dream never materialized, I turned to men to erase my misery. A church upbringing took the back seat as I threw myself at everyone I could. Some men were much older. And married. Many had dubious backgrounds. Nothing mattered. I only wanted to escape and knew someone else must lead the way. When I finally reached a tipping point, feeling I'd suffered too many disappointments, I had a severe nervous breakdown, which led to a diagnosis of bipolar disorder.

Years later I related my story to a friend, Irene. She had driven out to our condo in Carpinteria, California for lunch. She responded to my story in her signature New Jersey accent: "I had bipolar disorder once, but I got over it. When I knew something was broke, I fixed it."

As I listened to her, I felt dismayed. Despite the fact I always took my medication, I still exhibited symptoms that prevented me from holding jobs or forming meaningful relationships. My moods resembled a teeter-totter on steroids. Every so often I would hit bottom with a thud. Getting up and dusting myself off was never easy. Try as I might, I couldn't overcome my illness. I often worked hard just to get out of bed in the mornings. And, as always, I tried to keep the fantasy alive that someday—somehow—somebody was coming to put an end to my unhappiness.

I shared my friend's words with my husband. Gary suggested, "Maybe she didn't actually have bipolar disorder. You know how she exaggerates."

"I don't know why anyone would want to pretend to be bipolar."

"Maybe she felt she was being helpful."

"Well, she wasn't. After all these years, my mind is still like a stagecoach pulled by runaway horses."

Mood swings were the main problem. I wore my moodiness like a cloak that I could take on or off in an instant, changing my moods without warning.

When I was diagnosed, my life was in shambles. I had no money, no job and no emotional support from my family. I had always worked in the legal field, but never stayed at a job for long. Concentrating proved difficult as the voices inside my head constantly vied for my attention.

Thank goodness my husband loves me despite my illness. We moved to California, wanting some adventure in our lives. Living in a small beach town provided a lifestyle we greatly enjoyed, but my mood swings still didn't disappear. I had a meltdown at the law office where I worked and walked out. Gary was supportive, yet I could tell he wasn't happy.

He did go with me to a new doctor, though. I finally found a professional who seemed empathetic. In our third session, he said kindly, "After hearing your story, I think you could benefit from not working. Just until you get your life in order. I've prescribed some newer drugs that should be more helpful than those you've taken in the past." He looked at me intently as he continued. "It also sounds like you need to find out who you are apart from being bipolar. Your bipolar disorder is just a small part of you. But you've let the illness take over your life, denying those wonderfully creative parts of you that make you unique."

"It's funny you should mention creativity," I said. "I had writing talent years ago, but after my diagnosis, my voice was drowned out by all the other voices. I lost my ability to put pen to paper, and now I'm one frustrated writer."

"Creativity comes packaged many ways. Perhaps you will write again. In the meantime, stay open to any opportunity for growth. By the way, my patients call me Dr. Looney." The psychiatrist smiled. "You're welcome to call me Dr. Looney, too."

Taking Dr. Looney's advice, I stopped looking for work. Initially, I feared searching for the real me. What if there was nothing there to find? I'd lived with bipolar symptoms for so long that my teeter-totter behavior seemed normal. But, with time on my hands, I dabbled in scrapbooking and card making, discovering I had an eye for color and design. Seeing a finished product helped me realize I could accomplish something. I befriended other women with the same interests and enjoyed the camaraderie. Their praise and support made me feel like a member of the human race.

I also spearheaded the creation of a neighborhood newsletter, which gave me skills that paved the way to writing short articles. I even went beyond my comfort zone and taught a self-esteem class for young girls. My own self-esteem had been in tatters for years, but while encouraging those precious preteens, my own self worth was unveiled. I had talents to offer the world after all.

Eventually, my husband and I moved to Oregon. A new doctor prescribed an even better antipsychotic that helped me focus. And once it got into my system, words started raining down in torrents. If I had ideas, I quickly wrote them in a journal so I could later spin them into inspirational stories. Some of those stories have been published. But all of them make me a bona fide writer, a longstanding dream come true.

One day when Gary and I went walking, he asked unexpectedly, "Do you think you've overcome mental illness?"

I couldn't formulate an answer right away. Finally, I said, "I don't think I'll ever overcome mental illness. But look at all the hurdles I've cleared so I can be the person God wants me to be! It's not important to be an overcomer anymore. Instead, I'm living with this disease one day at a time. Staying in the present moment is the healthiest thing I can do. And it's the best way I know to explore more ways to enjoy life."

I remember hearing as a child in Sunday school that Jesus Christ directed His disciples, "Be of good cheer, I have overcome the world." I figure if He's already overcome the world, then there's no need trying to overcome bipolar disorder. He's done it! I may never get over it the way Irene said she did, but there's no reason for this disability to wreak so much havoc. With proper medication and people supporting me, I'm up for any challenge. And I don't entertain delusions anymore. As far as I'm concerned, the knight in shining armor already came. Ever since Gary whisked me away to the West Coast, things just keep getting better.

~Jill Davis

42

It's All in Your Head

To conquer fear is the beginning of wisdom.
~Bertrand Russell

I was sleeping soundly when, for no reason whatsoever, my eyes snapped open and I jumped out of bed. Something was wrong. My heart raced and my hands shook. My legs felt like jelly as I stumbled toward the hamper to grab my jeans, because I was obviously headed to the hospital. I was gasping for air and my mind was a roller coaster of scary thoughts:

I'm losing my mind.

I'm going to be sick.

I am sick.

It was two in the morning, and I was alone in my apartment. My boyfriend lived just down the road, but he hated cell phones and refused to carry one. My closest family members were twenty miles away, not close at all.

Should I call 911? And if I did, what would they do with someone who was obviously losing her mind? Take me to a hospital? To the psych ward? This thought only made me shake more.

Miserably hot, I rushed to the bathroom for a cool washcloth. I touched my face. My neck. My arms. It helped some, and I went to my tiny living room. I paced. I cried.

Needing company, I grabbed the remote. The television flickered to life, and I watched in a bewildered daze while Sam and Diane flirted with each other behind the bar on *Cheers*.

It helped.

By the time the credits rolled, my shaking had subsided. I was exhausted and still a little anxious, but the racing thoughts had stopped, so I felt brave enough to venture back to bed. Unfortunately, sleep didn't come easily. I was too afraid that whatever had just happened would happen again.

At the age of twenty-eight, I had experienced my first panic attack.

A few days later, I was grading papers while my sixth graders finished their assignment when I felt it. My heart raced, my hands shook, and my mind screamed at me to RUN. In that moment, my fear wasn't having a heart attack or dying. My greatest fear was losing my mind in front of my students.

Thus began a vicious cycle of sleepless nights, scary thoughts, and sometimes paralyzing anxiety that lasted nearly ten years. During that time, I was prescribed a sleeping pill that made me hallucinate and anti-anxiety drugs that made me a zombie. I didn't want to go anywhere because I was too afraid of having the mother of all panic attacks in a public place, especially in my classroom. Or at church. Or at the store. If it weren't for the fact that I had to work, I probably wouldn't have left the house at all.

The human brain is incredible. It can convince you that you're a bad person. A bad wife. A bad teacher. A bad friend. It can make you afraid to drive, fly, or simply walk out your door. Things you used to do without a second thought now seem too overwhelming to even imagine.

Anxiety may not be a disease, but it still eats at you until it affects your daily life. You feel guilty, depressed, and scared... all the time.

When I tried to explain my panic attacks, I heard things like:

"You have no problems. You have a great job and a fantastic husband. What do you have to worry about?"

"Suck it up and deal."

"Stop scaring yourself."

And my personal favorite: "It's all in your head."

I was always a good student, so if I was going to have this condition,

I wanted to be an expert. I started doing some research, and that led me to make some changes. I found a new doctor who understood that I hated taking anti-anxiety medication (it never really helped me anyway). Once she confirmed that I was physically fine, this actually gave me confidence. I could say to myself, "You are not dying. You are not having a heart attack."

And for the first time, I believed myself.

I also started seeing a therapist. When I told her my greatest fear was that I was going crazy, she simply looked at me and said, "Crazy people don't know they're crazy."

Oddly enough, those words were a comfort to me.

Through my research, I learned a lot about panic disorder and myself. I learned that, for me, the keys to controlling my anxiety are in my breathing. I have stopped anxious episodes from turning into full-blown panic attacks simply by slowing down my breathing and distracting myself with some kind of simple task that makes me focus on anything but me.

I have learned that anxiety can be hereditary, but it doesn't have to be.

I've learned that a panic attack won't kill me. I may have to excuse myself from a social situation to get some fresh air, but I won't die. If panic attacks were deadly, I would have died a long time ago.

I've learned not to feel guilty about having panic attacks. Anxiety is real, and it's frightening. Feeling guilty only feeds the negativity, and that is the opposite of helpful.

I've learned that, unless someone has actually experienced a panic attack, they cannot understand how it feels.

I've learned there is no cure. No magic pill that will make it go away forever. It is an ongoing process that requires you to take better care of yourself, mentally and physically. It encourages you to think positively, to pace yourself, and to breathe deeply. It requires you to be a little selfish. It teaches you that it's okay to say no.

Most importantly, I have learned that anxiety is, indeed, all in my head. It's the way I think and react. It's a message my brain sends to my body, telling me to take better care of myself. To get more sleep.

To eat better. To get more exercise. To relax. To say no when I already have enough on my plate.

Anxiety is my little reminder that it's okay to not be perfect at everything, and that sometimes, good enough is good enough.

~Sydney Logan

43

Still Good

Happiness is a function of accepting what is.
~Werner Erhard

How does a young man in his twenties keep moving towards his goals when he's going to have to do it in a wheelchair? How does a mother not fall into a canyon of depression—and stay there—when her son is fine one day and paralyzed the next? And how does a friend find the right words to comfort that mother, when really, no words will ever make things right again?

For years, Darice and I bragged about our boys. My friend had three, but Aaron was her youngest. Ian was my baby but also my only boy. Aaron and Ian headed off to college the same year; they both played sports with unbridled enthusiasm; they both majored in therapy (Aaron in physical therapy and Ian in music therapy); they both graduated college with honors. I figured we would continue to share and tally up our maternal joys—uninterrupted—until they were too numerous to count.

I was wrong. One spring morning, when Aaron's wife had already left for work, a young man broke into their home. When the intruder found Aaron still in bed, startled, he told Aaron to lie back in bed. My friend's son refused. He refused to just lie there and die. After wrestling over a gun, Aaron was shot several times. The most devastating bullet lodged next to his spine.

In the hours that followed, all I could do was pray and worry at home while Darice and her family sobbed and paced during the examinations and surgery. In the days—and then weeks—that followed, she didn't live; she existed. Taking turns sleeping in a chair next to Aaron's hospital bed, taking turns crying in the bathroom so no one shed tears in front of him, their lives revolved around X-rays and surgeries and catheters. Family flew in from California and surrounded them, but so did the police and nurses and doctors.

When something horrific happens, people who are not directly touched by the tragedy sometimes say, "I know how you feel." But I couldn't, because I didn't. I didn't have any idea how Darice felt because my son was still healthy and whole. I could imagine the hysteria, the anger, the sense of loss my best friend felt, but in reality, I didn't truly know what she was going through. However, a part of me was sure that if it had been my son, I would still be in a crumpled-up heap on the floor. Deep down, I wondered if I would still be screaming—for weeks—if it had been my boy.

Phone calls, texts and e-mails kept us close. Only family was allowed to visit, so Darice and I would meet in the hospital lobby for a few minutes. Offers to help were appreciated, but there was nothing anyone could do. I felt helpless as a friend.

When the young man who paralyzed Aaron turned himself into the police, we all breathed a sigh of relief. One hurdle was crossed. The security was loosened; now friends could visit. By that time, he had been moved from the hospital to a rehabilitation facility where he would learn how to live as a paraplegic. A circle of college friends would come, all of them joking and laughing, and no trace of tragedy was present. Aaron popped wheelies in his wheelchair and spun around the room like he had been doing it his whole life.

When the trial was over, I wanted to go to the prison and spit on the kid. He had taken so much from my friend. I wanted to shriek at him, to make sure he knew the ripple effect he had caused. My friend's son was paralyzed, which devastated an entire circle of people. A couple would no longer be able to have a family in the same easy way they had envisioned. The home they bought, renovated and decorated had to be sold—there were too many nightmares from that morning.

I asked Darice how she kept her rage under control, and what she said blew me away: "That young man's youth is gone. He's going to be imprisoned for a long time." She saw what that young boy had lost. And she also saw what her son had never lost.

Aaron is still the most charming man I have ever met. He can put anyone at ease with his affable chatter and his genuine smile. After wheeling across the stage when he graduated with his master's degree, he continues to move forward. While looking for a job, he volunteers helping other paraplegics. He still plays basketball—on a wheelchair team. He and his wife found a new home and worked on it for weeks, retrofitting the basement stairs so Aaron can do his own laundry. He worked right alongside their church friends, college friends and family as they put down new flooring and constructed a shower stall and set up the kitchen so Aaron could cook. Aaron sat on the floor and scooted around, painting and installing the trim.

Now when I ask about Darice's sons, when I ask about Aaron, a smile spreads across her face. The light in her eyes, the grin, the simple two words say it all: "He's good."

They're moving forward—on a different path, but forward nonetheless.

~Sioux Roslawski

Hope in Miracles

There are two ways to live: you can live as if nothing is a miracle;
you can live as if everything is a miracle.
~Albert Einstein

t was the last summer of my childhood—right before the stress of college applications and shopping for prom dresses. But after seventeen years of near perfect health, my expectations of entering adulthood were crushed by a crippling illness.

It began with headaches and a fever. Nobody thought anything more of it until one day when I opened a book and found that I could not read.

"What's wrong?" my mother inquired with concern.

"I don't know how to read," I mumbled through frustrated tears. I started to panic. I couldn't imagine a world without reading! And how was I going to graduate with honors if I could not read?

But the words looked foreign to me, as if written in a different alphabet.

"What do you mean that you can't read?" my mother asked, perplexed. Seeing that I was not joking or exaggerating, she telephoned my aunt, a family doctor. My aunt gave me a quick neurological evaluation over the phone.

"What is your full name?" my aunt questioned.

"Chelsey... ummm... I don't remember," I responded.

"Can you count to ten?"

"One... two... four... umm..."

After failing these basic questions, I passed the phone to my mom. My aunt instructed her to bring me immediately to the hospital.

En route to the hospital, the fog in my brain increased. My last memory is the car pulling over to the side of the road and paramedics transferring me to an ambulance.

That night, I slipped into a coma. For the next month, the ICU would be my home. The doctors were bewildered, as every test came back negative and my body continued to deteriorate. I was intubated since I could no longer breathe on my own. At one point, I was losing so much blood that I needed multiple transfusions. The doctors prepared my parents for the worst: I only had a ten percent chance of survival. Even if I did survive, they warned my parents that I would be a vegetable or live with severe neurological disabilities due to permanent brain damage.

My aunt had flown in during this time to help support my family. She pored over research articles in the hospital, searching for the answer that my doctors could not find. Finally, she found out about an extremely rare illness that seldom occurs in children: central nervous system vasculitis. This is a neurological disorder that happens when the immune system attacks and inflames the blood vessels in the brain and spinal cord. It presents itself in a variety of neurological symptoms. She pushed my doctors to do a brain biopsy to confirm my diagnosis. Finally knowing the name of my disease, they gave me the protocol of chemotherapy and steroids.

After thirty-two days in a coma, I finally woke up.

I opened my eyes to a world of unfamiliar faces and strange sensations. Why couldn't I move? Who were these people? Where was I? The next couple of weeks were a flurry of medical specialists, brain scans, and visitors who wondered if I would recognize them. Thankfully, the chemotherapy worked to control the vasculitis and my prognosis improved each day. Within a week, I could speak in full sentences. Later on, tears welled in my eyes when I found that I could independently read my get-well cards.

My road to remission literally began with my first step. My body had lost muscle memory and therefore had forgotten how to walk.

The physiotherapist visited me each day to help me sit up in bed and eventually learn how to stand. My feet felt like a pile of bricks as I tried to lift one in front of the other. But after two and a half months of living in the hospital, I proudly took my first baby steps outside the hospital to finally go home.

It's not easy being a teenager with a new illness. The steroids had made me gain forty pounds. I was partially bald from my brain biopsy. My voice box was strained because of some damage from the breathing tube.

If this was supposed to be a miraculous recovery, I didn't want it.

One day, a Tim McGraw song came on the radio about a man who changes his life after being diagnosed with an illness. A piece of the lyrics caught my ear: "And he said someday I hope you get the chance, to live like you were dyin'."

That one line in the song triggered the turnaround in my attitude. Instead of viewing my illness as unfortunate luck, I could choose to value it as an opportunity to live life in an extraordinary way. Too many people live life forgetting the value of love, hope and joy. My illness showed me the power of love from supportive family and friends. I have recognized the significance of hope, even when it was only a glimmer. I also found joy when I traded my anger and blame away.

I wish I could tell you that I was miraculously cured; but to be cured means that the illness will never return. I experienced six years in a wonderful state of remission. Unfortunately, three years ago, the illness came back with new devastating symptoms. My brain went into a state of constant subclinical seizures. The vasculitis also began attacking my visual cortex, forcing me to live through terrifying hallucinations. It was not until the doctors restarted the chemotherapy infusions and steroid doses that my immune system regained control. And once again, God had let me survive without permanent brain damage.

I discovered that my illness was not finished with me yet and I became disconsolate again. What was the point of plans and dreams when I could not predict my flare-ups? How could I look forward to the rest of my life when my immune system was a dormant volcano?

I did not feel like much of a miracle anymore.

But then I remembered that I have a choice in how to live. I will not let my life be defined by my diagnosis, but I can also let my diagnosis be part of my story of hope. I may not be able to control my symptoms, but I can control my spirit. The real enemy was not my disease; it was the fear that made me choose not to live.

Today, there is still no cure for CNS vasculitis. Some people with this diagnosis live with disabilities. I have been blessed to have no permanent damage. I still live each day with the possibility that my immune system might attack my brain again. But for every challenge I have overcome, I have gained strength and resilience to help me appreciate the little miracles in my life.

Every step I take reminds me that I can still walk. My ability to write this story means that I still can read and write. But sometimes the most important miracle is not the one that saves your life, but the miracle of choosing to live with hope every day.

~Chelsey-Ann Alissa Lawrence

Finding Life's High-Five Moments

Grasp your opportunities, no matter how poor your health;
nothing is worse for your health than boredom.
~Mignon McLaughlin, The Second Neurotic's Notebook

never thought it could happen to me — getting diagnosed with a disease or losing my job. People all around me were finding out they had cancer, diabetes or other chronic ailments. I felt blessed to be healthy. The nightly news was filled with stories of big company layoffs and a high unemployment rate. I slept soundly knowing my job was safe.

Then, amid winter's wrath, both happened to me. In January of 2010, I was diagnosed with multiple sclerosis. Three years later, as my MS symptoms worsened, my company reorganized and my position was eliminated.

My heart ached. I felt betrayed by my former company and by my boss for leading me to slaughter. How could they let me go when they knew I had MS and it would make it that much harder to find a new job?

Discouraged, depressed and confused, I spent my days on the couch crying and blowing my nose. My eyes were so swollen I had to hold ice packs on them. The couch was my raft drifting though the days waiting for a rescue boat, which came in the most unusual way.

About a week after I lost my job, my husband and I were sitting on the couch watching the news when they announced another snowstorm was headed our way. This one was going to dump half a foot of snow just in time for the morning commute.

"At least you don't have to drive an hour in the snow anymore," my husband said.

He was right. Before, I had to commute an hour on roads that weren't always well maintained, past farms and through small towns to get to the big city where I had worked.

My spirits lifted just a little as we high-fived, and a tradition was born. Any time I felt sad about my situation, I found a little blessing in my life to celebrate.

I was no longer on the committee I didn't like. High-five!

I didn't have to pay for parking. High-five!

No more ten-hour days. High-five!

This became a joke between us. Out of the blue, one of us would realize a small blessing about my situation, say it out loud, and high-five. After weeks of doing this, the tears dried up for good and I felt motivated.

My former company had set me up with a job coach. I got started right away on creating a new résumé, branding myself and applying for jobs. The job market was still discouraging. I got only one interview for about every ten jobs I applied for, but I kept my spirits up by focusing on the good things in my life.

I made lunch and dinner plans with former colleagues so we could stay in touch and network. High-five, because I lost my job but not my friends.

I got to make healthy homemade dinners. High-five, because I don't like eating out all the time.

No getting up at 5:30 a.m. High-five!

I used my time off to catch up on doctor and vet appointments. It was nice to be able to say, "Anytime will work," and be seen sooner. High-five!

I played around with new recipes that I had been too tired to attempt and found a few winners. High-five!

I got the broken washing machine fixed and replaced the broken printer. High-five!

Things that I would have put off doing until tomorrow, next week, next month or never started to get done. High-five!

Focusing this positive energy on my job search got me interviews and opened my eyes to new positions in industries I would not have previously considered. My world expanded as I saw the full scope of possibilities in front of me. I never would have left my last job willingly. Although I had thought a couple of times that I might like something better, or closer to home, fear of the unknown held me back. Best of all, the time off allowed my body to heal and my MS symptoms completely went away. For the first time since my diagnosis, I didn't feel the grip of a chronic disease anymore. For the first time, I felt free.

High-five!

~Valerie D. Benko

46

Beauty Worth Praising

I learned there is a blessing sent from God in every burden of sorrow.
~Sherrie A. Hundley

My husband played professional football in the NFL for eleven years. It was an industry that made it easy to be consumed with tanning, mani/pedis, gyms and spa treatments, just to mention a few. Glamorous girlfriends and wives consistently raised the standard of beauty.

Early in my husband's career we were involved in a freak kitchen accident resulting in third degree burns from the hot oil in a fondue pot. I sustained the greatest trauma, so the doctors life-flighted me to a burn unit. After a month-long stay, a few surgeries, and four skin grafts, I went home. Forty percent of the front of my body, including my face, was burned. The doctor prescribed compression garments for me to wear from my toes to upper abdomen for a full year.

My confidence was challenged by the new normal I faced. I grew up playing sports and always took care of my body, but this time I was not able to work off my scars in the gym. Make-up made me feel like a clown. Our tragedy stripped me of the beauty that made me feel accepted, normal, and worthy. I had to grieve my old looks to make way for a new confidence that was not dependent on my appearance.

Wearing my compression garments for a year had its challenges because we lived in hot, sunny Florida at the time. My new wardrobe consisted of long sleeves, pants, socks, closed-toe shoes, and a hat.

Not only did I have to forego fashionable clothing, but the sun I once loved became unbearable for my tender skin. I would sweat rather than expose my unattractive compression garments.

For many reasons, it was a trying, difficult time in my life. Getting out of bed was just plain hard. I had a sweet friend who would meet me at a nearby gym every day, and we would work out or take a boot camp class to stay in shape. When I woke up each morning, I immediately put on my running shoes. My actions told my brain, "I will follow through with what I know is good for me today." This simple act of putting on my shoes got me out of bed and on the right track.

My confidence was severely shaken but over time my faith helped me find the strength to develop a new confidence based on my inner beauty, not on my outward appearance. "I am a burn victim" became "I am a dearly loved child of God" (Colossians 3:12). When I became confused and leaned toward unbelief, God's word reminded me, "I have the mind of Christ" (1 Corinthians 2:16). I chose what to set my thoughts on and which thoughts I believed. When I felt alone, God whispered, "I am with you" (Joshua 1:5). When my physical reality screamed louder than God's eternity, the "God of all comfort" would break through my isolation and comfort me (2 Corinthians 1:3-4).

I cried out to God, and He answered. Joy filled one day, and discouragement the next. God continued to teach me, love me, and encourage me. My circumstances wanted to define me, but God gave me a new identity. My desires morphed into the desires of God's heart. My thoughts centered on Him rather than on myself. Instead of allowing my past to push fear into my mind, I chose to focus on what God had to say about me. God's word directed my thoughts and focused my mind.

As I focused my thoughts on God's truth and sought His hand in my every day, God created a new heart in me. My heart began to love deeper and trust more easily. My confidence was in Him alone, and He became my strength, allowing me to love others.

It took time for the compression garments to smooth out my scars, and it took time for me to learn how to capture my thoughts and replace them with God's truth, but it was worth it. A stubborn joy grew inside of me, proclaiming that God will use everything for His good. Charm is deceptive, and beauty is fleeting; but a woman who fears the Lord is to be praised (Proverbs 31:30).

I would not wish for anyone to be burned. But on this side of my healing, I am grateful for the spiritual muscle I developed because of my burns. My old confidence that had been based on my looks faded, replaced with my new confidence based on who I am and what I believe. My new reality brought new freedom because I chose daily to surrender it to God. It was a tough process not performed perfectly, but God used my baby steps of obedience to create a confident heart in me. My appearance in no way affected my husband's success on the football field. A trip to the Pro Bowl and Super Bowl rewarded my husband's hard work, but gaining inner strength remained our greatest reward.

~Kasey Hanson

47

The Crucial String

Courage doesn't always roar. Sometimes it's the little voice at the end of the day that says I'll try again tomorrow.
~Mary Anne Radmacher

y husband and I had grown increasingly uneasy about our second child, Mickey. Though a warm, engaging baby, he showed no interest in playing Peekaboo, How Big Is the Baby, or waving bye-bye. At monthly visits the pediatrician assured us all was well. But by eighteen months, Mickey had only three words, and that's why we finally found ourselves sitting in a cubicle at a major teaching hospital. A team of unsmiling experts spent two hours poking, prodding, and measuring our son, asking him to draw a straight line, stack cubes, put pegs in boards. I leaned forward to catch the doctor's words more fully, hoping to hear how adorable, how promising, my child was.

Instead, she said, "Don't expect higher education for your son."

It felt as if we were looking down an endless, dark tunnel. Our radiant little boy had just been diagnosed with an autism spectrum disorder. How could she make such a prediction about a child not yet two? There was no doubt, she said, that he was "special." A puzzling word. For if he was special, did that make our other, older son Jonathan ordinary?

Just as you go through predictable stages of grief and recovery when someone you love dies, so too, learning to scale back your expectations and dreams for your child is an equally painful process.

We began the endless rounds: speech therapy, occupational therapy, sensory integration therapy, physical therapy, vision therapy, auditory integration therapy, behavioral therapy, play therapy, dietary and biomedical interventions. At first my mood was only as good as the last therapy session had gone. I felt isolated as friends and relatives rushed to dismiss my fears. "Einstein didn't talk till he was four. Give him time and he'll snap out of it. Boys talk later. Don't compare your children."

In the next year and a half, Mickey learned to recognize letters and numbers, and he showed a keen interest in reading signs and license plates. I was waiting for a "Miracle Worker" moment, a breakthrough where he would suddenly begin speaking in paragraphs. Naively, I still assumed that with enough intervention he'd be fine by the time he reached kindergarten. One night at bedtime, he offered a first full sentence: "Mommy, snuggle me," and my eyes filled with tears.

Disability seeps into all the cracks, the corners, of one's life. It becomes the emotional center of the family. Sometimes I felt as if other, "normal" families were feasting in a great restaurant, while the four of us were standing outside, noses pressed to the glass. Birthday parties for other children were sometimes unbearable, as my child, so clearly different, was unable to bowl, do gymnastics, or participate in any other activity. People often stared at him. Equally painful were Mickey's birthday celebrations; I couldn't help remembering just how much his older brother Jonathan had been able to do at a comparable age.

I was adrift in a foreign country, without a guidebook, and I didn't know anyone else who lived there. Those first few years with Mickey were like living with someone from another culture, and it was our job to teach him the ways of our world. Slowly, we learned the language, as I dogged my son's therapists with questions and requests for more information and articles, reading voraciously, going to workshops and conferences, acquiring a new vocabulary.

You adapt. Mickey was impulsive, and would often dart away in public or dash out of the house; we put a special lock on the front door. He frequently dumped every book and toy from his shelves; we stripped his room to a minimum of play materials. Loud noises—even the whir of elevators—disturbed him so much he would cover his ears and hum; we avoided crowds and learned to take the stairs.

And yet, for all that he could not yet do, there was so much about him that was intact. He was unfailingly sweet, carrying his collection of Puzzle Place dolls everywhere, hugging and kissing them, feeding them pretend food. He would line them up under the bed covers, whispering, "Shh, take a nap." Given the depth of his issues, his warmth and his sheer vibrancy seemed extraordinary.

The summer before kindergarten, Mickey lost his first tooth. We hadn't even known it was loose, because he still lacked the words to tell us. It was a bittersweet milestone. I remembered vividly the flush of excitement when his brother Jonathan had lost his first tooth. Though Mickey seemed pleased to show off the gap in his teeth, and we cheered for him, there was no elaborate celebration this time. The tooth fairy was too abstract for him.

The age of five was also the magic cut-off point I'd always imagined when all would be well. But the first day of kindergarten, I stood in a huddle with the other mothers and watched through the window of the special ed classroom as Mickey lay on the floor and said repeatedly, "I go home." In the next year, though, he learned to follow classroom rules, and began to read. That year, when he told us his first knock-knock joke, we celebrated.

As the years have passed, I have learned to wear emotional blinders. I stay tightly focused on Mickey, celebrating every change I see. I try to tune out what other, neurotypical kids his age are doing, because the gap is still too painful. Mostly, I try not to compare him with his brother Jonathan, an excellent student who is athletic, funny and well liked. Their trajectories are so different. It was hardest when Mickey was a toddler; if I did not remember every one of Jonathan's developmental milestones, there they all were, lovingly chronicled—by me—in his baby book. Comparing the boys is sometimes tempting, but dangerous. I must have separate, realistic expectations for each.

Most support comes, not surprisingly, from other parents of children with special needs. When I finally connected with them after those first hard years, it felt as if I could take a deep breath after holding it too long. Today we talk eagerly, like war veterans sharing their foxhole experiences. And though each of our tours of duty is different, we all long for our discharge orders.

I am often asked how I do it. I give the same answer each time. I wasn't given a choice. I just do it, one foot after the other. I have to be his advocate, because as wonderful as the therapists and teachers are, they go home every night. We are his ultimate teachers, the ones who are in it for the long haul. There's nothing particularly noble about it. We do it because it has to be done.

Acceptance doesn't mean giving up, and it isn't a constant state. Grief and anger still rear up unexpectedly. I still get tired of the relentless effort, the struggle for normalcy, the endless round of therapies and school meetings and fights with the insurance companies. This process of healing is a destination without an arrival. There is no cure, no magic bullet. Joy and grief are joined in lockstep.

Ultimately, what buoys our family is hope. When I look at this child, I do not see "autism." I see my child: an animated, endearing, and handsome fifteen-year-old with a mischievous sense of humor, who despite the early dire predictions, has learned to speak and read and do math. Parenting this trusting, gentle boy has deepened me immeasurably. But would I trade in my hard earned equanimity and expertise if someone could magically make his autism go away tomorrow?

In a heartbeat.

A few years ago, I heard a story that changed the way I framed my feelings about having a child with a disability. Itzhak Perlman was giving a concert. He made his way on crutches to the stage, seated himself, and took up his violin. He began to play, when suddenly a string snapped. Perlman looked around, seeming to measure the length of the stage, how far he would have to go on crutches to fetch a new string, and then seemed to decide that he would do without it. He lifted his violin and began to play, and even without that string, this man with a physical disability not only played; he played beautifully.

This is what it is like to have a disabled child. It feels as if you've lost a crucial string. And then, painstakingly, you must learn to play the instrument you've been given. Softly, differently, not playing the music you'd intended, but making music nonetheless.

~Liane Kupferberg Carter

Where's Dad?

There are things that we don't want to happen but have to accept,
things we don't want to know but have to learn,
and people we can't live without but have to let go.
~Author Unknown

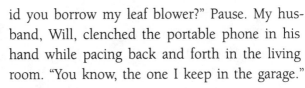

"Did you borrow my leaf blower?" Pause. My husband, Will, clenched the portable phone in his hand while pacing back and forth in the living room. "You know, the one I keep in the garage." He sounded exasperated.

Will was talking to our son, Matt, who lived a few blocks away. I was cleaning up the breakfast dishes and not paying much attention until the heat in the one-sided conversation escalated. Of course, I couldn't hear Matt's responses, but I had participated in the bargaining process last Tuesday when Matt asked to borrow the leaf blower. Warning bells went off in my head. The same warning bells that had jangled in my ears over the last few months. Lately though, they were getting louder.

"Irresponsible kid!" Will shoved the phone back into its holder and turned to me. "Now if Matt had joined the Army like I expected him to, this never would have happened. He'd have learned some discipline, some respect for other people's property." In recent months, this recurring theme popped up whenever Matt somehow failed to meet my husband's expectations.

Words deserted me. At thirty, our son was hardly a "kid," but my husband seemed to be regressing into one himself. Will quickly forgot the incident and moved on to his daily routine. However, later in the day when Matt stopped by to return the leaf blower, facing the issue became important — if only to clear the air.

"Jeez, Mom! It's like we never had a conversation about borrowing the damn leaf blower. You know he agreed to let me use it. What's going on with Dad?"

What indeed? The hurt look in Matt's eyes pained me. Truth time. As much as I've tried to avoid it, I couldn't any longer. Will, thankfully, had left for the office, something he did less frequently of late. He's a real estate broker and sets his own hours. It was just the two of us, my son and I, looking at an uncertain future. A future that we needed to discuss.

"It's way past time we talked about this, Matt. Blame me for turning a blind eye to the situation, if you want. I think your father needs professional help."

All the color drained from Matt's face. "You know it too?"

"Afraid so." All along, I'd been trying to shield my family from the truth but they were way ahead of me. "Now, what are we going to do to help Dad?"

Will and I had been going about finding answers in a piecemeal fashion. He'd suffered a bout of depression for several months over the decline in the real estate market. Depression wasn't new to him. Over our thirty-year marriage, this was his third go-round with it. When counseling and prescription drugs failed to turn him around in a reasonable amount of time, my suspicions grew. As time passed and his behavior became more and more erratic, the situation could no longer be ignored. The catalyst that brought me to my senses turned out to be Will's lapse of memory about agreeing to lend the leaf blower and his escalating anger with Matt over the incident.

My decision to conceal the truth from family and friends played a huge role in our evolving crisis. I hadn't wanted to discuss my worries with "outsiders" who would in all likelihood make judgments, or worse, shun us. At least, that is what I believed. We socialized less, limited our activities and generally kept a low profile. Withdrawing from the world limited my options.

Facing the seriousness of the situation was the first step in this long journey. What would we do? Doctors came to mind. Unfortunately, not many of them had a good grasp of what we were up against. They hadn't witnessed the changes in behavior that turned the man I loved into, if not a stranger, then almost certainly an alien presence. At first, the changes were so subtle that I hardly noticed, or maybe was trying to ignore. Even so, that ugly word—Alzheimer's—painted a scary picture. Then I watched as the changes wormed their way into an otherwise well-ordered life.

Knowing I wasn't alone helped. But there was fear, doubt and hopelessness until we were ready to reach out and find solutions. My path led me to our local Alzheimer's Association chapter. It was amazing how much lighter the burden felt when it was shared. At an Alzheimer's workshop, the lady sitting next to me described her husband's symptoms with such dignity, compassion and humor that I knew that my world wasn't coming to an end—just changing.

~Lizbeth Tarpy

Choosing Hope

If you knew that hope and despair were paths to the same destination,
which would you choose?
~Robert Brault

I thought I knew what to expect. But, I was hoping against hope. Hoping the first opinion was incorrect. Hoping they perhaps had seen something that wasn't really there.

I went to get a second opinion. Entering the neurology department, I checked in. I took a seat amongst the others who sat waiting. The wait, for a doctor's office visit, was unbelievably short. My name was called within minutes and I followed the nurse to the room I would frequent for the next few years.

When the doctor came in, his smile was infectious as he stretched out his hand to greet me. Dressed in slacks and a sweater, his dark curly hair was pulled back neatly into a ponytail and topped with a knit beret. As I studied this doctor, I immediately felt at ease. I knew that even if the first doctor's diagnosis was correct, I'd be returning to this doctor.

He introduced himself. Being the newest on the neurology team at the clinic, he told me where he had come from and where he studied. Then the moment of truth came—the testing.

Close your eyes. Start at sixty and count backwards with your eyes closed. Now, arms out in front, palms up, palms down, tap thumbs and second fingers together, etc.

He made notes throughout the thirty-minute examination. Then he put down his pen, sat up straight and pulled his chair closer to me. Looking right at me, he put his hand on my shaking right hand and said, "I have to agree with Dr. A's diagnosis. You have Parkinson's disease. In fact, I think, after reading your records, that they misdiagnosed you twelve years ago and you've had it since then."

Twelve years earlier they told me lupus. I could have flushed all that Plaquenil down the sink instead of my throat. But Parkinson's disease? I was only forty-three. Wasn't this an older person's disease?

I have since learned that Parkinson's disease doesn't care how old you are. It doesn't discriminate. It doesn't matter what nationality or gender you are.

I thought I knew what to expect when I drove thirty miles for that second opinion, but looking back, I think I wanted to hear something else. Something like, "Well, I'm not sure what Dr. A was thinking, but you're the healthiest person I've ever met in all my years as a doctor." Hope springs eternal.

Ah... hope.

At a recent seminar I attended on Parkinson's disease, one of the speakers stated that the greatest medicine we have in fighting any disease is hope. Hope for a better day. Hope for a breakthrough in research. Hope for a cure.

It's so easy to get down, to feel like giving in or giving up when faced with a challenge that you have no control over except for how you respond to it.

After my appointment that rainy winter afternoon, I walked across the wet pavement, stepped in some unavoidable puddles, got in my car and closed the door. The cold, damp feeling permeated into the very depths of me. I shivered. And then, I cried.

My doctor didn't tell me I was the healthiest person he had ever met in all his years of medicine. He didn't tell me that Dr. A was wrong or that I was going to get better. But what he did say was that he'd be there with me to the end.

Now, I know that you can't literally hold a doctor to a statement like that, but hearing that from a doctor who cares gives you hope. Knowing that you have someone who understands what you are going through; knowing they are on your side through your journey and that you are not alone gives you hope. And hope is great medicine. It brings purpose back into view. It shuts out the "what ifs" and turns down the dial of doubt. It disables the feelings of despair and enables you to not only have a confident expectation for a coming cure, but also the ability to find the blessings in the curse and have faith for a brighter future than you might have imagined.

I started the car, and as snow began to fall a peace came over me. A peace that all would be and was well. A peace that assured me that even though I couldn't give back this disease, I could choose how I was going to react to it. And I chose to do it with hope.

~Sherri Woodbridge

One Day at a Time

It is a mistake to look too far ahead. Only one link
of the chain of destiny can be handled at a time.
~Winston Churchill

"Dear God, I cannot do this! I cannot take care of everything by myself!" I sobbed as I collapsed halfway up the stairs. The despair and fear came from the depths of my soul, and it was so intense that it felt like physical pain.

My husband Dave's funeral had been the day before. My daughter had returned to her home five miles away and my brother-in-law and his wife had left just moments before for their home a thousand miles away. I was alone in the house where my husband and I had lived for thirty-six years and raised our children. I felt the weight of the world on my shoulders. I also felt like the most "alone" person in the world!

How could I take care of the acre of property, the big house, and the vehicles? Who would I call when I needed a repairman? What would I do if something went wrong after regular business hours? I had literally crumbled under the weight of these fears as I lay sobbing on the stairs. How long did I lie there? I do not know. What were my next thoughts? I cannot remember.

This was my reality until I realized that I had a choice to make and a challenge to overcome. I could either curl up in a ball and let life pass me by, or I could somehow face the hours, days, and weeks ahead. I knew I would have a helpful support system in my church and personal friends, but that did not alleviate my anxiety about stepping into widowhood. I even had difficulty checking the "widow" box the first few times on insurance and medical forms.

Dave, a healthy man who never knew what it was to be sick, had died just six weeks after being diagnosed with cancer. The suddenness seemed to make the shock even greater as I struggled with all the responsibilities of my new role. Dave was one of those unique men who could do almost anything—painting, plumbing, wiring, framing in a new room, mowing the property with the tractor, and keeping the vehicles in pristine condition. We never had to call a repairman. I had one living with me! Now I had the responsibility of finding the right people for the jobs.

A few days after his funeral, I recalled a conversation that Dave and I had several months before. Out of curiosity, I had asked him what attracted him to me all those years before when we initially met in college. I expected him to say something about my appearance or my outgoing personality, but he surprised me with his answer. "I saw a strength in you that told me you could carry on with our family if anything ever happened to me."

Dave had faith in me. Now I needed to have faith in myself. I knew it would not be easy, and it would not come overnight. I also realized something else that was adding to my burden. I was looking too far into the future—to the weeks and months and years ahead. That "distant vision" was defeating me, and I knew I had to take one day and one circumstance at a time.

"Lord, help me to take one day at a time because You know I always look into the future. You will have to help me reprogram my way of thinking, but I know I can do it with Your help," I prayed.

I returned to work after three weeks, although I was still reeling from the shock. My co-workers and supervisors understood when I would break down in tears and have to leave my work area to pull myself together.

During a counseling session that dealt with grief, the counselor explained a very helpful visual concept. She asked me to hold both arms out in front of me, which I did. "Now take one arm away. This is your situation now. All these years, you and Dave worked together as a team, each balancing your share of responsibilities. Now one member of that team is gone, and you would not be normal if you didn't feel as you do. This is an abnormal situation, and you are behaving quite normally." Her words gave me reassurance and made me realize that I was not, after all, losing my mind. I left her office that day with a renewed sense of my capability.

The weeks slipped by, and I found myself feeling a little more comfortable in my new role. I kept remembering Dave's words about the strength he saw in me, and I wanted to honor his trust. As each situation arose that needed a repairman, I would find the right person. My daughter took over cutting the acre of grass, and I continued to do the "prettying up" around the house with flowers. I knew that our inner emotions can often be affected, either negatively or positive, by our outward surroundings. I did not want my surroundings to reflect the difficult situation to which I was adjusting.

The initial twelve months were especially difficult, as it was a year of "firsts" for everything—holidays, birthdays, anniversaries, and special events. Each time I reminded myself that it would be the only "first" and that each one coming after it would be a little easier. Some days were better than others. I was able to traverse situations that I had expected to stop me in my tracks, but other times I would feel immobilized by the smallest task or comment. I came to realize firsthand that the healing process is like a roller coaster ride. You see some of the dips coming, while others take you completely by surprise.

As the adjustment continues, I keep reminding myself of the two valuable truths I have learned. First, I cannot look far down the road and try to anticipate things to come. That will keep me from making the first small steps necessary in the healing process. It will also burden me with all the situations that I know will eventually arise. I absolutely have to take it day by day.

Secondly, I have a strength within myself that I can call up when necessary and, when that strength is not sufficient, I can ask God to supply the added courage that I need. I also know that because God loves His children beyond measure, He will not fail me when I need Him.

As I look back over Dave's and my years together, I have come to realize that what seemed like small things at the moment have turned into precious memories that will last my lifetime. I will make it — one day at a time!

~Carol Goodman Heizer

51

Stormy Weather

For I have learned, in whatsoever state I am, therewith to be content.
~Philippians 4:11

I was a calm person on the outside, but on the inside I battled stormy weather. The atmosphere in my home was turbulent and it kept me on edge. It made me anxious and nervous. I didn't even want to go home after work.

I knew it wasn't healthy to live this way, but I couldn't do anything to fix it. I had no control over the situation. I lived with a son with a mental disability and it affected his temper and emotions. At times Jacob could be perfectly normal and other times his rage would shatter the peace in our home like a rock crashing through a window.

It was not unusual to hear shouts of profanity in the middle of the night.

"Where is my cell phone? I need to find it right now!"

He would flip on the lights in our bedroom and demand we help him find it.

Then there were the times of dread — when I sensed upheaval coming. I felt nervous while cooking dinner. There were not many things that he liked to eat. If I served something he didn't like, he would insist I make a different dinner for him. And he would not give up on his request. He followed me around as I cleared the table and prepared to do the dishes. "You're starving me!" For some peace, I would have to slip out the door and into my car and take a drive.

I loved my son and I tried to do everything I could to keep the peace between us. He actually wanted to get along, and would accept a hug and sometimes even apologize. My heart went out to him as I thought of the strong emotions he must wrestle with—and the friendships lost and the loneliness he must feel.

I felt lonely too.

I could not easily go to my husband for support, because he was hurting too, and we did not always agree on how to handle Jacob's issues. Our tempers would flare and leave us feeling distant from one another.

When I'd share with my friends about my difficulties with Jacob, they didn't know what to say to me. They would often respond:

"I'd hate to have your life."

"You are such an angel."

"Kick him out!"

So I stopped talking about it. It was a hard thing to bear alone. On some nights I would log into my computer and search for forums—looking for anyone who might be going through a situation such as mine. I came across other voices crying out, only to find their comments were labeled "three years ago."

Deep down I knew the only person who really understood was God. He knew exactly what I was going through because he could look down and see me every day. I prayed and asked him for strength. I re-read his promise in the Bible, "I will never leave you or forsake you."

Not long afterwards, a well-meaning friend reminded me that living under constant stress could do serious damage to my health.

"It can kill you."

Her words haunted me. I tried to shrug them off, but deep down I knew I had to change things. I lay awake at night and worried about it. I had to take care of myself. But how?

I knew I couldn't kick my son out. He would not be safe walking the streets. As I contemplated and prayed, a thought drifted into my consciousness.

Accept your situation. You need to accept it as part of your life.

But I did not want to accept the fact that my son might never recover. Nor did I want to accept that my life would never be quite "normal." And I wasn't ready to accept the possibility of my son living with me the rest of my life.

But the more I thought about it, I knew what I had to do. I had to face reality. And I had to make the best of it.

And so one day at a time I began accepting the situation. As soon as I changed my attitude, I felt myself relax. I didn't need to fight my circumstances anymore. I didn't need to wallow in self-pity. I didn't need to compare myself with others.

This situation was not going away. It was part of my life and I would have to work with it, and also learn to work around it.

I knew my first priority should be thankfulness. So I began to thank God for everything that was right in my life, even if it was just the purple pansies blooming in my garden — or an affectionate lick from the dog.

Second, I made sure I carved out some time for myself. At first I wasn't sure what to do. I was so accustomed to focusing on my son that I had forgotten about the activities I had once enjoyed. I heard a voice in my thoughts: Go back to your roots — what have you always enjoyed since you were a child? Warm memories of playing the guitar, writing, hiking, and tennis filled my mind and lifted my spirits.

Today, I spend a few hours a week doing at least one of these activities. And if that time doesn't work out, because of an emergency, I don't sweat it. My life will have emergencies, and I will get through them.

The days are better now, because I look forward to "me" time and I'm becoming more aware of my blessings. In addition, I don't feel so alone anymore. I've joined a National Alliance on Mental Illness support group for people who live with loved ones with mental disabilities. My husband and I are doing better, and every day God gives me new strength.

I wish I could say things have improved with my son. But it's hard to tell. On some days the skies are clear, and on other days the weather is wild. But there is one thing I do know. If I take a deep breath, relax, and accept my situation, life gets better—both for me and for my loved ones.

~Elizabeth Waters

52

Victory Over Death

Forgiveness does not change the past, but it does enlarge the future.
~Paul Boese

The phone rang. And then came the words pouring from my mother's mouth that no one ever wants or expects to hear: "They think she's dead."

Sometimes life throws something so big at you that time stands still for months. When you finally remember to look up, you sincerely wonder how the rest of the world has just kept going as if this life-altering event never occurred.

Something so traumatic that it changes how you keep time. All other events are now remembered as "before" or "after" it happened.

My sister. My eighteen-year-old fiercely compassionate, justice-loving, blond, blue-eyed, too-smart-for-her-own-good, picks-dandelions-for-her-niece's-hair, beautifully flawed little sister. Gone?

The information slowly came in as the homicide detectives made progress with their case. We were warned to stay away from the news for our own emotional health, but morbid curiosity drew me to the screen and the papers day after day. The news didn't sugarcoat things the way the detectives or my parents did.

He killed her. We'd known him since he was a boy — quiet, sweet, respectful. We'd played hide-and-seek together. We trusted him with her. And he killed her.

After it happened, I couldn't stand the color red because it reminded me of blood. I hated the dark and the night. I only slept during the day.

I wouldn't leave the house at all, unless it was to go to court or the police station.

Once I was finally able to leave the house, I would drive miles out of my way to avoid having to drive by the place where it happened.

"Time heals all things" felt like a lie.

We were faced with a never-ending stream of flowers, cards, phone calls, doorbells, and casseroles in dishes we'd have to return. Relatives and strangers took over our home, cleaning, answering phones, asking questions, crying with us.

Well-meaning people would say they "understood," as if they ever could. And then as if to prove it, they'd tell their own terrible story. Or worse, they'd offer the advice of "moving on" or "getting past this."

My favorite people were the quiet ones. The ones who let me remember my sister for who she really was. My opinionated, creative, annoying little sister, whose small frame somehow housed a strong, bold personality that so often got on my nerves.

I realized that there were a few people who actually could understand. They'd stood in the exact same spot I was in, and they'd somehow come out the other side. Forever altered, but alive, offering hope that I would survive this, too.

I was once asked if time really does heal all things. I didn't know how to answer — how to offer hope and honesty in the same sentence. I finally answered, "Time changes things."

You may never feel fully healed, but you won't always feel so raw. You never get over it. And every loss after that seems to compound on top of that one big one.

You feel like you'll never be okay again. The "okay" you're expecting belongs to the person you were before it happened. But there is a new normal, a new "okay" ahead for the person you are now.

And you will find it.

One day you'll be surprised to discover that you've learned to breathe again.

I remember one day realizing that I hadn't thought about her at all for an entire day. I felt confused and guilty, like I had inadvertently betrayed my beloved sister.

But I could not go on living in the past, wishing things were different. I would not create a culture of sorrow and festering agony and make my children suffer the immeasurable loss and horror along with me. She was an aunt they would never remember and I would not allow generational trauma to rob my children of their joy.

But this loss was two-fold. I had the death of my sister to face. And I had her killer to face.

The sweet, shy boy we'd known since he was a child turned out to be a cold-blooded murderer. I could let the parasite of hate and bitterness crush my spirit and poison my future... or I could face it head on.

How do you face a killer after he's been sentenced and sent to prison?

The turning point for my healing was in the scariest F word I've ever encountered: Forgiveness.

Forgiveness is not a feeling that just happens one day. It's not forgetting what's been done, or excusing it. In fact, forgiving is the opposite of excusing. The fact that forgiveness is necessary means that what happened was inexcusable.

Forgiveness is letting go of my need for revenge. It's refusing to allow anger, bitterness, and hatred to rule my life. It's a very deliberate decision. One I've had to make several times for the same offense. One I expect I'll have to make several more times over the course of my life for this one terrible crime.

It's been ten years now, and I still find unforgiveness in my heart. It's been ten years and I still miss my sister. I wish she were here to know my husband and children. But I can't live my life in the past, thinking of what might have been.

It's okay that I miss her.

It's okay that I sometimes go for days without thinking of her.

It's also okay that I remember.

It's okay that I talk about her and about what happened. And it's okay that I'm still heartbroken. But it's also okay that I'm happy. It's okay that I live.

~Genevieve C. West

Bananas for Harry

When someone you love becomes a memory, the memory becomes a treasure.
~Author Unknown

t seems that the little things in life pull at your heartstrings the most. Who would have believed that buying bananas at the local suburban Philadelphia Shop Rite would have a fifty-three-year-old woman in tears? But it does every week.

My husband of twenty years, Harry, died last year of congestive heart failure. We were together twenty-two years and we thrived on being together. We shopped, cooked, laughed, traveled, argued, embraced, loved, and planned for a future with our six-year-old son — our miracle child — together.

And now the first thought when I am awakened by a loving and rambunctious child each morning to get him ready for the school bus is that for the first time in decades, I am alone. The quiet in my four-bedroom house is deafening. The sadness that enveloped me is enough to make me double over in physical and emotional pain.

Well-meaning family and friends give advice: sell your house, date, don't date, buy a new couch to replace the downstairs bed where Harry convalesced for three years after a near fatal car accident, stop crying so much, have more fun, smile more, redecorate, take some of the photos of him down, talk more about him and the fact that he has died to your son, talk less about him, pack up his clothes to donate to charity, find a new life. And most of all — stop buying bananas.

My husband loved bananas. He did the grocery shopping before his car accident and I did it after he became ill. But we always had three to six ripe bananas sitting in a blue bowl on the kitchen counter. I don't really eat bananas. But I buy them each week at Shop Rite, bring them home and end up giving them to friends and neighbors.

If I stop buying bananas, it would mean that he is really gone. And while I saw him in his hospital bed for the last time, I said goodbye, arranged the funeral and watched his casket lowered into the ground, the thought that he is never coming back—for a hug, a loving kiss, to admire my new haircut, to help me buy new appliances, to fix my computer, to give advice, to take trips to the Jersey shore, to cheer our son at his horseback riding show, to put our son on the bus for his first day of kindergarten, first grade and more—is all too unbearable to imagine.

I have learned a few important lessons from Harry's death. You plan and God (or whatever higher power you believe in) has his own ideas. When one door slams shut and spins you around, another door or window may not open for a very long time. Nothing prepares you for how sad and overwhelmed you can feel when the love of your life is taken from you. Sleep is now a battle. Keeping the TV on at night is like having a new friend. Making new friends at my age is difficult—and who would I hang around with? Families? Couples? Single moms? Younger people with six-year-old children? Older people with grown children?

I wish I could report after six months, nine months, more than a year later, that the crying has stopped and that my heart will feel whole again—but none of this is true. All I know is that I want and yearn for Harry as much as I did twenty-two years ago, ten years ago and the day before he died. Maybe more.

My new and unimproved life and world will never be the same without Harry and his many idiosyncrasies. The trips to his favorite diner, the mall, a beachside resort, and others may one day become less painful. But I will still hear his advice, and love and concern.

Yes, I was lucky. I found my soul mate, my one true love twenty-two years ago. And dating services will never understand that we loved one another in spite of our differences. I watched James Bond movies,

House and *NCIS* and he watched endless romantic comedies, *The Good Wife*, and *Desperate Housewives*, because that's what you do when you want to spend time with someone you love with all your heart.

Harry and I believed in unconditional love, which makes watching fairy tales of any kind so much more painful than I ever could have imagined.

So I will keep buying bananas. Maybe I will eat one for breakfast, make my own banana chocolate chip muffins, or my son, now seven, will develop a taste for them. But it actually makes me smile through my tears to buy them and remember bringing them home to the man I loved.

~Debra Forman

Chapter
6

Find Your Inner Strength

Accepting
What Makes You Different

54

Bag of Hope

There is no hope unmingled with fear, and no fear unmingled with hope.
~Baruch Spinoza

t was five o'clock on a Friday afternoon when Nathan came to the door. His blond hair was cut short; his blue eyes matched the warmth of his smile. It was his eighth birthday.

Instead of receiving gifts, he was bringing them. He brought with him his parents, his younger brother, and on his shoulder he carried a Bag of Hope.

My six-year-old son, Kaipo, greeted them at the door.

"Show Kaipo what's in the Bag of Hope," said Nathan's father.

The boy spilled the contents of the bag onto the couch. He didn't save the best for last. He started with the best, a teddy bear named Rufus.

"I sleep with mine every night," Nathan told Kaipo.

Rufus, the Bear with Diabetes, comes complete with a medical identification bracelet to show that he has diabetes and patches on his body to show where he takes insulin shots: his arms, legs, abdomen and buttocks.

"I give Rufus shots, just like I have to take," said Nathan.

He went through the rest of the items in the Bag of Hope, giving some to Kaipo and some to me — kids' books, coloring books, a video, and some literature for parents. Then he took out his blood testing kit and showed Kaipo how he tests blood from his arm instead of his fingertips.

Earlier that day, Nathan's father had called me to set up a time to meet. The Juvenile Diabetes Research Foundation had hooked them up with my son and me.

Nathan had been diagnosed with diabetes six months earlier, his father told me.

"When was your son diagnosed?" he asked.

"Two weeks ago," I said.

"You must be a basket case."

He understood. Here was someone who could actually relate to me in a way that others couldn't.

"Yes," I told him. "Sometimes I just start crying in the middle of a conversation."

He knew the fear I felt, the grief, the sadness, the loss. He could identify with my pain.

It was amazing how much life had changed overnight. Suddenly I was a nurse checking my son's blood at least four times a day, giving him shots of insulin twice a day, making sure he had the right amount of food to eat six times a day. I dropped my son off at school with worries that were so magnified from what they'd been just days ago. Would my son know if his blood sugar level was too low? I recited the symptoms over and over to him.

Our three-day stay in the hospital had been intense. It was a crash course in diabetes, and it was overwhelming. I knew that once we got home, I wouldn't have the nurses there to answer my questions. I was on my own. What if I couldn't remember something I'd learned over the past few days? I didn't have the other parent in the home to help me remember all the information that had poured into my brain.

My worry was constant and extreme. That's the part of single parenting that I find the hardest — taking on 100 percent of the fear and stress of the situation. The other parent isn't there to take on half of it. Nathan's mom said she worried about her son's blood sugar level getting too high. His dad worried more if it got too low. I worried about both, but was more scared of hypoglycemia (low blood sugar). It happens quickly and can lead to unconsciousness. If it became low in his sleep, would he wake up?

Parents like Nathan's say, "Call anytime," and they mean it. They let me know that I'm normal.

"It was bedtime and his reading was low. I gave him extra carbohydrates and had him sleep in my bed."

"We've all done that."

When I first called JDRF, the woman I spoke with told me, "I cried every day for three months after my child was diagnosed." With time, the tears eventually dry, replaced with experience and knowledge.

Nathan's Bag of Hope brought more than its contents. With it came experience, kindness and sympathy. I'd heard that most parents say it takes them a year to feel comfortable with their child's diabetes. Just six months into their own son's diagnoses, Nathan's parents were out offering support—that alone gave me a lot of hope.

That evening after I gave Kaipo his shot of insulin, he took the used syringe and gave Rufus a shot. As a matter of fact, Rufus had several shots that night. It must have been the right dose—he slept peacefully in Kaipo's arms all night. The dose of hope was just right, too—Kaipo's been holding that teddy bear tight every night since, just like Nathan.

If it's true that in giving we receive, Nathan had the best birthday ever.

~Jo Eager

Being Fat Set Me Free

It took me a long time not to judge myself through someone else's eyes.
~Sally Field

For much of my adult life, I've had what many consider a fatal flaw. However, unlike others who can hide their flaws behind a shiny façade, mine is out there for the world to see. What's my flaw? I'm fat. Some people feel that tells them everything they need to know.

Yet fatness describes nothing about me beyond physical appearance. My weight doesn't demonstrate who I am: a mother, wife, friend, daughter, sister, aunt, volunteer, author, artist, and musician. Some might suggest I am quite accomplished in my own right — something I was told by a woman I'd just met.

Here's what she said: "Wow! You've had a really interesting life! You're really accomplished, in spite of... you know."

I could hear the pause where she caught herself, and I watched her eyes quickly shift from left to right. Her voice trailed off in a whisper as she realized she was about to approach a taboo subject.

"In spite of?" I asked politely.

Her eyes roamed up and down my body, settling on my ample midsection and behind. She looked tortured and embarrassed.

"You know," she said again, looking like she'd rather be anywhere else than where she was at the moment.

I let her off the hook. I smiled and changed the subject.

It's a sentiment I've heard before, and probably one I'll hear again.

In a society obsessed with how we look, there are many aspects of a woman's appearance that are not okay, including being fat, wrinkled, old, unattractive, or gray-haired.

It's no secret I'm fat. I see it in the mirror and feel it in the jiggle of my arms when I wave goodbye.

I haven't always been this way, but with Hashimoto's thyroiditis I've struggled with my weight most of my adult life. In my early twenties, I seemed to have a handle on it. I was active and ate very little.

One morning, I woke up feeling ill and my head was foggy. It was as if someone had flipped a switch. Suddenly I was chronically exhausted and constantly in pain. No matter how little I ate, the weight piled on. It took me the next several years to receive an accurate diagnosis. By then, the damage was done.

I was overweight by the time I was twenty-five. The size I wore slowly crept up from a 3 to a 24. I was constantly hungry, in pain, and exhausted, but it was my life.

Once, for a period in my early forties, a doctor prescribed a medication for migraine headaches. Something with the medication reacted with my body chemistry, and weight started dropping off quickly. Unfortunately, the medication also robbed me of my emotions, creativity, and intelligence—all of the things that made me who I was. While I loved that it made me skinny, I didn't love anything else about it. I stopped taking the medication, and the weight immediately reappeared.

When I was that tiny size 3 in my early twenties, I did everything I could in pursuit of matching an unrealistic ideal. I exercised incessantly. I constantly dieted. I tanned, toned, plucked, and waxed. I wore body-conscious clothing and painful shoes with impossibly high heels. I had many superficial relationships based on looks and little substance. I wasn't a happy or accomplished person.

Today things are different. I still cringe sometimes when I look in the mirror, and I still occasionally feel the need to explain myself to others. Sometimes, I also feel I have to be better, smarter, faster, stronger, and more talented than someone else half my size so people will accept me, but those are issues on which I am working.

The things I value most about myself have little to do with how I look or how much I weigh. Instead I value who I am—the mother, wife, artist, author, volunteer, and friend. Those are the aspects of my life that bring me joy. In many ways being fat has set me free to be that person.

I was headed in another direction until that switch flipped in my early twenties. I spent an inordinate amount of time and energy trying to mold myself into what I felt I should be instead of who I wanted to be. I was becoming an object in order to please others—a pretty doll that sat on a shelf without an ounce of joy or an original thought.

Then the switch flipped and all that went away. It ceased to be attainable, and I could no longer accept the superficial as a way of life. Once the ideal of beauty to which I aspired truly became unobtainable, I was free to focus on what really mattered. It was a bucket of cold water waking me from a nightmare of my own creation. I was an intelligent woman who'd bought into something I was conditioned to believe. When it became clear I could not be that, no matter how hard I tried, I was free to become what I truly desired. Without the Hashimoto's and weight gain, I'm not sure I ever would have gotten here from there.

I want to go back to that young girl I once was and wrap her in my arms. I want to take her chin in my hands, look deeply into her eyes, and tell her she doesn't have to do this. She doesn't have to be a physically idealized version of herself, because that will never make her happy or fulfill her.

Even with how happy and centered I am now, I would be lying if I said I'm always completely comfortable in my own skin. My conditioning about appearance runs deep, and I'm still not a huge fan of watching myself on video or seeing myself in photographs. I recognize my own biases that lead me to judge on the basis of appearance, but I also know from my own experience one must go a little deeper in pursuit of the real person who lies within.

We often make assumptions, no matter how incorrect they are, about what being fat must mean emotionally. Insecurity. Poor self-esteem. Gluttony. Sloth. Loneliness. Sloppiness. Poor self-control.

I'm here to tell you this: I may sometimes feel a twinge when I look in the mirror, but none of the adjectives above describe my emotional life. I have a different set of adjectives by which I describe myself. Vibrant. Compassionate. Passionate. Joyful. Funny. Fun. Honest. Talented. Creative. Loving. This is who I am, and it is who I choose to be.

Being fat set me free. It freed me from pursuing a physical ideal. It challenged me to be a woman of substance and to find my bliss in what truly matters. For that, I am grateful.

~Karen Frazier

56

To Be King

Be content with what you have; rejoice in the way things are.
When you realize there is nothing lacking, the whole world belongs to you.
~Lao Tzu

s I took my seat at the pep rally, I looked around the packed gymnasium and thought this was completely and absolutely ridiculous. The four other boys sitting with me were the captains of the football, basketball, soccer and track teams. They were also voted best dressed, most athletic and best looking during the senior superlatives. I, on the other hand, was none of those things. I ran cross-country and, while I always tried hard, I wasn't really good. I could also guarantee that I wasn't going to get any votes for best looking or best dressed anytime soon. I wondered if this was all some sort of weird joke, because I could not comprehend what I was doing sitting with them.

During the ceremony, my mind wandered and I thought back to the last six months. I know that high school students tend to over-dramatize things, but I honestly can say that those six months had more highs and lows than most high school students experience in such a short time.

It all started in April when I and three other boys were selected to represent our high school at a national conference on politics in Washington, D.C. While the trip was fun, I had a hard time connecting with people and by the end of the week felt pretty lonely. A few weeks later I ran for the only thing I had ever wanted in school—Student

Government President. It was a very close election, but when it was over, I had lost. That night was brutal as I spent hours on the phone with, of all people, my chemistry teacher. I wondered if there was something else I could have done, and he tried his best to reassure me. But still it hurt.

Things got better a few weeks after that when I and three of my classmates were chosen to represent the school at Boys State, a leadership program intended to bring the best and the brightest male students together. That week, though, was a disaster. I was ridiculed by almost all the other boys except for my own classmates. In a blatant attempt to ridicule me further, I was nominated for the position of State Treasurer. I knew it was only to give my tormentors another chance to poke fun at me, as I'd have to speak to the whole group of a few hundred students.

So with the help of a friend from school on the trip, I gave a speech where I called them out on their behavior and expressed my disgust at what the supposed best and brightest had done. Shockingly, the speech was almost unanimously well received. I received a standing ovation, and the award for best delegate.

The summer passed by fairly uneventfully, until August when I was T-boned while driving my father to the airport. I was lucky to escape with minor injuries.

Through all of these events, I grappled with a choice. I had been presented with an opportunity to change myself, but it was not going to be easy. To put it bluntly, I'm short. I stand barely five feet tall, and have been since I was probably thirteen years old. When I was younger it wasn't that big a deal. But as I went through my teenage years, I stopped growing while everyone else continued to do so. The choice was to undergo a complex surgery. It involved breaking both my legs and then inserting pins between them to lengthen the bones. If it sounds painful, that is because it is. I would need to take a year off to deal with the medical issues. During those past six months, I wondered if things would have been easier if I were taller. Would I have won the election? Would I have not spent a week being ridiculed by a couple hundred teenage boys? Would that have somehow prevented the accident?

I snapped out of my funk and my mind stopped wandering when I heard my name called. I needed to run one of the pep rally contests. As I walked to the microphone, I searched the crowd for a particular young lady. I had fallen for her and was hoping she would go to the senior prom with me in June, assuming I'd get the nerve to even ask her. Dating for me was nonexistent. While I had some good close friends, I was never part of the "popular" crowd and spent many nights at home. The school had a semi-formal dance every year in which the girls ask the boys, and I had never been asked to go with someone, even as a group thing. I often wondered if girls would be more interested if I were taller.

The contest was over and I went back to my seat. Thankfully, this whole ceremony would soon be over. A short time later, I heard a shout from the crowd and the girl sitting next to me elbowed me and whispered, "Stand up, we won!" For a second I didn't move, but as the throng of people came to congratulate us, I realized what had happened. Somehow, I had been elected Homecoming King. The rest of the afternoon was a blur until I got home and my chemistry teacher was on the phone. He remembered our conversation from that past May when, in tears, I had asked him if I would have won the election if I were taller. This afternoon, he wanted to make sure that I finally realized none of that mattered.

It has been twenty-one years since that day. I'll never really know why the students voted the way they did. But to each of them that did, I owe a big thank you. They taught me that the biggest obstacle I needed to overcome wasn't being short. It was being okay with who I was. And that if they were okay with it, then I should be too.

We all have our strengths and our weaknesses. For many of us, the challenge is seeing the good in ourselves. I had been myself during high school and that had been enough. My classmates saved me from choosing an unnecessary and painful surgery. I opted not to have the surgery and graduated on time with my classmates. When the senior superlatives came out, I didn't get best dressed or best looking. But I got something just as good: friendliest. I also did ask that particular young lady to the prom and she accepted.

~Rajkumar Thangavelu

57

Toes

I cling to my imperfection, as the very essence of my being.
~Anatole France

'm going to tell you a story about my toes. Yep, really. My toes. You know how some people have a second toe that is longer than their big toe? Well, I was cursed with the longest second toe known to man. In fact, all of my toes are pretty long. As my boyfriend's son recently told me, "You could play piano with those things."

So, yeah. I'm kinda known for my horrendous toes. And you know what I used to do? I used to hide them. I dreaded summer. All the girls would pull out their cutesy little flip-flops and sandals, but not this girl. Nope. I was sporting tennis shoes no matter how warm it was. There was no way I was going to show the world my hideous toes.

But one day, that changed. And I don't mean that in a generic sense of the term "one day." I mean, I remember the exact day.

It was a particularly hot summer day and I was sporting my tennis shoes, as usual. I was standing in line at a gas station to pay and looking down at the ground while I waited. I noticed the feet in front of me. They were some chick's cutesy little toes in a pair of cutesy little flip-flops. Why, oh why, couldn't I have feet like that? Why couldn't I have the cutesy little toes and wear the cutesy little shoes? Why did this chick get the cute toes and not me? What a lucky, lucky girl she was.

And then I looked up.

Along with the cutesy feet, you know what else this girl had?

A bald head.

She was a cancer patient.

Suddenly, a million memories came flooding back to me. A few years prior to this, I too had been a bald cancer patient. And, at the time, I was absolutely mortified by the fact that I was a seventeen-year-old girl with no hair. I didn't have the maturity yet to realize that being bald was a small price to pay for the medicine that was saving my life. No, I was too self-conscious and insecure for that. I was just worried about how I looked. I wouldn't let anyone take any pictures of me without my wig on, so I have no documentation whatsoever of that time in my life. Once I was finally able to return to school to finish my senior year, I remember a lot of the kids telling me to just take my hot, itchy wig off and wear scarves or something to make myself more comfortable. But nope. Silly me. I wasn't ready to uncover something that I felt was a flaw, even though I knew that I would be loved and embraced regardless.

I have often looked back at that time and wished that I would have just taken that thing off. It was silly to hide behind it. It was hot; it was uncomfortable; and I would have felt so much better if I had just stopped worrying about how I looked and let my bald head shine for all the world to see. It was nothing to be ashamed of. I couldn't help it. I was beautiful—not in spite of my bald head, but because of it.

And now, here I was, hiding something else. My stupid toes.

I silently applauded pretty-toe-girl for her confidence and strength. When I got home, I took off those uncomfortable, stupid tennis shoes and started wearing flip-flops and sandals.

So, why am I telling you this?

Do you have something you're hiding? Well, stop that. Maybe it's something physical like ugly toes, or maybe it's something a little deeper. Some part of you that you think people wouldn't accept if they "saw" it. Either way—stop it right now. There is no logical reason to hide something that makes you who you are. Whatever it is, own it. One day you'll look back and wish you had.

Be comfortable. Be confident. Be you.

Show your toes.
Got it?

~Melissa Halsey Caudill

58

The Enemy Within

suffer from a self-diagnosed disease. It's called self-hatred, and it's a writhing serpent that has infested my brain since my teenage years, continually attacking me, releasing its venom and paralyzing me. I conspired with this entity to create a stream of propaganda against myself in a twisted pattern of reverse psychology. No one could reject me because I had deemed myself unworthy of love.

I must first present some backstory on the origins of my self-hatred. Shortly after entering high school at age fifteen, my family physician referred me to an endocrinologist. I had complained to my parents that the other kids were sprouting while I had remained the same height as the year before.

The endocrinologist ordered a battery of tests, including a skull X-ray to determine my biological age. The scan showed a gray spot that was later diagnosed as a craniopharyngioma, a benign brain tumor near the pituitary gland. This type of tumor can cause headaches, hormonal imbalances and vision problems if left untreated.

Surgeons at Upstate University Hospital in Syracuse, New York removed the tumor in 1984. The surgery was successful, but it left me with panhypopituitarism, a deficiency of all of the hormones the pituitary gland produces. Puberty was delayed. While my friends continued to grow and mature as we headed for college, I remained physically unchanged.

I looked like a fourteen-year-old boy when I began my freshman year at St. John Fisher College in Rochester, New York; some of my classmates mistook me for an academic prodigy. I had to explain to them I was of normal intelligence — only scoring 970 on the SAT — but appeared young for my age due to an illness.

No female at the school took me seriously as a potential boyfriend, as I was considered cute in the way a teddy bear is cute — soft and safe — the antithesis of sexy.

My self-hatred festered during this period.

Without testosterone and growth hormone, my body was a soft shapeless mass and I loathed my round baby face with peach fuzz on the upper lip. My feminine features and a high-pitched voice meant people would sometimes confuse me for a girl.

While waiting to order a drink at a college bar near campus one night, I drew the attention of two mustached men, dressed in jeans and Carhartt jackets, who were sitting at the bar, nursing draft beers. One of the men looked at me and then turned to his friend and asked, "Is this a guy or a chick?" I caught the second man gazing at me, and he whispered to his friend, "I'm not sure." I left the bar right away. I walked back to campus in the cold night air with hot tears stinging my face.

I retreated into a world of shame, unable to control the revulsion I felt when a mirror or photograph reflected my image back at me.

And I could do nothing to shed my child-like exterior.

But the endocrinologist prescribed growth hormone and testosterone shots. In time, my body grew and my face matured, if only slightly.

I graduated from college, earned my master's degree and began working in the journalism field. My self-hatred simmered, but I was able to keep it under control.

A series of health crises then altered my perspective. One of the most memorable happened while I was living in Phoenix in 2004. Over the course of a Sunday afternoon I began vomiting and my legs became heavy and weak. I still intended to go to work that night at my job as a copy editor. But as I got ready to take a shower, I fell in the bathtub and struggled to climb back out. I called in sick and my roommate drove me to the hospital.

Blood tests revealed dangerously low sodium levels. Doctors in Scottsdale determined my blood had become diluted because the dosage of desmopressin I had been taking to replace vasopressin, a hormone that controls urine production, was too high while the dosage of cortisone was too low.

I spent a week at the hospital with IV fluids pumping through my veins. My sodium levels rose and I left the hospital on a bright sunny afternoon with clear blue skies overhead. Woody, a volunteer with white hair, a white mustache and muscular forearms, wheeled me outside to the curb; the sun felt warm and the desert smelled clean, with hints of sage and wildflowers wafting in the air.

As I waited for my roommate to bring the car around, I talked with Woody, and his positive attitude and the joy he expressed in helping people made an impression on me. I felt thankful for being restored to full health. I was alive. I could walk and I didn't have a serious disease that required surgery or further treatment.

And I made the decision then to stop hating myself, to turn off the negative thoughts I had allowed to flow into my brain. The futility of my self-defeating philosophy became clear to me. I asked myself, what good had all this self-hatred brought me? How had it served me?

It had controlled my existence but produced nothing of value, while robbing me of energy and time, time I lost and could never recover.

My parents' deaths from lung cancer—my father in 2007 and my mother in 2011—solidified my thinking. Seeing them wither as the cancer spread made me realize that our bodies are only finite machines. They hold no power besides the functions they are able to carry out.

I have tried to put aside my obsessions with the self. I've come to the conclusion I can't rearrange the molecules of my being and construct a new face, a new body or a new voice. This is who I am, and I need to stop rejecting myself or wishing for a better version.

In 2011 my craniopharyngioma returned, only this time with greater intensity. The tumor pressed against my optic nerve, causing headaches, a drooping right eye and double vision. Surgeons at Upstate performed a transsphenoidal (through the nose) decompression of the tumor and my vision was restored. I could see again and gratitude swelled inside me.

And although I would never claim victory over my self-hatred, gratitude cancels it out; the two cannot share the same space. You can't hate yourself if you feel lucky to be alive, if you celebrate the gift of life, breath, body and mind.

The bad thoughts about myself are still stored inside, archived for future use, and they can be accessed anytime.

In order to dispel negativity I often repeat a silly slogan in my head. It's a variation of Popeye's mantra of "I yam what I yam and that's all what I yam."

An adapted version I started using in 2004 goes, "I am who I am and I can't hate this man." I have since revised it to: "I am who I am and I must love this man."

I don't always succeed at taking this advice, but I also don't condemn myself when I fail.

~Francis DiClemente

59

What Makes Her Special

True beauty is the flame of self-confidence that shines from the inside out.
~Barrie Davenport

When my twin daughters, Melody and Jessica, turned seven, I stopped by their school to drop off birthday cupcakes (for Jessica's first grade class) and doughnuts (for Melody's). Mrs. Connelly, the principal, spotted me and asked me into her office. She must have seen the look on my face—or perhaps she's merely accustomed to how people react to being called into the principal's office—and set me at ease, saying, "I need to brag about Melody."

"Did Melody tell you what happened last week?" she asked after we were seated.

"I don't think so." Both my daughters had told me a lot of things that had happened the previous week, but none of their stories featured anything principal-worthy.

The principal told me that one of her fourth graders, normally a sweet boy, had been acting up recently. In one incident, he sat next to Melody at lunch and asked her what happened to her face. Melody began to cry.

At this point in listening to the story, I began to cry too, which made the principal join in. Before I continue with the tearfest, let me give a little background.

I don't think it's merely maternal pride that makes me think that both Jessica and Melody are pretty. They are identical twins, but by developmental happenstance, Melody was born with a frontonasal dysplasia, or a facial cleft, similar to a cleft palate, but higher in her face and not affecting her palate. Jessica was born without the cleft. Melody has been seeing a craniofacial specialist since birth. The appointments were every three months at first, then slowly changed to yearly, and are now every two years.

She hasn't needed surgery, and there's nothing wrong with the function of her nose. It just doesn't have a defined tip. The cleft also causes her eyes to be wide set and has given her a widow's peak hairline. All of it combines, in my mind, to give Melody an adorable china doll look.

Melody's doctor warned us that, even if there was no functional issue with her nose, kids get mean about appearance around age seven. We could always opt for surgery if it was needed for Melody to have a healthy self-image. Honestly, I never gave surgery much thought. Melody is a well-adjusted kid.

It's not like Melody's unusual look has never come up before. When kids have asked why she has a "funny nose," I've responded by saying it's so that we could tell her apart from her sister. When I overheard a little girl telling Melody that her nose was "too small," I responded by focusing on its purpose. "Does it breathe?" Yes. "Does it smell?" Yes. "So is it too small to do its job?" No.

I've told Melody that she has the world's most kissable nose, and she permits me five kisses exactly at bedtime on her "kissy nose." A while ago, Jessica told someone that a good way to tell her apart from her twin was her pointy nose, in contrast to Melody's flat one. I considered taking her aside to have a serious discussion about thinking before we speak, but realized that she wasn't attaching a value judgment to one look over the other. She was just stating a fact.

Part of me worried, though, that having an identical twin would come to show Melody what she would have looked like without the cleft, and that she would resent Jessica. It's never come up, though. I hope it never does. It helps that, while my girls value their twin relationship, they also relish being individuals and having some differences from one another.

Let's return to the principal's office. As you may recall, we were crying.

The fourth grader had been mean, and Melody had cried in front of all her friends. It took a while for the older boy to admit that he'd acted wrongly and with intent to hurt. By the time he was ready to deliver a real apology, Melody was back in class. The principal called her out into the hallway, and the fourth grader apologized.

"It's okay," she told him. "You already said sorry, and I forgave you. People say that stuff to me all the time. It's fine."

Now it was the little boy's turn to cry. He was ashamed.

"It's not fine," the principal told her. "You're a beautiful girl, and it's not okay that people say mean things."

"But I forgive them," said my amazing, extraordinary child. "I love this school!" And she skipped back to class.

That night at dinner Jessica was distracted by her dessert, so I took the opportunity to talk to Melody about this whole thing. "I heard you were extremely forgiving at school. Mrs. Connelly was pretty proud of you."

Melody beamed.

"Do you want to tell me about it?"

She told me essentially the same story I'd heard in the office. I reiterated what her principal had said, that she didn't need to just accept people's cruel words.

"But Mommy, it's okay. They can say what they want. It's my job to forgive. I just don't get it. I don't understand why they would want to be mean about what makes me special. My kissy nose makes me special. What's wrong about that? I don't know why it's like this, but it makes me special."

There was nothing wrong with that, I told her. By a major act of self-control, I kept my tears at bay this time. Would she like to know why her nose was special? She did want to know, so I explained in very simple, objective terms the nature of her cleft. I also pointed out that it was responsible for her widow's peak, which she calls her "heart hair," since it helps give her a heart-shaped face.

"I love my heart hair!" she said. "That is part of what makes me special too."

She went on to tell me that her teacher had told her about being teased as a child for not speaking English well. Her sister's teacher told her about being teased for having a big nose. I added my own story about being teased for my eczema. I told her that I'd never realized I was pretty until I was eighteen.

She gasped. "But Mommy, you're beautiful."

"So are you, baby girl. I'm so glad you already know it."

"Me too. I've known ever since Nicole [her friend from infancy] told me I was beautiful when I was very small. That's why she's such a good friend," she said.

There was nothing more to say.

~Sadia Rodriguez

60

Finding My Place

Every blade of grass has its angel that bends over it and whispers,
"Grow, grow."
~The Talmud

"Well?" my teacher prompted. "Do you know the answer?" I shifted uneasily in my seat and glanced around the classroom.

Forcing myself to meet her eyes, and in a voice I hoped was nonchalant, I said, "No idea." Not noticing the tears in my eyes, she continued the math lesson. The rest of the day dragged on slowly, until finally the last bell rang. A signal of freedom, until the next day.

A throng of kids flew past me. I felt out of place at school, and I found no comfort with my family either. All the pain, frustration, anger, and embarrassment I had to face in school only intensified at home.

What would my parents, who raised my five older brothers, all budding intellectuals, want to do with a nothing like me? Me, the failure who had to be in a separate class because he couldn't learn? The one who needed to repeat kindergarten when most of his brothers had already skipped a grade.

I always had a tough time in school. My father had put it best: "Some kids are good in school, and some aren't. You're just one of the kids who isn't." But I wasn't satisfied with that answer.

Ever since the first day of school, it had been drilled into my brain that I must strive for academic success. Our principal talked to us many times about striving for greatness. Pictures of past scholars and professors adorned at least one wall of almost every classroom.

But school wasn't the worst of my troubles; my time at home had the greatest effect on me. Whether it was the glowing reports on my brothers, or even the A's and B's on their report cards, I felt I wasn't as good. That I was inferior. (It was only later that I realized I had blown things a bit out of proportion.)

By fourth grade, my self-confidence had shrunk considerably and I became depressed. As I only had a couple of friends, and I wasn't even sure they liked me, I had no one to talk to. I would lie awake at night and wonder if my life had any meaning. Weren't my brothers embarrassed by me? Did they see me as the failure of the family? The black sheep? Tears would soak my pillow. Eventually I would drift off into an uneasy sleep.

I had been tested three years earlier, and they found that I had several learning disabilities. I had to review constantly to keep the information in my brain, and I was always two to three years behind my grade level in math.

As the work became harder, and the shame too much to bear, the depression I had suffered the past two years snowballed into suicidal thoughts. I would wonder, long after I should've been asleep, if life was worth living. Thankfully, I never acted on those thoughts.

Rarely did I accept a compliment on achievements in school or at home, always shrugging it off and telling myself that they didn't really mean it. To make matters worse, my brothers had all gone to the same elementary school. So all the teachers had known them, and I thought I had to keep up the "winning streak." I was living with the ghosts of their pasts, and I simply couldn't keep up.

In high school, without special ed, I had to find new ways to help myself do better in school. But the strain from the past six years had caught up with me, and I loathed working. I had had enough failure in my life. Why add more salt to the wound?

After school one night during my sophomore year, I was working with my tutor. I just wasn't getting it, and it had been going on like that for a few weeks. My tutor had finally had it, and started yelling at me in front of the entire crowd of kids (each with their own private tutor). "How dumb can you be? We've been reviewing the same four math steps for three weeks now. If you don't start shaping up soon, you'll end up being a failure."

That was the first time someone had said "you're a failure" right to my face. Until then, my failure had been my private despair. I stormed out of the room and hid in a dark corner right outside the school. I stayed there for a half hour, crying and asking God if the pain and disappointment would ever end.

I left that school shortly afterwards, hoping to find a place where I could get away from the pain and find the greatness buried deep within me. And I did. My new school has allowed me to see myself in a better light and recognize how much I have grown. The academics aren't as intense as my previous school and I've opened up to others, no longer scared of what they'll think of me. I have built new bonds—not based on academic skill but on true friendship.

I can look in the mirror and see, not what I should be, but what I am. That it doesn't matter who gets the good grades, but rather how I conduct myself and act that matter most. I realized that I had been looking at it all the wrong way—evaluating myself on my abilities, not on my potential to grow into a wonderful person. I had been so wrapped up in the academic side of things that I forgot to look at the person underneath.

People greet me cheerfully each morning because they see my inner spark. They see that I'm a friendly and caring person. They don't care if I fail my classes or don't do well on tests. They care about the person, not the achievements. They want to be with me because of who I am as a person. Me! The person who tries as hard as he can in class. The one who works to make himself into the best person he can be.

This year has breathed new life into me.

~Louis R. Cardona

On His Own Terms

While we try to teach our children all about life,
our children teach us what life is all about.
~Angela Schwindt

s usual, I'm awash with anxiety. We're going to a graduation party for our neighbor's son. It's not because of
the sadness I feel that my twenty-year-old autistic son,
Mickey, isn't going to college too. Well, okay, maybe it is
just a little. Mostly I'm worried because tonight there will be fifty or
so people there, many of them teenagers who've never met our son.

Mickey, however, is eager to go. He is so keyed up he doesn't
even balk when we tell him he can't wear a T-shirt. He pulls on a pale
blue polo shirt without protest. "Can I bring my Muppet album?" he
asks.

"No hon, not appropriate."

"Okay," he says agreeably. "Next time."

Without even waiting for us, he strides confidently across the
street. He greets people happily, working the crowd. I shadow him;
even as I stop to chat, I keep my eyes on him. He walks out to the
deck; I'm right on his heels. He walks back into the kitchen; I stand
close behind.

"Can I have some water?" he asks the caterer.

"Please," I prompt him.

"Don't follow me Mom," he says, irritated. I'm startled. But really,
who can blame him?

I get it. He hates my hovering. But I'm not only monitoring his behavior.

He's excited to be here. Maybe too excited. That can trigger a seizure. I remember a dinner in this same house two years ago. Mickey beside me at the table. How his head pivoted toward me as his eyes rolled back. The room went eerily still as I cradled him. "I've got you, you're safe," I'd whispered to him over and over until the seizure subsided.

But do I really need to be this vigilant? No twenty-year-old wants his mother policing him. I take a deep breath.

"Okay, Mick," I say. "I won't follow you."

Mickey plunks down at a table filled with teenage boys I don't recognize; one of them slides over to make room. Mickey has always wanted to connect. I think back to the time a behavioral therapist observed him in the elementary school cafeteria. Her report had been gutwrenching. Each time Mickey sat down at a lunch table, all the other kids got up and moved. Mickey doesn't have much small talk in him; he still struggles to sustain a complex conversation. But I watch as he listens intently and hangs in there. No one stares; no one points; no one moves away. Later I see him in the back yard with the other boys, somewhat awkwardly whirling a Frisbee back and forth. I feel a rush of gratitude. The other kids have absorbed him into their group without question.

I'm not kidding myself; I know there are many times he still stands out. Does this bother me just for his sake? Isn't it also about my own abiding discomfort when it feels as if people are judging him — and by him, I mean us — so critically?

I long for him to fit in. But I also want him to be exactly who he is: his playful, endearing, unfiltered self. How do I reconcile the two? Is it even up to me any longer?

Our neighbor's daughter Ali joins me. "I had a great conversation with Mick," she tells me. Ali is studying to be a special education teacher.

"Was he talking about the Muppets?"

"Not at all," she assures me. "He told me he's been working out at Planet Fitness and asked if I wanted to go with him."

I love that he's mustering up appropriate conversation. Yes, he can only sustain it for brief periods. But how far he has come since that day eighteen years ago when his first speech therapist told me he might never speak at all.

My husband Marc joins me on the deck. Together we watch three handsome young men tossing a football in the twilight. Our son is one of them. He is holding his own.

"Look at him," Marc says softly. "You know what's remarkable? How unremarkable this looks."

~Liane Kupferberg Carter

Chapter 7

Find Your Inner Strength

Learning to Reach Out

Finding God in Reality Television

You have power over your mind—not outside events.
Realize this, and you will find strength.
~Marcus Aurelius

L et me start by saying that I am not a particularly religious man. I have spent a large portion of my career working in reality television, where God is a concept reserved for those devout contestants casually referred to as "Jesus freaks." The last place in the world I expected to be divinely inspired was on the job. But nevertheless, it was during my time working on *Survivor* that I was witness to a series of events that radically changed my view on belief in a higher power.

Three years ago, as a Segment Producer on *Survivor*, I was given the opportunity to produce a new twist for the show called Redemption Island, which altered the most basic rule of the game. When contestants were voted out by the tribe, they were no longer out of the competition. They went to the Redemption Island, where they would live in solitude, waiting for the next eliminated contestant to join them. Once there were two residents on Redemption Island, they would compete in a Duel, or a challenge combining physical and mental skills. The winner stayed alive on the Redemption Island, waiting for his or her chance to go back into the game with the other contestants. The loser went home.

In the conceptual meetings, we imagined Redemption Island as a vicious place. Ideally, contestants would be so bitter about being voted off that they would do anything to get back into the game for vengeance. We dreamed that the first exile would monopolize the food and shelter and leave the second resident out to dry in order to weaken his or her opponent in the Duel.

The first *Survivor* to be voted off was a woman named Francesca. She was a sweet-natured and smart woman, but she had been blindsided at the first Tribal Council. By the time she arrived on Redemption Island, she was upset, embarrassed, and angry (not to mention starving and freezing). She rationalized and did all the self-preservation typical of those experiencing rejection, but by the time the second arrival came, she was still angry and bitter.

Matt was the second person voted out and the second resident of Redemption Island. He was a twenty-two-year-old devout Christian from Nashville who had promoted his love of Christ too much for his fellow Survivors. His good nature was taken advantage of, and he was also blindsided.

Francesca did exactly what we hoped when Matt arrived on a cold and rainy night. She had built a small roof of palm fronds within the shelter to protect herself from the rain, but she didn't let Matt join her under it. She told him that she was still upset that he had been a part of the alliance that voted her off. Matt didn't fight the decision. He slept in the rain.

An unexpected thing happened when I interviewed Matt the next morning, right before the first Duel. While he was extremely upset about being lied to by his "friends," he wasn't filled with anger or the need for vengeance. He said that everything that had happened was for a reason and it was all part of God's plan. As much as I tried to get it out of him, he wouldn't give me the sound bite I wanted, which was "I'll do anything to get back into the game to get vengeance." He said he would keep fighting, and he hoped to get back into the game, but it wasn't up to him.

Matt won the first Duel, and the second, and the third. He kept winning, but the motto remained the same. He was God's servant, and the results of the duels were in God's hands. He had a calm and relaxed energy in the Duels that deeply contrasted the obvious nervousness and exhaustion of his opponents. He stopped talking about getting voted out and simply concentrated on the next Duel. Not only that, but Matt convinced almost every contestant who was voted off after him to join him in his faith. Instead of a place of anger and vengeance, Redemption Island turned into a place of peace and love. You can imagine the reaction of the producers when they saw this happening. Every arrival was the same. The contestants arrived angry and embarrassed, but within hours, Matt had them reciting Bible verses. Even the most notorious *Survivor* villain of all time, Russell Hantz, laid down his devious tricks and shared a meal and Bible study with Matt on the morning of the Duel. When the Duel was over, the losers repeatedly hugged Matt and thanked him on their way out of the game. In a lot of ways, it was the opposite of what we wanted for our TV show, but through our frustration we couldn't help but notice that Matt was turning into a great story.

Matt won six Duels before he was let back into the real game, right when the two tribes merged into one. He went back to the tribe mates who blindsided him with a renewed sense of hope, not out for vengeance but not necessarily opposed to it either. Then came a shocker. Matt was taken back in by the same people who had blindsided him and was promised that he would be taken to the finals with them. Hesitantly, he believed them, and then they blindsided him again. He was the first person voted off after the merge, and he went straight back to Redemption Island after only three days of being away.

Matt was completely overcome with emotion when he got back. The betrayal went against everything he believed in. He was embarrassed, depressed, and visibly broken, and remained so for the next few days. He didn't want to be in the game anymore, and yet he wouldn't quit because that wasn't God's will. He still firmly believed that he was there for a reason and everything that had happened was part of a plan, however perplexing that plan might be. After a few days, he regained his footing. He came to realize that he was actually better off on Redemption Island than in the real game. He was still in the competition, but he had a personal haven, free from deception and backstabbing, where he could show new arrivals how to leave behind their anger.

Gradually, Matt found strength again, and he kept winning. Bible study continued with each new arrival, and after every Duel the loser continued to hug Matt goodbye and thank him. He had given them a way to leave the game in peace, something that had never been possible on previous seasons of *Survivor*. Matt won another four Duels and returned to a state of satisfaction, even joy. Then, on Day 36 out of a possible 39, in the last Duel that decided who went back into the game to face the final five survivors, Matt lost.

It was an endurance challenge where each of the duelers had to balance a platform that held a vase with their foot. If their foot moved, and the vase dropped off the platform, they were out. Matt went into the duel with the usual peace and confidence that I had seen for most of the twenty-nine days we spent together on Redemption Island. He was so at peace that at one point, while he balanced the vase, he looked over at me, behind the cameras, and gave a little head nod and a smile. This was the end of our time together, regardless of the outcome, and I actually found myself getting a bit sad. He hadn't given us any of the dramatic twists and turns that we wanted as television producers, but I couldn't help but admire him for what he had done with Redemption Island. On a practical level, it simply made more sense. His belief that everything happened for a reason had allowed him to unload his negative emotions onto the shoulders of a higher power and therefore regain his strength.

I smiled back at Matt as he balanced the vase, and a few minutes later, his foot moved ever so slightly and the vase dropped. He was disappointed, but not entirely. I knew that a part of him didn't want to go back into the game, where he would undoubtedly fall victim once again to the backstabbing and deceit that he hated so much. I knew that he was happy to exit on his own terms, with his dignity and his beliefs. And even though his departure from the game was part of God's plan, I had a suspicion that maybe, at that pivotal moment, he had willed his foot to move.

That was my last season working on *Survivor*. In the time since, I have not become a highly religious man, but in times of adversity I do think about my experience on Redemption Island. And what I tell myself is this: There are always going to be negative experiences in life, rejections and tragedies and disappointments. At some point, we all get voted off by our tribe mates, but in the aftermath of those experiences, we get the same opportunity as Matt. The chance to set the tone for our own redemption islands. We can make our island into a place of anger and bitterness by seeking blame or vengeance, or we can create an island of peace and acceptance by believing that it's all happening for a reason. In Matt's case, the results showed that the latter works far better for surviving.

~Nick Fager

A Life of Her Own

Don't wait for a light to appear at the end of the tunnel.
Stride down there and light the bloody thing yourself.
~Sara Henderson

The knocking at the front door seemed insistent. My mom hurried to answer, only to encounter Merle, the man next door. "Mary," he said, "Bill's fallen out back!"

Mom stood confused, but then understanding dawned: Merle was speaking about my dad. As Mom ran through the house Merle dialed 9-1-1, but it was already too late. Dad had gone out to garden early that morning and now lay stricken on the ground, dying of a massive heart attack right in the middle of his back yard.

Mom, needless to say, was devastated. Her life with Dad had been her whole world. Always a bit shy, she was used to letting Dad take the lead. But with Dad gone, everything changed. For the first time ever, Mom faced living alone, a situation compounded by the fact that my two younger sisters and I resided with our families in cities hours away.

I worried so much about Mom in those early days. And while I spent weeks with her after Dad's funeral, the time came when I had to go home. My heart broke as I started the four-hour drive. I was still grieving Dad, of course, but I also just couldn't banish the image of Mom standing there all by herself, waving goodbye to me from the front doorway of her home, her lovely white hair touched by the morning sun. I cried for miles.

A few years after Dad's passing, Mom decided to relocate to the city where I live. I was delighted with her decision, but it concerned me too. She had lived in her hometown her entire life. How would she fare in a different place, a larger city, where she knew no one but my family and me? Yet we didn't see she had much choice. An ice storm that winter had proved that to me when it left Mom's house without power for almost two weeks. As my husband and I traveled through the storm to pick her up that January to bring her home with us for the duration of the power outage, I knew the time for change had surely come. Though Mom was in fairly good health, she was beginning to need more help than my sisters and I could provide remotely.

It took months to accomplish the move, but we finally got Mom settled into a new home five minutes away from me. The home was just what she needed, perfect in size, and close enough that if she had any problems, I could be there in a flash. At first, she depended on me to take her places, but as she began to learn the area roads, she started venturing out on her own. She was trying so hard to be independent, but I knew she was lonely. "If I could just make one friend," she told me many times, "I'd be happy."

"I'm praying for that, Mom," I said.

"I am too."

And then one day when I called to check in, she was out of breath as she answered the phone. "Everything okay?" I asked.

She laughed a bit sheepishly, as if I'd caught her in some grand misdeed. It was odd to discover that somehow, over time, Mom's and my positions had switched. Here was the woman who had made me, in seventh grade, call the boy I'd secretly asked to the sweetheart dance and tell him that I couldn't in fact go with him to the dance because I wasn't yet allowed to date. As a girl, I just knew my mother had the proverbial eyes in the back of her head! She'd always seemed one step ahead of me, but now I was the one watching out for her, making sure she was safe and well. "I was actually just looking out my front window," Mom said. "I'm not trying to be a nosy neighbor... you know I'd never spy, but..."

She went on to tell me about the woman living across the road, little more than a hundred feet away. Mom would see her every day walking out to her mailbox. "She looks so nice," Mom added. "I have the feeling we could be friends."

"Why don't you go introduce yourself?" I nudged.

Mom hesitated, but only for a moment. "Maybe I will.. someday."

I knew that would be the hard part for her—working up enough courage to turn "someday" into "today" and "I will" into "I did." It's such a simple thing, really, but stepping outside our comfort zone can sometimes feel like such a big deal. My dad used to say that if something is worth having, it's worth working hard to attain, and that sometimes, to get started with anything new, including friendship "You've got to dust off your britches and just go for it."

Mom ultimately did just that. She summoned up her courage, put one foot in front of the other, strode across the road, and murmured that most wondrous of words: "Hello."

"Guess what?" she said to me the next morning, her excitement bubbling over the phone line. "I did it! I walked over yesterday and met her."

"Oh, Mom, that's great!"

"Her name is Carol. She's widowed too."

From that time on, Mom and Carol became fast friends. They now regularly go out to eat, take in plays, and see movies. They've joined a women's club and travel together on field trips. Mom and I recently met Carol's son, and as he shook Mom's hand, he said to her, "Thank you for being my mother's friend."

His words stunned us. All along, Mom and I had believed that Carol was a gift from on high, never considering that Carol and her family might also feel the same way about Mom.

"Oh goodness, Carol," said Mom, "thank you for being my friend too.

As the two women beamed at each other and hugged, I knew without doubt that this was a sacred connection. Mom and Carol's friendship had been cosmically crafted. Their paths were destined to cross.

I've heard it said that God can envision greater things for us than we can envision for ourselves, and I know that's true. With a little faith, a little nurturing, and a little courage, Mom has not only persevered, she's blossomed. She has not only made a dear friend, she has become a dear friend as well. Mom has overcome a challenge that rocked her very foundation, and in so doing, she has been transformed. She has taken what could have been a lonely, fearful existence and fashioned a life of her own.

~Theresa Sanders

64

The Good Deed Challenge

Good actions give strength to ourselves and inspire good actions in others.
~Plato

The summer of 2011 marked my first summer as an alumnus of Central Michigan University. The idea of a "big kid" job made me nervous and I had an itch to travel before I became tied down by the nine-to-five grind. As a friend and I sat and indulged in small talk, I mentioned my desire to travel. This friend told me that her boyfriend was working at a restaurant in the beautiful state of Alaska, and he could get me a job as a seasonal server for the summer. I put in my application the next day, and was interviewed the day after. Within one week, I accepted a job in Alaska and was on a plane for the adventure of a lifetime.

I was fortunate enough to receive a job as a server at the end of the summer season, lasting only two months. Seasonal jobs usually last four to six months, with the last two months becoming competitive. Within those last two months, employees try to make as much money as they can before they either fly home or depart for their next seasonal job. I arrived during this competitive time, not knowing a soul; I was an outcast. Because of the competition, a few of the other servers would try to get new people to quit or get fired. How could they get someone to quit or get fired? Workplace bullying, and I was the victim.

With this job, everyone worked and lived together, making it impossible to escape. I had awful cell phone reception, making it difficult to call family and friends. It was nearly impossible to get on the Internet, so I was stuck and couldn't talk to my friends or family about what to do. I was isolated and alone with my struggle.

There were two bullies in particular who made a valiant effort to get me to quit. If I asked, "Hey, how are you?" the response I got would be, "Why are you talking to me? I hate you! I don't ever want you to speak to me again! I can't wait until you're gone!" There were times when one of the bullies became physically abusive, but I was too nervous to tell my boss. I didn't want to look like a rat, and I was intimidated.

Every day, I thought about how easy it would be to quit and go home. Get back to my friends, get back to my family, and get back to my life.

But life throws you in a mud puddle once in a while and your character is developed by how you get back up and clean yourself off. I realized this situation was my mud puddle and my character would be defined by how I climbed out of it.

I took a step back and looked at my situation from a different perspective; I started to make observations on why I was being bullied. Broken souls and past demons have a way of causing permanent damage to people. These people sometimes allow bitterness and hate to govern their lives. I realized that the average age of employees was eighteen to twenty-two, but the main bully was thirty-one. I began to question why he enjoyed working with younger individuals and what his goals were. I then thought back to the first day he bullied me.

The first time he bullied me was in a group. As he said an incredibly mean comment to me, everyone laughed, including me. I wanted to act like this comment didn't have an effect on me, but I didn't think about the outcome it would have on the bully. He realized that his mean comment made people laugh, making him friends. I then realized that the only way he knew how to make friends was by picking on others. If he hurt one person to make five others laugh, he was winning. My goal was to change this habit and outlook. I decided to start a good deed project! This response to my bullies ended up changing my life in a way I could have never imagined.

My good deed project was a bit of a case study. I decided to do a good deed every day for my bullies, one in particular. I made sure I knew his schedule so I didn't miss any days. I opened the door for him when I saw him, and I did everything I could to make his life easier. After I began making a conscious effort to do daily good deeds, I noticed he stopped acting as rude and hateful. As I did these good deeds, I studied how my bully's persona would change from an individual setting to a group setting. After a couple of weeks, one of the bully's friends made a statement that helped strengthen my backbone.

"You don't deserve the way people are treating you; you deserve better than this."

After that, I started making friends, some of whom were friends of the bully. Being accepted made me a much happier person, showing me the importance of inclusion. I was finally enjoying my time and believing in myself.

Having mutual friends with the bully created a conundrum for him. My bully was faced with a tough situation: be nice to me and hang out with me and *our* friends, or continue disrespecting me and risk losing all of his friends. Remember how he thought bullying made him friends? Now was the moment he had to explore a new path to friendship. This was where the light bulb turned on, and the case study worked. He gave me respect, and it saved me. I climbed out of that "mud puddle," had a great summer, and learned a valuable lesson on how to handle any bullies that come into my life in the future.

~Andrew J. Nalian

65

The Very Bad Diagram

We either make ourselves miserable, or happy and strong.
The amount of work is the same.
~Francesca Reigler

When you're twenty-three, you don't expect to discover that you've been harboring a tumor that's determined to kill you—a tumor that's a rare form of advanced ampullary pancreatic cancer.

But that's what happened to me. It was 2008, and I'd fainted at work in what turned out to be a grand mal seizure. Then after a few days of stubbornly insisting I was just tired, I'd stumbled into the emergency room with my friend Hartman, still hoping I only needed a vitamin or two.

But nope. I was actually dying.

Within seventy-two hours, I had an official diagnosis: a massive pancreatic tumor that was bleeding into my abdomen.

It all felt unreal. A few days earlier, I'd been a typical twenty-something, a young woman still new to Vegas and ambitious to build a business. Now everything was upside down. I had a massive tumor and faced a surgery called the Whipple procedure that would basically reconstruct my digestive tract. And then, of course, I'd still have to find out whether it was actually cancer.

Okay, I thought, I can do this. But it felt like a lie. I did not feel like I could do this at all. But I just kept saying it, hoping for belief.

I'd taken the news well at first—as well as I could. Dr. Casey had been kind but also no-nonsense about the fact that I'd need the surgery—and that was when I began to panic. I'd been poked, prodded, and scanned, alternating between fear and frustration on a constant basis. Now Dr. Casey was back, and without much preamble, described the tumor they had found.

"So that's the situation," he said quietly. "We need to act fast. Alicia, we have to do the Whipple."

I thought I'd be brave. But I wasn't. I started to cry.

Dr. Casey sat there, quietly, listening to me cry. Then after a few minutes, he picked up a marker, and drew a big scrawly diagram on the whiteboard on the wall at the foot of the bed. He was showing me in the simplest way what the Whipple procedure would entail.

He wasn't a good artist. He was actually a really bad one. But bad drawing or no, he was getting the point across. And it looked like a huge surgery, as he drew a shaky human figure—me—then drew the lines resecting my stomach, my pancreas, my gallbladder, and drew more lines on my small intestines. From the looks of this, they were going to cut me in half.

"You want to do that to me?" I asked.

"Yes," he said quietly. "Because this is the best option we have to save your life, me and Dr. Lau. It will remove the tumor that is killing you."

"Or it'll kill me," I said.

He nodded. "Which is why you need family here," he said. "Where's your mother?

I looked at the diagram and took a deep breath. I hadn't wanted to involve my family from so far away. I'd wanted to be strong.

But he was right. "She's in Florida."

"She should be here." He waited for me to respond. "Right?"

"Okay," I said. "Schedule it. I'll call her."

Dr. Casey smiled. "Good," he said. "I'll see you Thursday morning." He patted my shoulder, then left.

I cried a little more, then looked at that terrible scribble of a drawing on the whiteboard and steeled myself. I picked up the phone, and did what I should have done sooner—I called my family and asked them for help. I called my mom, my grandma, my Aunt Sherry, needing the connection of family. They were all so far away—I was in Vegas, Mom was in Jacksonville, my aunt in Boston. They were upset by the news, but I felt the love and support flowing through the phone.

And on Thursday morning, Mom was there, next to my friend Hartman, after flying all night to get there for my surgery. I opened my eyes to the sight of my exhausted mom, cherishing that we had these moments together before the operation. We just held hands and smiled at each other, but her presence was exactly the comfort I'd needed.

Then came the moment of truth. Nurses and aides came in to prepare me, adjusting and disconnecting my IVs, tubes and wires so that they could wheel me into surgery and then transfer me to the operating table.

Mom and Hartman said their goodbyes, looking scared and worried, and I hugged each of them as hard as I could, awkwardly from the gurney, telling them I loved them. "See you on the other side," I told them, trying for cheerfulness.

Mom smiled through her tears. "We will." She nodded. "We'll see you soon."

I didn't want them to be afraid for me. I wanted them to think I was confident. But I had never been so scared in my life. I kept trying to breathe naturally, kept telling myself, "You can do this!"

Then a very strange thing happened.

As they began to roll me into the operating room, I experienced a huge wave of calmness, and a certainty I had never felt before.

I heard my own voice in my head: "I can do this. I'm going to be fine." The certainty was as strong as the fear had been. I felt calm, protected. I felt almost eager, wanting to see what would happen next.

In a blaze of light and swinging doors, I entered the operating room. Even as they moved me to the operating table, I watched the incredible precision of the activity around me. It was very organized, quick and calm, a kind of dance.

"You okay?" asked Dr. Casey.

"You bet," I said. The room buzzed with activity. So many people in scrubs and masks, that sharp smell of antiseptic in the air, the shiny instruments that would soon be cutting around in my abdomen. It didn't feel real.

"Alicia? You ready to do this?" asked Dr. Lau. His eyes crinkled above the surgical mask.

I looked at my brave doctors who were so confident they could save me. I looked around the room, at these talented people who would fix me and remove my tumor, the terrible invader that I wanted out of my body. I felt a wave of calmness and trust. It was out of my hands and into theirs.

I smiled, gathering everything I had into this feeling of strength, joy and absolute certainty.

"Absolutely," I said. "Let's rock this."

I saw the surprise in their faces, then they glanced at each other and smiled. Dr. Casey laughed. "That's exactly what I wanted to hear."

I was still smiling as I fell into the warmth and darkness of anesthesia. This wouldn't defeat me. I was made of stronger stuff. And I knew it was the truth.

I can do this. I took a deep breath, smiled, and slept.

~Alicia Bertine

Other People

Hope is the physician of each misery.
~Irish Proverb

We became those "other people" the night we received the knock on our door. You know, the people who bad things happen to, the ones who receive devastating news in the middle of the night. That kind of thing wasn't supposed to happen to us. Losing a child, that unimaginable heartache, only happened to "other people."

Our daughter Kyley was sixteen when she died in a car accident down the road from our home. She was on her way home from work. She was so close. It almost made it worse knowing she was just down the street, as if being in that close proximity to her home, to her family, should have somehow protected her.

The first week, as we planned for her services and received visitors to our home, I was conscious of the fact that I felt very little emotion at all. It was as if I were playing a part in a movie. I dutifully went through the motions while impatiently waiting for this awful scene to be finished. I realize now I was in shock and I remember the exact moment that shield of protection crumbled. The pain and despair washed over me and I became inconsolable.

My mom was at my home visiting one day. "Why don't you go talk to someone, Melissa? Like a counselor."

I was surprised by the flash of anger I felt. I had always prided myself on being able to fix whatever problem came my way. The only acceptable resolution to my grief was to have my child back. I couldn't make that happen. Certainly no counselor was going to make that happen. My response was a resounding, "Absolutely not!"

I suppose that's where a lot of people would have tiptoed back from the angry, grieving mother, as to not upset her any further. Not my mom. She was persistent and I finally gave in.

I may have had a little bit of an attitude in the therapist's office that first day. I sat with my arms crossed, barely making eye contact as I informed her that unless she could bring back Kyley, we were both wasting our time.

She was surprisingly tender when she responded. "You're right. I can't bring back your daughter. My job is to help you move forward without her."

Up until that point the thought of "moving forward" had never occurred to me. I didn't want to move forward without Ky! Everything I knew of Kyley, everything I remembered about her, was prior to that day in December when she left us. If I picked up and lived life, wouldn't I be moving further away from my child? How could I possibly do that?

My friends and family appealed to my spiritual side. Kyley now resided in my future, where she was waiting for me in Heaven. Every day I lived was a day closer to being reunited with her.

I looked at my eleven-year-old-son and my husband. I was only thirty-five years old. I had many years ahead of me and I knew I didn't want to spend them consumed by heartache and bitterness. I was in such pain and I didn't know how to make it go away. I couldn't see an end to the hurt, but maybe that therapist lady could.

She didn't let on whether she was surprised to see me at that second visit. She just steered our session with the exact confidence and compassion I needed her to show. I left her office that day with a list of a few additional resources. She encouraged me to seek out services for my family.

The Children's Bereavement Center of South Texas was on that list and I called to schedule an intake appointment. We interviewed with them as a family and were informed of the services they felt might benefit us. The center was designed to help children process their grief and give them a safe place to express their feelings among other children their age who had experienced a similar loss. It was a beautiful facility and the staff was wonderful.

We arrived back at the Center on our assigned group night. The center director had let us know what to expect: we would eat dinner with the other families and then the adults would separate from the children into their own support group headed by a trained grief facilitator.

All of the children at the facility that evening, my son included, had lost a sibling. Our group was comprised of other parents who had also lost a child. We didn't know any other families at the time who'd experienced the same type of loss as us. I didn't know quite how to feel looking into those other parents' faces and seeing the same hopelessness I felt.

My heart had been softened towards this type of therapeutic process by my experience with my own therapist and I tried to keep an open mind. I participated in the group, sharing my feelings with the other parents. It was reassuring to hear that some of the feelings I was experiencing were normal, and nothing to feel guilty about. It was healing.

It's been nearly five years since my family and I first visited the Bereavement Center and since I sat in my therapist's office with my arms crossed, practically daring her to try and help me. We are no longer clients at the Center but I recently visited and spoke with its director. There was something I wanted her to know.

When I first visited the Center, I was in so much pain that I could not see outside my own heartache. I knew I would never feel joy again and I even doubted that life could feel normal after such a tragedy. I did not dare hope for something I could not see as a possibility. That's the wonderful thing about hope: its existence is not dependent on one's ability to see it or feel it. Those special people at the Center knew it was not lost. They gently ushered me towards it as I healed, until I could finally see it for myself. They did that for me.

My "therapist lady" and the staff of the Bereavement Center celebrated when I, a self-professed reluctant client, walked into their offices and proclaimed, "Thank you, but I don't need you anymore."

I'm living my best, most joyful life. And yes, life feels normal again. Hope is never truly lost. Sometimes we just need a little help seeing it.

~Melissa Wootan

It Takes a Village

We cannot live only for ourselves.
A thousand fibers connect us with our fellow men.
~Herman Melville

Thirteen is an awkward age for anyone, but it proved to be an especially stressful time for me. My family life imploded, and we learned that keeping secrets could be a dangerous, even life-threatening, practice.

My father had always been a heavy drinker. That was nothing new. But when he lost his job, a downward spiral began, with threats of violence against my mother and us kids. I never thought I'd feel so helpless or so afraid. Unfortunately, that was only the beginning.

When my mother went back to work full-time, my father was left to care for my baby sister. The day I came home from school to find my father passed out on the couch and my sister crying in her crib, with a diaper that had obviously been full for hours, was the last straw. My father couldn't be trusted to look after a child, so my mother paid our next-door neighbour to babysit. Of course, she wasn't about to admit the real reason why. She pretended my dad couldn't child-mind because he was looking for another job.

Violence escalated in our household until my mother found the courage to kick my father out and seek divorce. Sounds easy enough. It wasn't. My father refused to leave our family home and my mother had no choice but to take out a restraining order against him. She did what she had to do to protect us.

The police escorted my father from our house, but that didn't keep him away. He phoned so often that we stopped picking up. He filled tape after tape on the answering machine with death threats. He sent us pictures in the mail of all the guns he had access to. He sent photos of himself holding those guns, aiming them at the camera.

My mother took all this to the police, but they shrugged it off. Tapes of death threats and pictures of guns didn't qualify as evidence, they said.

Still, we kids were too ashamed to tell anybody what was going on. My mother talked to our lawyer, the police, and a few family members, but my siblings and I? We had only each other. Keeping secrets is prevalent in households with rampant substance abuse. We were secretive to a heartbreaking degree.

After a while, it wasn't enough for my father to threaten us by phone and through the post. He smashed a window and broke into our home, entering when my mother was at work and we kids were in school. When I came home that day, with my younger siblings in tow, I knew we needed the police. But, in a time before cell phones, how could we make an emergency call? In our suburban neighbourhood, no payphones were close by.

We had to break the silence.

My siblings and I went next door, to the neighbour who babysat our youngest sister. We told her everything—about my father's drinking, his neglect, his death threats and his guns. She helped us call our mother, and Mom phoned the police. My father was taken away in handcuffs for violating his restraining order.

If only the ordeal had ended there.

But that was just the first of many times my father broke into our house. When we put bars on the windows, he broke down the door. We couldn't hide what was going on from the neighbours anymore, not with the noticeable police presence at all hours of the morning. There comes a point where you can't lie any longer. You can't cover for a family member who has wronged you.

When we told our neighbours the truth, something incredible happened.

The next time my father came to "take back his house," he gave us warning. He even gave us a date. My mother called the police right away, but they said he wasn't in violation of his restraining order yet. There was nothing they could do in advance. She'd just have to call them when he got there.

We were all afraid, but my mother, in particular, was beside herself. She'd done everything she could to protect us kids. But if she waited for my father to arrive before calling the police, it could be too late.

This time, when she vented her concerns, it wasn't to my grandmother—who often didn't believe the things Mom told her—but rather to our next-door neighbour, the woman who cared for my baby sister during the day. My neighbour was a loud and opinionated woman, and when she called the neighbourhood to action, the neighbourhood listened.

If my father was afraid of one thing, it was exposure. He trusted us to keep quiet, to keep his secrets. He shouldn't have. Because, on the day he said he'd take back the house, our neighbours came to our rescue. They all joined hands and formed a human barricade across our driveway.

My father drove up the street, and his car slowed almost to a halt when he saw us—the whole neighbourhood standing alongside his kids, showing him they were there to support us, that his threats and behaviours were unacceptable, that he needed to leave.

And he did.

When his car pulled away, my mother thanked the neighbours and told them we'd taken up enough of their time. They were adamant. He wouldn't give up so easily. What if he came back and they were all gone? No, they would stay as long as it took. They'd camp out on our front lawn all night if they needed to. Now that they knew what we'd been through, the neighbours were going to protect us.

They were right, of course. My father circled by the house, again and again, until my mother called in the restraining order violation and the police apprehended him. The neighbourhood, which had never been terribly close or cohesive before that day, worked together to protect us kids and our mom.

Through the whole ordeal, the most terrifying obstacle we faced as a family was an internal one: the fear of admitting the truth, of worrying what others would think. The shame seemed insurmountable.

This horrendous situation was in no way my fault, but it sure didn't feel that way at the time. I thought we were the only ones. I thought no one else could possibly understand.

It took an incredible strain before my mother, my siblings and I cracked the veneer of normalcy. When we told our secrets, we expected the neighbourhood to view our family with contempt. Instead, they became our shield. When the police failed us, our neighbours stepped up. They stood alongside our family, and we finally realized we were not alone.

~Foxglove Lee

Poison Ivy

As your faith is strengthened you will find that there is no longer the need to have a sense of control, that things will flow as they will, and that you will flow with them, to your great delight and benefit.

~Emmanuel Teney

Two days before major surgery, I faced an overwhelming to-do list featuring my arch nemesis, poison ivy. The vines had not only overrun my rose garden, they had begun to thread their way through the geraniums and up the side of our house. In long sleeves and gloves, I pulled and clipped every vine and creeping root I could find.

Staring up at the noon sun blazing down on me, I said, "On top of all I need to get done, Lord, why do I have to deal with a bumper crop of poison ivy?" It seemed like a never-ending battle, a symbol of the obligations and responsibilities that were tying me in knots.

As I worked well into the afternoon, I couldn't help thinking about what lay ahead in the next few days — a hysterectomy, removal of endometriosis, and colon surgery. It was as if the operations were just another chore on an endless slate of things to get done. As I yanked at the tenacious plant, I thought of how the doctors had cautioned me about my recovery. They'd ordered no driving and no work in the office or at home.

I piled the vines by the curb and looked at my car, wondering how I would survive without driving. I couldn't ask my busy husband,

Allen, to chauffeur our eight-year-old daughter Meredith to and from school and dance lessons. That was my job.

When I finally quit the ivy pulling and went inside, my friend Caroline called. "I know how independent you are, but you need to let your friends help you," she said. "Please—at least until you're back on your feet."

"I'll call if I need anything," I promised. "But I think everything's covered."

I could hear her sigh as I hung up.

The next day was "liquids only" for me, crammed with last-minute meetings and errands. There wasn't enough time to do everything. That night, after I took Meredith to a sleepover, I lay in bed and thought of my sixteen years of marriage. Careers had been important from the beginning. Then came Meredith and a promotion for me to Vice President at the manufacturing company where I worked. Allen had added being mayor to his busy life as a real estate agent. We seemed so entangled in our responsibilities, our lives so overrun with duties and tasks. I felt as choked as my rose garden.

I must have slept eventually because the blaring alarm clock woke me at 4:30 to get ready for the hour-long trip to Savannah.

"I can drive while you nap," I said to Allen.

"Don't be ridiculous," he countered. "I'd like to drive you."

In no time, the anesthesiologist set up an intravenous line and asked me to turn on my side. "Just a little stick," he muttered. The next thing I remembered was opening my eyes and feeling Allen's warm hand holding mine.

"I was worried," he confided. "It took so long."

"I'm fine," I said and tried to turn toward him. I felt the tangle of tubes and wires like a net thrown over me.

"You're so pale," he whispered, stroking my face.

"Well," I said, smiling. "You don't look so hot yourself."

He laughed. As I drifted in and out of sleep, I kept telling Allen he didn't have to stay, that he had too much to do. "You need me," he said, "and I'm here."

Something about his simple declaration gave me an incredible sense of peace, like a long-overdue surrender. God, why couldn't it always be like this? Why did I think I had to take care of everything? Why did it seem I was forever spinning my wheels?

The questions nagged at me, even after I left the hospital. Once home, however, Allen handled the errands and drove Meredith to her activities. Meredith made sure I took my pills. For the first time in my life, I didn't allow myself to schedule anything. I looked out the window at the poison ivy, half admiring its strength, half admitting I couldn't get rid of it by myself. It was strange, but depending on family and friends seemed like a kind of truce with my lists and duties.

My life felt different. Better. I found Allen at home more. He insisted on driving me to my doctor appointments. Meredith completed her homework without my nagging. Friends brought casseroles for the freezer.

Caroline, who'd called before surgery, stopped by with a new book and flowers. "Thought you'd enjoy these," she said. Then, as she turned to leave, she thanked me. "When you let someone help, you allow them to feel needed."

For six weeks, there was no to-do list at all. I allowed myself to be cared for and, in doing so, I felt a freedom I'd not known for many years—a freedom from the constant turmoil of living up to my expectations of myself. I'd always thought that depending on others would be tantamount to admitting I was inadequate. Yet there was something incredibly generous about asking for help, something almost spiritual.

Though the poison ivy had once again crept up the south wall of my house, my days didn't seem so entangled and choked. By the time I could drive again, driving wasn't so important anymore. None of the old tasks that filled my hours seemed so urgent. Even as our lives gathered speed and momentum again, I stepped aside and let others carry some of the weight.

One sunny Saturday afternoon, three months after my surgery, I took Meredith to the mall. When we returned, Allen was in the yard with the wheelbarrow and hedge clippers, a smile widening across his face.

"Daddy," yelled Meredith, "what're you doing?"

He came over to us, wiping the sweat from his brow. "Just working on your mom's poison ivy." He laughed, slipped an arm around my waist and kissed the top of my head.

"Thank you, Allen," I said, stunned by his actions, hoping he realized how much I needed him.

In retrospect, I'd allowed responsibilities and obligations to strangle the life out of my relationships. Accepting help turned out to be the cure. The simplest lessons, I decided, are sometime the hardest to learn.

~Debra Ayers Brown

The Gratitude Wave Pool

[Gratitude] allows us to reshape the meaning of any situation,
so we can choose the perspective from which we view a joy,
a sorrow, a disappointment—even success.
~Dr. Robin Smith

I t wasn't yet 8:30 a.m., but instead of entering my workplace, I was leaving it. Along with my purse and lunch sack, I carried a plastic shopping bag of my personal items—framed photos of my husband, my dictionary, ancient packages of microwavable popcorn, packets of tea, and other miscellanea collected throughout nearly four years. I could still hear the hollow sound of "goodbye" ringing in my head. I stumbled to my car, threw in my stuff, and drove home sobbing. I had just been fired.

A half-hour later, I pulled into my driveway still crying. I walked inside and sat down, my tears sporadically interrupted by silent moments of staring into space, forgetting to breathe. I called my husband's cell phone. I knew he was attending a conference, but I had to call. When he picked up, I told him the news.

"I'm coming home," he said immediately.

"Oh, thank you," I said, sniffling, "but you don't have to do that. I don't want you to miss your conference. I just needed to talk."

"No," he declared, "I'm coming home. I'll be there in half an hour."

When he arrived, I was marginally calmer, but only because I'd taken my "as needed" prescription medication for anxiety. He drove us to a nearby café and consoled me as I ate a breakfast burrito. The melted cheese and emotional support were comforting, but just for a little while. Over the next few weeks, the aftershocks from being fired continued.

I was troubled by the repercussions of my termination: What about the people who would be affected by my abandoned projects? What about the critical job information only I knew? What would my co-workers hear, and what would they think of me? What about all those suddenly severed relationships and the people that I'd come to care about over the years? Would I ever get another job with this black mark on my record? For weeks I struggled with anxiety, shame, and sudden outbursts of tears. At night in bed, I fought alternating battles with insomnia and nightmares.

Over dinner on the patio of a bistro, I told three of my close friends how disoriented I felt. I was conscientious, hardworking, and honest, and being fired had come as a shock. I felt as if I'd been told I was going to jail — my first reaction was, "But that doesn't happen to people like me! I'm not a bad person!"

As my friends and I talked, I learned that two of them had been fired before. The third friend had been, as she put it, "the equivalent of almost fired" when an employer was so dissatisfied he refused to pay her (though he later relented). I was surprised; I had known all of them for nearly a decade, and I knew they were good people, smart and caring. Clearly, my "fired equals bad person" thinking was flawed. It was reassuring to realize that these successful, kind people had firings in their pasts too.

About a month after losing my job, I read that Chicken Soup for the Soul was seeking stories on overcoming challenges. The submission deadline was a little more than four months away. There was no question my unemployment was testing my emotions, finances, and even my identity, but I hadn't overcome anything yet. Then I realized something tantalizing: I had four months to turn my life around and share my story. Challenge accepted.

As I read the writing prompt — "What changes did you make to help you cope with these issues and turn negative into positive?" — I realized it was an excellent question. Although I was researching and applying for jobs, I could do more. I wrote down three additional goals: I'd go to a networking night, investigate continuing education, and start acknowledging the people who were helping me on my journey.

Easier said than done. I found an upcoming networking night and asked my friend Nicole to join me. She said yes, and I felt relieved and hopeful—until I read that the event was cancelled for that month and the next. We agreed we'd go the month after that, but my enthusiasm waned. For my continuing education, I researched opportunities for classes on graphic design software and social media. Although I discovered useful articles online, I had yet to find the low-cost overview training I wanted.

Thankfully, the third of my goals was easy to achieve. I decided that once a week for ten weeks, I would handwrite a thank you card to someone who had helped me either with the emotional support of losing my job or in my search for a new job. Each week, as I pulled out my box of thank you notes and put pen to cardstock, I was inspired by others' generosity. In addition to having a financially and emotionally supportive husband, I had references who would praise me if called by potential employers, family who sent encouraging cards and e-mails, and friends who helped me network and sent me job leads. Writing thank you letters kept me feeling positive, mindful of my blessings, and grateful—emotions easily lost in the face of joblessness.

My friend Nicole had done an enormous amount for me, and she got my first thank you card. Black ink filled the page as I tried to squeeze in a comically long list of all the ways she'd helped. Feeling appreciative, I mailed the note and didn't think about it again until about three weeks later, when I got her e-mailed response:

"I was never into giving or getting thank you cards until we started hanging out. I wasn't against them exactly, just sort of thought of them as frivolous. Now I am starting to see how valuable they are. I have one from you posted in front of me at my work desk, and it has a list of ways you saw me supporting you through this job loss mess, and it makes me feel appreciated and noticed. But in addition to feeling appreciated and noticed, I get to see the good stuff you liked RIGHT

IN FRONT OF ME. It is a reminder of the ways I can be a good friend (to you). I didn't do any of the things you listed because I thought I was 'supposed to,' but I can see from your list that I did things you appreciated. This means so much to me."

I was delighted to get Nicole's message. Soon after that, another friend battling her own unemployment thanked me for writing to her. Like a wave pool of gratitude, the thankfulness that flowed outward was rippling back to me and lifting me up. Writing thank you notes was the best thing I could have done to dissolve my negativity and move forward.

Shortly before my self-assigned weeks of note sending were due to end, I got a job that fit my skills and interests. I also made a decision: I would continue sending thank you cards until I had sent all ten. My happy ending wasn't only being employed, it was putting on a swimsuit and jumping into my gratitude wave pool.

~Alaina Smith

Chapter 8

Find Your Inner Strength

Rising to the Challenge

USA vs. My Mom

*The turning point in the process of growing up is when you discover
the core of strength within you that survives all hurt.*
~Max Lerner

In 2012, 1,276,099 people were arrested for possession of a controlled substance in the United States, according to one website that I researched. My mother was one of them. I would have never thought my mom would end up in prison over prescription medication. I didn't know you could get addicted to something a doctor prescribed. But ever since my parents separated in 2007, my mom had abused her prescription medication.

Mom has been diagnosed with a number of things, including scoliosis and depression. Along with those diagnoses came several medicines: Oxycontin, Percocet, and Xanax are a few that come to mind. These are highly addictive medications. I believe her addiction started when I was in sixth grade. Her friends would come over, and she'd tell me to go to my room because they were having "adult talk." I wasn't ignorant as to what was really going on; I knew she abused her medicine. She crushed up her pills and used a straw or a broken pen to snort them. Once I asked why she didn't just take them by mouth and she replied that they worked faster when she snorted them. I didn't really understand why she needed the medicine.

Mom had a new boyfriend when I was in seventh grade. He paid for our apartment, bought her a car, and always made sure we had food and necessities. He seemed like an okay guy, but then I found out that he abused prescription medication too. They were both looking for a better life and somehow they thought that abusing drugs was the answer. They were always nodding off. Holding a conversation with them was nearly impossible. They would drool and mumble things to themselves. Their eyes would roll back and their bodies were lifeless at all hours of the day. If they even started to come down from their high, they would do more drugs.

My mom wasn't my mom anymore. I became angry; I was tired of watching her do that to herself. It was as if she had just forgotten about me, like she didn't care about me anymore. I would come home from school and find her passed out. I would run to her with tears rolling down my face because I thought she was dead.

Then my mom and her boyfriend started to sell prescription medications. A guy would give them a certain amount to sell, and they would bring the money back to him and get a piece of it. They claimed it was just "easy money" until they got back on their feet and got real jobs. We always had random people coming and going at our house. This happened throughout the day and even during the night.

Sometime after they started dealing, my mom and her boyfriend began making trips with groups of people to Florida. In Florida, they would all visit multiple doctors' offices as new patients, get prescriptions, and then go to multiple pharmacies to get the scripts filled. My mom made these trips several times a year. She was trafficking drugs across state lines, a federal offense. In 2011, a group of six people including my mom, split up into two vehicles and drove down to Florida. On their return, the Georgia State Police pulled over one of the vehicles—one that my mom wasn't in.

I don't know exactly what happened, but they were released and drove back to Kentucky. About a month later, they were arrested in Somerset, Kentucky and held in Pulaski County Detention Center. The police offered them a deal—if they named the others involved in the drug activity, they would get reduced sentences. So, they spoke out against my mom and the others involved. On January 31, 2012, a U.S. Marshall found my mother and arrested her. I found out via text message that my mother had been taken to jail. It was the worst day of my life.

I would go to Pulaski County Detention Center about twice a week to see my mom. You were only allowed thirty-minute visits, and you had to sit behind a glass window and talk through a nasty telephone that didn't work half the time. Most of our visits ended in tears or fights.

My mom went before the judge on September 11, 2012 and pleaded guilty to the drug charges. I went with my grandmother to watch the trial. We sat in the last row and saw my mom enter through the side door in handcuffs and foot cuffs, as if she were a dangerous criminal. She started crying when she saw me, and I did too. I will never forget when the judge asked her if she had anything else to say. Despite the judge's warning not to look into the seats behind her, my mom turned to face me. With tears rolling down her cheeks, she apologized and told me how much she loved me. It absolutely broke my heart.

The judge sentenced her to fifty-seven to seventy-one months in prison, due to the counts and her criminal history. At first it didn't hit me that it would be a long time until my mom was back in my life. But now, two years into her sentence, I realize how much time together we have lost; time that we will never get back.

My mom used to be a powerful, independent, lovely woman. She was a single mom, had a job and a house. She was even thinking about going to college to further her education in childcare. Now, she is residing in a federal prison camp, about eight hours away from me. We usually get five-minute phone calls once a week. I haven't seen my mom in over a year. I haven't hugged my mom since January 1, 2012.

I can't help but wonder what our lives could have been like if she hadn't used prescription drugs. I watched her ruin her life with prescription medication, and because of that, I will never have a normal life. My mom hasn't had a chance to see me go to my high school proms. She hasn't been there to help me through the most important times in a teenage girl's life. I graduated high school in May of 2014, and my mom wasn't able to see it. I started college in August of 2014, and she missed that too.

It has had a huge impact on me, but I have come out on top of this situation. I took AP classes in high school, while also holding down a part-time job and participating in extracurricular school activities. My family has told me that they don't know how I'm living with this, that they would break if they were put in my position. But in all reality, you can't stop living when you have a life-changing experience. Life goes on, and someday it's going to get better. I don't feel sorry for myself. I accomplish a lot more that way.

~McKenzie Vaught

71

Teachings of a Clown

Those who bring sunshine to the lives of others cannot keep it from themselves.
~James Matthew Barrie

I listened closely to the nursing report for my newest hospice assignment. The more Tina told me about the patient, the more doubt I felt. The nightmare list of patient problems seemed endless: amyotrophic lateral sclerosis (ALS), quadriplegic, limited mobility remains in right arm and torso, unable to speak, feeding tube. How could I possibly be of help to this man? Where would I start? What would I say? How would I say it?

I'd been an RN for three decades and had cared for similar patients, but volunteering for respite care as a layperson is another ball game. Respite care involves going to the patient's home and assessing how I might support both the patient and the family. Being an RN, I am often assigned the more challenging patients. I think this new one fit the bill.

The next week found me driving to the country to see the daunting mystery man. After several wrong turns and a lot of dust, I pulled into the correct driveway. It took several knocks for a spry, gray-haired lady in jean capris to open the front door. She was warm in her welcome but politely let me know I'd chosen the never-used door assigned to strangers and the UPS deliveryman. Not the best first impression I wanted to make.

Mary introduced herself as the patient's mother. The warm smile and twinkling eyes soon absolved me of my wrong door sin.

Why was I so nervous?

Mary showed me to the living room couch while she finished getting her middle-aged son up to a recliner with the aid of a Hoyer Lift. Her agility spoke to her having done this before. Then I remembered a piece of my earlier report, "Patient's sister also died of ALS." Mary had cared for her daughter, and now cared for her son, while watching the cruel, progressive disease chip away pieces of her own flesh and blood. I cringed with uneasiness and guilt.

Next, I met my new patient, who presented as a paradox. The handsome six-foot-four man barely fit the oversized recliner. His eyes had the same sparkle as his mom's, his hair was combed precisely, and his right hand clasped a wadded red farmer's handkerchief while his body involuntarily leaned a bit to the left. But it was his long legs that really caught my attention. They stuck out from his lap blanket and showcased one-of-a-kind knee-highs with horizontal stripes of red, yellow, blue, and neon green.

Glancing up to see the big mischievous grin on his face, I could only chuckle and shake my head. He was the one making me feel at ease in his home. My doubt, fear, and nervousness were gone. I'd just met Wul-wee, a professional clown. Oh, yeah, we'd both be fine.

We quickly found much in common: we were hard workers, country-raised, faith-filled, writers, and both were trying to live life well with a chronic illness. I have multiple sclerosis.

We once talked about how we grieved for our losses. Wul-wee calmly stated, "I miss walking in the woods and talking out loud to the person next to me."

I replied, "I miss being a nurse."

Along the way, my new friend Wul-wee became a patient teacher and mentor. He taught me how to talk with a person who can't talk. Looking closely and listening well are the basics. Wul-wee could say a lot with a gaze, squint, nod, tiny shrug or a busy index finger. If body language didn't suffice, he'd resort to a hunt and peck on his iPad that converted his entry into a tinny, robotic computer voice. Pretty cool. I learned butting in to guess his thoughts while he typed did not help. It was rude and no different than interrupting someone speaking out loud.

As the ALS thief continued to rob my friend of functioning body parts, he continued to write daily with his right index finger. During the time I knew Wul-wee, he completed a biography, *Balloons N Stuff*, and began his second manuscript, an autobiography.

I teased him: "You are such a show off and make me look like a slacker." My first book was published that year and during the next eight months I had written a total of three chapters of my second book.

He volleyed with one shoulder shrug: "You're a slow poke." There was no need to use the keyboard for that one.

So we talked a lot about books and a lot about clowning. Clowning had been both a passion and ministry for Wul-wee. He taught others in clown school and received honors nationally. His antics and balloon sculpting touched the lives of children and adults. I know his outreach ministry will continue with his book. It saddens me he did not get to see that happen.

One time when I arrived for a visit, Wul-wee greeted me with, "I'm having a party, a celebration today."

"Well, you got me, what are you celebrating?" I asked.

"It's my two-year anniversary of ALS." He grinned widely, paused, and waited for my light bulb to go on.

Aaaah, I got it. He had beaten ALS for two years and he was "still kicking." Remarkable. That was powerful for me. Could I ever be that strong?

Wul-wee taught me so much, the biggest being to make the most of what you can do and celebrate life every day. I appreciated my time with David W. Ritzert, but it was too short. David, his devoted wife Vi (alias Baggy Geenz, the clown), and I talked about the whole crazy process of death and dying. There is no road map. There is no magic. There is just living life well until you can't any more. These two got it. They were true role models for anyone meeting a life challenge. Their strong faith in God guided them daily and their love for each other ran deep. They knew there was a time for holding hands and crying, and a time to load up and head to a Pink Floyd concert.

The three of us discussed what the book cover of *Balloons N Stuff* might look like. I was shown a picture under consideration that looked a lot like David's wedding picture where he wore green and white clown shoes with his tuxedo. The picture's viewpoint is from the head of David's hospital bed, looking over white sheets and ends with the same two gigantic green and white clown shoes, sticking out and forming a really big V. It's perfect! When I think of my dear friend, David, that hilarious picture will forever be branded in my mind. Thank you Wul-wee!

~Mary Ellen Ziliak

72

Running for My Life

If you want to live, you must walk. If you want to live long, you must run.
~Jinabhai Navik

am sweeping my maple kitchen floor, my triathlon finisher's medal swinging back and forth in rhythm with the broom. Abbey, my five-year-old daughter, runs past me on her way to the back yard, her shoulder-length blond curly hair bouncing behind her. She stops and turns to me. "You still have your medal on. Did you know that?"

I laugh. "I am planning to wear it all day long." She giggles at her silly mom. "Tell me again, did you win?" I try to explain to her that I did not even come close to winning. She glances at my medal again, shakes her head and exits the patio door.

Did I win? I ponder the question. In my mind, I won the moment my face lowered into the lake water, cold enough to warrant a wet suit. Now I stand here having showered off the dried salty layer of sweat from my 750-meter lake swim, my 20K bike ride and my 5K run. What I have not showered off is the three-digit number marked vertically along my left arm or the sense of achievement. I keep glancing at the black numbers marked on my skin. I did it. I completed my first sprint triathlon. I feel strong and fit. I have demolished another mental barrier about my limits.

The phone rings and it is my sister-in-law calling to congratulate me and ask about the details. I put the broom in the closet and take the portable phone onto the deck and into the warm, sunny June afternoon. I hold the phone against my left ear, my left elbow and my right forearm rest along the railing of the wooden deck. I watch my dark-haired three-year-old son, Alexander, playing in the sandbox, sitting on the corner seat so he doesn't get too dirty. Abbey sits smack in the middle of the handmade, blue, wooden sandbox, running fingers and toys through the sand. My husband putters in the yard, staying close to Alexander, who can sprint to the road faster than any of the athletes that crossed the finish line ahead of me.

My sister-in-law is congratulatory and supportive. After I have broken down the three events and expressed my wonder at being able to do this, she asks, "Why do you do this? Why do you push your body this way?" She is curious and concerned, but not judgmental. We are the same age and she is a fit mom who likes to run but not race, so this level of commitment has her bemused. My tone is joking, but my words are dead serious. "I am running for my life."

How else can I explain it? Most simply, the endorphins bring me joy. But more than that, I need to complete something. I need something I can check off my list. I need something with a tangible reminder, like my medal. Motherhood does not offer many of these things. For all moms, motherhood is complicated, all consuming and never ending. For me, it has also meant one overwhelming medical challenge after another. My motherhood triathlon includes: Abbey's cancer diagnosis at eleven months, a life-threatening allergy for Alexander, and now, likely an autism diagnosis for him. I know my sister-in-law is worried that this athleticism is pushing my tired, middle-aged body too hard. Some days I wonder the same thing.

I struggle to explain how pushing my body is positive. Painful and tiring at times, yes, but positive. It is unlike the year I pushed my body while caring for Abbey when she was diagnosed with a rare form of leukemia that required a year of intense, tortuous treatment. It is unlike living in that hospital room with no windows for almost six months. It is unlike how my body managed to carry a pregnancy to term while living in that hospital. It is unlike when my infant son, my twenty-month-old daughter and I all slept in a single hospital bed for days on end while my husband returned to work to support us. It is unlike breastfeeding a new baby whose small, dark head lay cradled in my left elbow while my right hand caught vomit with a cardboard fish and chips container as my daughter on chemotherapy retched in bed beside us.

Running, biking, swimming—this pushing is good and necessary.

The exertion is rebuilding my body and my spirit, drained from that year of chemotherapy and the times my daughter almost died. My training flushes away the fear of a relapse, at least for the minutes that I am running, swimming or biking. What I do not say to anyone, even my husband, and what is only a whisper in my soul is that this exercise will make me strong in case I need to guide her through treatment again. If she relapses, I know I will need every ounce of strength I can mine from these muscle fibers.

The first time through cancer treatment I was naïve. I did not know the script. I did not know that my New Balance runners would sit ignored in the closet of her hospital room. I did not know that living in a windowless hospital room and dealing with daily, sometimes hourly, medical crises while growing a baby inside me would drain all my energy. I did not know there would be no time or stamina left for a rejuvenating run.

Now I know what childhood cancer looks like. That knowledge is terrifying. I know chemotherapy can erase my baby's lips, replacing them with yellow blisters. I know what it is like to change my baby's diaper with gloves because her waste is toxic. I know that some kids who leave the oncology ward do so with physical or mental handicaps. I know that about half the children admitted to that ward will die, no matter what the statistics say. I know that my only hope of surviving in that world again is to build my physical body into an endurance vessel.

So I swim twice a week—on Tuesday night when my husband can watch the kids and on Saturday morning at seven when I can be home before the family is out of their pajamas. My runs are squeezed in between my son's appointments with a speech therapist, Early Intervention and my daughter's kindergarten. My bike sits on a training device in my basement so I can ride when kids are in bed. In the pool, I don the mask of just another mom in the blue Speedo swimsuit, a woman in training, training for fun and fitness.

During treatment, another chemo mom assured me that I would carry the cancer experience with me as a medal of strength. "If you can do this you can do anything," she said. So I keep training to make sure that remains true.

~Sue LeBreton

Starting Over at Eighty

Travel and change of place impart new vigor to the mind.
~Seneca

I was all alone in Chicago at age seventy-nine, with a son in California and a daughter and granddaughters in New England. One by one, old friends had departed for warmer climes or had simply departed. "Mom, you can't live there by yourself!" became my children's almost daily mantra. That was ridiculous. Of course I could. It's not as if I were some emancipated teenager living in her first apartment in a questionable neighborhood, I reasoned.

Born and bred in suburban Chicago, I couldn't imagine living anywhere else. Leave the home that I loved in the town where my children were raised? Nostalgia blurred my reasoning. No more Wrigley Field, cheering on my beloved Cubbies between mouthfuls of Chicago pizza? No more short rides on the Metra to downtown Chicago, Michigan Avenue shopping, world class museums, theater, fine dining, the opera, magnificent architecture, a spectacular lakefront with miles of bike and jogging paths?

An unscheduled stay in the hospital with no advocate caused me to reconsider. I had to admit that catching a movie with a friend had morphed into a solitary time-killer. Shopping at boutiques and patronizing pricey restaurants were no longer doable on a fixed income. They had become instead sharp reminders of the past, where I had increasingly begun to live. Memories of past decisions taunted me with scenarios of a history impossible to rewrite. I was caught up in coulda, shoulda, woulda, seeing more ghosts than blue skies.

It was time to turn the page and begin a new chapter. Would it be the East Coast with the girls or the West Coast with my son? His frequent business trips and upscale location ruled out a move to California. My daughter and granddaughters, on the other hand, lived in a small Massachusetts town where affordable senior living was available. It was a no-brainer.

Selling the house was gut wrenching. Knowing that my new quarters offered a fraction of the space necessitated some drastic decisions. The first casualty was the eight-piece dining room set. In the weeks before the move, I pared down to the essentials. In the days before the movers arrived, my treasures were whittled down to three piles—keep, discard and don't-know-yet. A lifetime's worth of possessions changed places like dancers in a Virginia reel, jumping from one pile to another as I wrestled with the decisions. Renouncing earthly goods is difficult!

Finally the day came. Armed with a carefully detailed itinerary and my ten-year-old Malibu, equipped with new belts, hoses and tires, I was on my way. My companion was a caged Parakeet riding shotgun. Forging eastward with the morning sun in my eyes, unaccustomed to reading the overhead signs in high-speed traffic, I prayed: Dear Lord, don't let me take the wrong off-ramp and end up in Tulsa. An uneventful thousand miles later, my daughter and I exchanged hugs and kisses.

Some time has now passed and I've made adjustments. Frequent street name changes and mastering roundabouts instead of driving the familiar grid patterns of my Midwestern past proved challenging at first. More than once I lost my way in forest-like settings on unfamiliar country roads. Instead of meeting stereotypical flinty New Englanders who respond in terse monosyllables, I have found them to be friendly, helpful and responsive to my overtures. Funny how that works. The library's book of the month club provided introductions to fellow bookworms. I found several kindred spirits who enjoy *Scrabble* as much as I do. My energy level is higher now, thanks to gym classes with my Silver Sneaker health aficionados. Ask me the names of my favorite restaurants and I can rattle off five. Fenway Park and the Red Sox have claimed my new allegiance. Patriots fever has me in its grip.

Being happy in my new life was never a question. It was a statement. Forsaking the familiar for the unknown has brought many rewards: spontaneous lunch dates with my daughter, granddaughters who have folded me into their lives, and above all, a new great-granddaughter to cuddle, see her first steps, and hear her first words.

One door closed and another opened. All I had to do was take that first step. I'm so glad I did.

~Joan Dayton

A Hand Up

The only thing that overcomes hard luck is hard work.
~Harry Golden

"There was a fire yesterday." My mother's voice was matter of fact. "The shop and the apartment are in pretty bad shape. You can't come home. There's no place to come to right now and we don't have money to pay for you to stay in college. So you have to decide what to do."

Stunned, I asked a few questions, hung up the phone and fled to the Resident Advisor's room in tears.

I was nineteen years old, in my sophomore spring at the University of Michigan, 600 miles from my New Jersey home. A home that no longer had a place for me.

"No one died," the RA soothed. "It's only stuff. In two months the semester is done. Then you can figure out what's next." At about twenty-two or twenty-three years old, she probably hadn't dealt with anything more traumatic from her undergraduate charges than a breakup with a boyfriend or disagreements between roommates.

No one died, except I felt my dream of a degree from this university slipping away. And I was on my own to keep it alive.

Since I'd been twelve, the third daughter of a family in a blue-collar mill town, my father had supported my dream to pursue a science degree at a big university. Less than a quarter of the students from our local high school went on to college. Most who did stayed nearby and became teachers, nurses, learned a trade, or took a factory job. A mere handful of the two hundred in my senior class ventured away from their roots, yet Dad never questioned my decision to leave the state for a campus I'd not even seen, and he promised to help as much as he could.

As soon as I was old enough I'd worked at jobs ranging from writing a newspaper column, sales clerking at department stores, dispensing ice cream at Dairy Queen, and lifeguarding at the Y, socking away as much as I could toward my goal. I also graduated as valedictorian with an assortment of small scholarship awards. That, plus what Dad could send me from month to month, had gotten me to that April of the second year, and that phone call.

I confided my plight to a favorite professor, one who really took time with students who shared his passion for biological sciences. "Go to the Dean of Women," he advised.

The Dean of Women? In a huge university, what was one undergrad in the grand scheme of things?

To my surprise, she was approachable and sympathetic, but skeptical. "Unless you want to drop out and put off finishing a degree until you are in a more stable situation, I'd advise you to enroll in summer school. You don't need to stay in the dorm; you might find a cheap apartment. I don't know how you're going to make it."

"I can't drop out. I have nowhere to go and I'd still need to find a job and a place to live. And I'm afraid if I quit now, starting again will be even harder." Threaded through my desperate anxiety I heard my father's voice from all the times life had thrown us a curve: "We'll always manage." And we did.

"Okay," the Dean said. "Here's a deal. If you can get yourself through summer classes, I'll give you a tuition grant for the fall and allow you to move to an approved rooming house. You'll pay rent, but can probably economize on meals and piece together some jobs."

Piece together jobs and study? Economize? That sounded familiar from the prior six years of my life. I was flooded with gratitude for the chance to continue toward a degree and I understood her clever challenge. If I could manage the next four months myself I'd have earned her faith in me plus the grant-in-aid she held out as a reward in the autumn.

"Deal," I said. "I'll make it somehow."

After final exams that June I took the train for a brief trip to New Jersey. My dad's one-man glass and picture frame business had indeed been heavily damaged. But true to his nature, he'd cleaned up the debris and taken out a bank loan to replace the inventory, which was not insured, then hired carpenters to make the apartment livable. My younger sister had moved in with the family of a high school friend in exchange for babysitting and housework. I'd have to replace the summer clothes that weren't with me in Ann Arbor, and years later I came to the strange realization that I had almost no documented past. No high school yearbook, no family pictures, keepsakes, artwork, or award-winning essays.

Back in Ann Arbor that summer, I housesat in the basement apartment of a professor on sabbatical — rent-free, worked in the cafeteria at my former dormitory, took classes, and scoured the bulletin boards on campus for psychology experiments paying subjects twenty dollars in any study concocted by a grad student.

Also, for the rest of my college career, I sold my blood once a month for thirty dollars to a medical research team who needed fresh, not bank, blood. And, of course, I borrowed money.

College wasn't the fun time for me that it is for so many young people. When I feel a tinge of regret, it passes when I measure it against what I gained in maturity and determination, self-reliance and ingenuity, which served me well when later employed in research. Those years were invaluable in coping with life's later difficulties. And they imbued me with a belief about what can be accomplished if you truly want it badly enough to work for it.

Recently, my husband and I endowed a modest scholarship granted each year, not to a high school senior, but to a student entering the final year toward any degree, one who has a student loan. This unusual scholarship reflects the Dean of Women's challenge to me that awful spring of the fire. It also reflects the attitude of my father and my husband.

"First show me how much you will do to attain what you say you want, then I'll help you."

~Ann Vitale

75

Just One More Step, Darling

The first step binds one to the second.
~French Proverb

f someone had told me in June 2013 that I would take part in a marathon event, I would have laughed. Yet there I was on October 6, 2013 with a medal around my neck.

Okay, it was the 4.2K race and I walked it more than I ran it, but I still did it.

Did I mention that I weigh around 300 pounds? I also have asthma, but it's not that much of a problem because I take good medication. Also, I haven't mentioned that I live with four anxiety disorders. One of which, my social anxiety disorder, makes me deadly afraid of people's judgment. Yeah, I know.

But somewhere in the middle of August I decided that registering for the 4.2K event of our local marathon would be a great motivator to get in shape. So I registered and started walking religiously.

I told only a few people—my family and some other people I trusted.

My training went well until the middle of September, when my work situation started deteriorating and left me too exhausted to do much once I left the office. I also had volunteer commitments for another local event. So the frequency of my walks decreased and that was not good.

I was able to keep my anxiety in check until it was time to get my race number. I kept wondering what the other participants and the volunteers would think. I didn't have the usual runner's profile.

I got my number without problems or comments, but I did skip the humiliation of the T-shirt table. It's very nice of them to provide a keepsake for everyone, but considering there were no shirts that would remotely fit me, I turned my back on the table and quickly left. That started me doubting myself again. What the heck was I doing? I had no right going there. The 4.2 is the "popular event," with families and young children participating. But I was willing to bet a hundred bucks that not many obese people had registered.

I had nightmares for most of the night before the race, which is NOT the best way to start a race day. When I got up, for a brief moment I considered not going. But I didn't want to disappoint myself or my family. Then I considered giving up again when I realized I had forgotten to wash my best pair of running pants. But Walmart, which sells them, opens at 8 a.m. My race wasn't until 10 a.m., and it was barely 9 a.m.

I had another fit of despair when I checked the weather. The sun was shining, but it was barely 32 degrees. But then I realized that with the appropriate clothing, I would be just fine.

No matter how hard I tried, there was no valid reason for me to give up. So, I drove to Walmart, bought a pair of pants and a running shirt, and headed to the starting line.

I quickly found that people didn't really care about me; they were too focused on their own experience. It appeased me a bit, but not completely. Once I ended up at the end of the pack, those real athletes would surely wonder what I was doing there.

But it was much too late to turn back. So I started walking, my earphones playing loud music to drown out the possible hurtful comments.

Pretty quickly my calf started hurting. I must not have stretched enough, but I pushed on. My nerves and my bad night also took a toll, and as I looked at people passing me, I panicked. I didn't want to be last. Then I took a deep breath, and told myself it wasn't a race.

Well, okay, it WAS a race. But since I had no chance of finishing first, the only thing that mattered was finishing. The only person I was racing was myself.

Just then something happened. As I relaxed, I started noticing that the people passing me on their way to the finish line were encouraging me!

All along the way there were "real" runners giving me a nod, a wink, a thumbs up, a "good job, don't give up." I didn't care why they were doing it. Was it pity? Was it (dare I say) a bit of admiration for the courage it had taken me to be there? Or (more likely) plain old good sportsmanship? It's not important, because it made me feel like I belonged.

As I walked I kept repeating to myself, "Just one more step, darling." That had been my motto in 2007 when I started battling my anxiety disorders and the severe depression they caused. That motto is how I try to lead my life now. When things get overwhelming or when life doesn't happen the way I would like, that's what I tell myself: Just one more step, darling—because every step takes you closer to your goal.

So I pushed on, one step at a time, and eventually I saw the big tent at the finish line. I tried going a little faster, but I was tired and hungry.

As the finish line got closer, more and more people lined the path clapping and cheering on the runners. I never thought I would be so grateful to see all these people.

Finally, the finish line was only a few meters away. I started running. That's how I crossed the finish line, running with the last bit of energy I had.

The moment I crossed the line, I heard someone calling my name. I would know that voice anywhere—my sister, who was there with my father, both beaming at me. I wasn't alone anymore.

Then I heard my name over the speakers, as they announced all the participants as we came in, and I felt incredible pride. One last high five to one of the local radio personalities who served as the announcer and it was over.

I had done it. I had the courage to register. I had the courage to show up and participate with everyone else. I did it with my head held high.

With a time of fifty-five minutes, I was neither the slowest nor the fastest. But it's not important; I was faster than if I hadn't gotten up from my couch.

I have already decided that next year I'll be RUNNING that same 4.2K.

~Genevieve Gosselin

76

Having Heart

Strength will grow from the heart, blossom as results,
and wither in others' hearts as seeds.
~Mikhael Dominico

W hen my husband of forty-two years died suddenly, I became one of those left-without-insurance widows. Bills began to stack up. It had been over twenty years since I had worked as a teacher and the thought of returning to the classroom scared me beyond words. What little income I made came from teaching gardening at the local community college, but there were often not enough students and the classes were frequently cancelled.

When a faculty member asked if I would be interested in teaching at a homeless men's shelter and informed me that most of the population were felons, I was afraid. Then when I was informed that this would probably be the biggest challenge of my life, I just didn't think I could do such a job.

Over the next few weeks, my financial situation got worse. On the brink of losing my house and my car, I decided to go back to work and conquer the fear one step at a time. At age seventy-seven, I wondered where I could get a job that would help me pay the bills. The first step would be to push through my fear and contact the college to see if that teaching position was still open. Following an interview, I was told, "You are exactly the kind of person we need for this job."

I struggled with thoughts of what might happen. A bunch of

"what ifs" filled my thoughts. What if I was attacked and raped? What if I was beat up? What if I was a failure in the classroom? But I knew I had to give it a try. I drove to the rundown section of town where the shelter was located. I pulled into the driveway and saw several men walking out from under a canopy of trees with only backpacks on their shoulders. Did they live in the woods? How did they survive? What would they think of me?

Slowly I walked towards the steps leading to a set of double doors. My heart pounded as the men walked behind me. Security was high. A guard stood behind locked doors and used a wand to detect any metal items when the men and I entered the premises. "Is this where I'm supposed to be?" I questioned myself. When I heard the doors slam shut behind me, I frightened myself to the point where I had to use the bathroom. Within seconds, a guard accompanied me to the restroom. I felt like a criminal who couldn't be trusted to pee alone.

A recurring question kept me wondering. Do I work inside these restricted walls or do I allow fear to overcome me and forget about this job? The answer didn't come immediately. I don't know if it was curiosity, my need to work or my desire to teach, but I managed to get through the next three hours of classroom teaching, and I became increasingly overwhelmed by the courteous responses to the questions I asked.

"Does anyone know how to plant a tulip bulb?"

"Yes, ma'am," came the answer from one man seated at the end of the table. "My gramma had a beautiful garden. I would like to plant a garden when I leave this place." He smiled.

"What is a sustainable garden?" I asked.

A voice from the back of the room replied, "I know, ma'am. It's when you grow your own food and feed the family."

Over the next three weeks the men began to share their personal stories and I listened. Each one had been dealing with hard luck including job loss and divorce. Some had committed crimes. Several were incarcerated for DUIs. Unannounced sobriety and HIV tests were frequently given. A group of jobless veterans who had returned from Afghanistan and Pakistan were living in the shelter. With so many men without jobs and little hope for the future, I forgot about my fears.

Here were people who didn't have a home, a family, who had not seen their children for a long time. I began to share my stories with them. Soon, we formed a bond. As more men arrived, the old guard began to look out for me. "We got your back, Miss Anita," I was told many times. "No one will harm you."

When I shared a story about my dog getting sick and being put to sleep, I was surprised when Alan, a jobless scientist, rose from his chair and approached me with open arms. "You will be okay, Miss Anita." He hugged me. "All of us will pray for you." Terry, a retired veteran, handed me a wildflower he had picked from the woods. "We love you. You have heart," he said.

When First Sergeant Glen heard about my need for money and food, he walked two miles to the nearest market one afternoon and, with his food stamps, bought me a loaf of bread, a tub of margarine, one dozen eggs and a raw cut-up chicken. "You don't have to be hungry on my watch." He smiled.

One day after class I found a crumpled $100 bill shoved into the first page of the teacher's guidebook. "Who gave this to me?" I asked. My eyes welled with tears.

"Read the card," came a voice from the back of the room.

I fumbled, hands shaking as I opened a folded paper napkin. It read:

"Nothing can touch the beauty of your soul.
Nothing can take away the love in your heart.
Nothing can stop the people who care about you.
From Your Family."

I dried my tears. "All of you are my heart," I told the men. "This is definitely where I'm supposed to be."

Sometimes others can see your heart and who you really are inside. You only have to find the courage and believe that you can thrive with those whom you fear.

~Anita Stone

77

Strength in a Child's Voice

If a man does not keep pace with his companions,
perhaps it is because he hears a different drummer. Let him
step to the music which he hears, however measured or far away.
~Henry David Thoreau

t was an ordinary summer day. People were milling about on the main thoroughfare, bikes zigzagging through traffic, cafés and pubs spilling onto the sidewalks, patrons sipping their way through a lazy Friday afternoon.

We were ordinary that day too. Just another family managing the hectic jumble of kids' lessons, bills, our careers, endless streams of birthday parties, too little sleep and the occasional date night.

But it was all shattered by a single word: autism.

"Your son has autism," said the child psychologist, who was neither gentle nor particularly sympathetic when she delivered the blow that knocked us flat for the better part of a year. I thought I had prepared for this moment. After all, we had long suspected our younger son, Casey, wasn't following the traditional path. At age three and a half, he was affectionate, happy-go-lucky and bright, but he was struggling to speak beyond two- or three-word phrases, and would happen upon a word or an activity and get stuck there with a seemingly endless "repeat" button. He also had fine motor skill difficulties, gut problems, sleep issues and some other behavioural challenges—things we would later learn are all associated with autism spectrum disorder (ASD).

But it was Casey's inability to communicate fully and fluidly that stung us the worst. It seemed cruel and ironic that our son would lack what the rest of the family had in abundance. His father is multilingual the master of three European languages, two Indian dialects, English plus a smattering of Swahili—the hallmark of an early childhood that spanned three continents. My elder son was already thriving in an early bilingual (French-English) school, and I was a writer by trade. We had a surplus of words and we spent them recklessly, unthinkingly.

That would all change.

We quickly learned that what other kids intuited—grammar innuendo, body language—Casey would have to study, as if a second language, except it would be his first. So the lessons began in ear nest—for all of us, really. A speech therapist came to our house twice weekly for an hour and taught us the building blocks of what we had been taking for granted. Piece by piece, she laid out the connecting fragments that we hoped would one day be the means through which our beautiful little boy could both find and express himself.

While our life settled into a comforting routine, albeit a full one with medical appointments and assessments and therapy sessions magically squeezed into the household calendar, I realized that as Casey was starting to find his voice, I was losing mine.

As any writer who is also a parent of young children knows, it is challenging enough to shave off quiet time for yourself every day to pause, and then write. Having a child with special needs made that challenge almost impossible.

Writing time quickly morphed into time spent ferrying Casey to various specialists, studying the mysteries of autism, discerning quackery from science, mapping out the byzantine structure of the publicly funded health care system, and complying with the demands of disability tax laws. All of this while making sure both boys had all the thoughtful attention and care that young children require. My partner was equally engaged. (How can you not love a man who on hearing his child has autism, goes out and becomes certified in Applied Behavioural Analysis?) But it was a serious challenge just to keep afloat.

Casey, on the other hand, was thriving. An integrated nursery school with a clever educative assistant and caring teachers kept him challenged and engaged every day, and his evenings and weekends were full of more therapy, lessons and social outings.

After a year, his few word utterances finally became five- or even eight-word sentences. Occasionally he could even be called "chatty." Sure, the grammar was, and still is, often a mess, and he can seldom communicate things in the abstract (ideas, thoughts or items that are not in his immediate, present environment). But the words come freely and aren't choked in his neuro-passages, and what he intends to communicate is usually clear.

Watching Casey's trajectory has often been thrilling. Hearing hard-earned words, phrases or constructs pop out of his mouth, after months and months of methodical teaching, coaching and practice, elicits rounds of applause from his family and puts a triumphant grin on Casey's face. He knows he's nailed it. I never thought I could be elated over a correctly selected pronoun or a subject-verb-object composition, but that's the way it is with autism: words are like gems dropping from your child's mouth—every one a treasure.

It's pretty clear that developmental milestones with Casey will never be mapped in a slow, steady upward arc of achievement, as with most kids. His development lags and sprints in abrupt and unpredictable bursts. For example, while Casey still struggles to answer simple questions like: "Did you have fun today?" he can easily recount all the stops on many of the bus routes in the city—and spot a hexagon at 300 metres.

Here's a boy who once, to our collective amazement, cracked a hotel safe at age two and a half, long before he could answer, "What's your name?" or "How old are you?" He still, now aged five, struggles with the appropriate response to these questions some days (or seems puzzled that the answers would be relevant to anything). Autism is one mess of developmental brilliance and delay, all bundled together, and you never know which bit will pop up at any given moment. Somewhere in all of this, Casey resides.

While he is finding his voice, step by painful step, and on his own particular path, we feel blessed, proud of his hard work and achievement, and exhausted. His journey has become our collective journey too.

Never would I have predicted this path. But it is the road I'm on and I walk it willfully, willingly, and with grace and thanks. When your eyes are opened to the world of children with physical and mental challenges — and there are so many — you never see the same again. You throw away concepts like "normal" or "ordinary" and you embrace possibility like a religion. No one works harder than a child who has to struggle to walk or talk or eat, yet still they engage the world playfully and lovingly and with an openness to marvel at.

I may have lost my voice for a while, or rather, the time to express it as I'd like, but need is slowly giving my voice a broader range, more depth and strength, with a tremor of pain and heavy understanding. So Casey's voice, as it emerges note by beautiful note, is changing mine and that's a positive thing. And in a strange twist, these days I find my writing often mirroring Casey's developmental surges: ideas and stories, when they decide to come, no longer appear in slow, steady arcs of completion, but charge fully formed onto the page.

I'll embrace it, as I have to, and relax into my own developmental journey as I help Casey along his.

~Kathleen O'Grady

78

A Journey of Healing

Turn your wounds into wisdom.
~Oprah Winfrey

On a sunny July day, my younger brother Terry was killed as he attempted to cut down a tree. He died instantly of traumatic brain injury. In the blink of an eye, I no longer had a brother.

As I grieved, I found I wanted to pay tribute to my brother's life. I enrolled in nursing school, got good grades and made the Dean's List. In my junior year, I began carpooling with Jeanne, one of the intensive care unit instructors. Driving fifty miles a day, we shared family stories. I explained how Terry's death affected my decision to return to school and how fearful I was just thinking about treating a patient with a traumatic brain injury. She listened intently and seemed sympathetic.

The day before our senior year ICU clinical experience, Jeanne—my instructor and carpool friend—assigned me a traumatic head injury patient. Thinking of what lay ahead, I prayed silently for help. I could NOT let my personal experience interfere with giving this patient the best care possible.

Upon entering the ICU, I learned that my patient was in surgery, having his second operation to relieve pressure from a blood clot on his brain. The doctors had given him little chance of survival. Terry had no chance at all, but this guy did. He was still here, fighting for his life, and I was going to do everything in my power to help him. I prayed for my patient and his family in the waiting room.

That afternoon and evening I studied the patient's chart. His name was Sam, he was nineteen years old, the youngest child of a large family, and his accident was eerily similar to Terry's. He worked for a tree-trimming company and while strapped in his safety harness trimming branches, a falling branch hit him in the head. He hung upside down in the tree for nearly an hour before being extricated. He suffered a fractured skull with a large blood clot in his brain. A device was in place to relieve and measure the pressure inside his skull. A ventilator helped him breathe, he had arterial lines, IVs and a urinary catheter. He had been given last rites. Twice.

The next day, just after dawn, I saw Sam for the first time. His head was swathed in bandages; he was unresponsive and his tall frame was motionless in the bed.

My knees were weak, but I knew every detail of his physical condition, medications, procedures and his monitors. In ICU, the details can mean the difference between life and death.

I can do this, I said to myself. All my hard work to this point came down to this day and this patient. I laid my hand on Sam's arm.

"Good morning, Sam. I'm your nurse for today. My name is Nancy." I told him the day of the week, the date, the time, what the weather was like. I chattered on while gently caring for him. There was no response.

Out in the waiting room, I approached a tired-looking woman and introduced myself to Sam's mother. She told me all about Sam and the family. I asked her to bring in a radio to play his favorite music and family pictures to tape in easy-to-spot places around his cubicle. I shared my plan to gently stimulate Sam in the hopes of helping him come out of the coma. She was pleased that she could help.

Each day we carried out the plan. I talked to Sam and played his favorite music. While completing all my nursing duties, I told him about the leaves changing colors and about the apples and cider for sale along the roadside. No response. It was hard to see this young man remain so still.

One day, as I struggled to put one of his heavy, long legs into his pajama bottoms, I said, "Sam, it would be great if you could help me. Can you lift your leg?" His leg rose five inches off the bed. I tried to remain calm. "Thank you, Sam. Can you raise the other leg?" He did! He could hear and follow commands; he had bilateral movement, but still, he had not regained consciousness or opened his eyes.

The next morning, I was told that during the night Sam had started breathing against the ventilator. As I came into his cubicle, I put my hand in his and told him I was there for the day. Sam squeezed it! I grabbed his other hand and asked him to squeeze again. He obeyed. I encouraged Sam all day. By the afternoon, he was breathing totally on his own and no longer required the ventilator.

Still, his eyes remained closed. As I worked with Sam the next day, he turned his head from side to side to follow my voice wherever I was. I brought his mother into ICU. "Sam," I said, as his face turned towards me, "your mom is here." A tear slid down his cheek. "Sam," I repeated firmly as I came to stand behind his mother, "your mom is here. Please open your eyes." We watched him struggle to lift his eyelids. His eyes fluttered open, he looked toward the sound of my voice. "Sam," I said, "look at your mom." Suddenly, recognition dawned in his eyes and he began to sob. I partially lowered the bed's side rail for a long-awaited mother and son embrace.

Sam continued to improve rapidly and was soon discharged from ICU to the rehabilitation unit.

A few weeks later, while walking through the rehab unit, I heard someone call my name. It was Sam's mother. We hugged. She was smiling. I saw a tall, handsome young man standing next to her. His previously shaved head had grown into a crew cut, beginning to hide the many scars.

"Hi, Sam, how are you?" I said.

He cocked his head and spoke haltingly. "Your voice sounds so familiar."

The lump in my throat only allowed me to respond, "I was one of your nurses in ICU."

His words came out haltingly. "You are Nancy. My mom told me all about you."

Here was a true miracle standing before me. For two weeks, my life was intertwined with Sam's as we each experienced miraculous healing.

One day, while Jeanne and I were driving to school, I gathered the courage to ask her why she blindsided me by assigning me a traumatic head injury patient when she knew my story. She explained that she believed in my nursing skills and even more so in my character. She wanted me to face my fear while she was there to watch over and support me. I was touched by her kindness.

A few months later, I received flowers from Sam's family. The card read, "To our Angel!" Sharing this journey of healing, Sam and I each had someone watching over us.

~Nancy Emmick Panko

79

Envelope of Hope

*If we had no winter, the spring would not be so pleasant: if we did not
sometimes taste of adversity, prosperity would not be so welcome.*
~Anne Bradstreet

cried when I opened the envelope. It was from a man I'd never
met. A check fell out, a very big check; and it was the first of
many from people who had heard about our fire.

"You like to write," said my friend, "You should write about
your fire."

"I write inspirational humor," I told her. "There is nothing funny or
uplifting about your business burning to the ground or about watching
your lifelong dream, as well as your livelihood, go up in smoke."

A forest fire had swept across our property, burning acres of land,
killing hundreds of trees, damaging our home, and completely destroying my husband's boat building business.

My friend said, "You have gone through tragedies before, and you
found something positive to write about each circumstance — your son's
cancer, your blindness, a serious accident, a chronic illness. You've
found humor and inspiring lessons in all those situations."

"Not this one," I answered. "It's too much. We've been knocked down
many times, but this time we won't get back up. We are defeated."

Our insurance coverage hadn't been nearly enough. We had trusted
our agent to know what we needed; and who really reads their insurance policies? We should have. We lost $300,000 in machinery, tools,
and property, but we were reimbursed only a tiny fraction of that; and

we had to hire a lawyer to get it. Much of what we were awarded went to the lawyer in payment.

"We've exhausted our life savings," I told my friend. "We're using credit cards to buy food and pay bills. We have no money to rebuild I'm unable to work, and my husband is sixty years old. Who would hire him? How can we start over? Besides all that, we lost treasured family heirlooms in the blaze, a lifelong collection of antiques, and ten rare, antique wooden boats. So much of what is gone can never be replaced. No, there is nothing positive to be gained from this dev astation. I will never see anything good come from it and I will never write about it."

Then that check came, and it was the first of many. The second came from a grandmother three states away. Her home had burned thirty years ago and a stranger had given her $200. She wanted to pay it forward and help someone else. That someone was me. I cried again. And I have cried more times than I can count, as check after check has arrived this past year. There were checks from neighbors previous employers, friends from grade school, our doctors, local businesses, long-lost relatives, and friends' extended family members Local churches gave us food and money, and even churches in other states sent us money. Friends told friends, and a magazine we had advertised the business in published a story on our loss. People who had read my book or had been helped by the charity I founded sent us help. We received donations, as well as words of encouragement from nearly every state. I was shocked when I received a phone call from a stranger in Hawaii.

So many of our son's musician friends volunteered to do benefit concerts that he had to turn most of them down. He organized two all-day fundraisers with music by ten bands, and our community came out to support us. More tears.

If we hadn't received so much from so many, we would have filed for bankruptcy and given up. But hundreds of people eagerly helped us, believing that we could come back from this disaster. Their confidence inspired us. We began to believe we could rise from the ashes and start anew. We determined that we would do whatever was required to overcome this setback. It has taken a lot of hard work, seven days a week, sometimes fourteen-hour workdays for over a year. And we haven't recovered totally yet, but we're getting closer; and we've managed to avoid bankruptcy.

We may never have the lifestyle we had before. After all, it had taken most of our lives to build up to that point before the fire. But I must finally admit that there was a silver lining behind this dark cloud after all. We learned that there are many more good-hearted and generous people in this world than we had suspected. And we have a new compassion for fire victims and try to help them whenever we can.

We've come to believe that with determination and the help of good friends, and even strangers, anything is possible, and we strive to share this belief with others who may be discouraged.

The story of Thomas Edison rekindled our hope. At the age of sixty-seven, after investing every cent he had (as well as ten years of work) on a particular invention, Edison's lab, records, and experiments were destroyed by fire. He was only insured for about ten percent of the value of what he lost. Yet, Edison looked at the ruins and said, "There is great value in disaster. All our mistakes are burned up. Thank God we can start anew."

Three weeks after the fire, Edison managed to deliver the first phonograph. His life proves that good can come from bad situations, and anything is possible to those who believe.

~Marsha Mott Jordan

The Road Less Traveled

The best way out is always through.
~Robert Frost

I t was a cool, sunny spring Saturday in our high chaparral community of Anza, California. My husband Steve planned on flying his newly painted powered sailplane. In the early afternoon, he rode to the airstrip in our community of Lake Riverside Estates.

Our greenhouse window off the kitchen provided an unimpeded view of the runway below. As our four children and I watched Steve taxi east, then take off to the west, we waved and the children returned to their lunches. For some reason, though, I continued to watch as he struggled to gain altitude, then plateaued and flew out of sight. Immediately, I saw dust trails from cars lining the runway racing towards the runway's end. I knew he must have crashed.

I yelled for Chris, my eldest, to run and get my keys, which he obediently did. As I reached for the knob on my front door, I knew my life would be altered forever. I would not see my children again for two weeks. My new reality would revolve around the intensive care wing of a hospital, while my children's reality would be living with close relatives and friends who cared for them in the ensuing days and weeks.

When I arrived on the scene, the terrifying scope of the accident lay before me. Steve appeared physically whole, but upon looking at the devastation of the plane, I knew he must be gravely injured, both internally and externally.

I knelt down beside Steve, and saw that his eyes were milky white. He was thrashing, mumbling incoherently, and crying out as an EMT, who happened to be on the runway looking at property that day, attempted to remove his boots to check for leg injuries. I did not know how long I had with him, and wondered whether I would be a witness to his death. But a sense of peace encircled me, and I was momentarily comforted. He was in good hands after all. What were the chances that an EMT would be on site in such a remote location at the very moment needed? It was providential.

After another twenty minutes, local emergency medical technicians arrived and monitored Steve's vital signs. It took an additional thirty minutes for Life Flight to arrive and take Steve to Loma Linda University Medical Center in Redlands, California. After a seemingly never-ending drive, a pilot friend and I joined him there. We checked in with the ER reception desk, and I was eventually led to Steve's room where medical personnel were attending to him.

His stay at Loma Linda turned into days, then weeks, then months. He was constantly in and out of hospitals those first two years following his accident. We lived two and a half hours from Loma Linda, where most of his hospital stays took place. But he also spent time at St. Mary's in Long Beach, and at Palomar too. It took a great deal of coordinated effort from family and friends to get the children to preschool and elementary school and church activities. We remain awed and grateful to this day for the blessing of extended family and friends in our lives during that difficult time.

As authorities began to unravel what had happened to Steve's aircraft that day, they determined that the engine had failed on takeoff when he was about one hundred feet in the air. As he attempted to correct the free fall by returning to the runway, a crosswind had stalled his left wing and taken him into an unrecoverable tailspin.

In the coming days, weeks, and months, we learned the extent of Steve's injuries. In addition to the not-so-noticeable injuries were the noticeable ones. In the hospital, after his first surgery, his face was littered with railroad track stitching from lacerations incurred when his face penetrated the plexiglass windshield upon impact.

I had to decide right then, in his hospital room, how I loved him, not why. I knew the whys. I determined that I loved all of him, then and always. William Shakespeare once said, "Love is not love which alters when it alteration finds." I took that insight to heart and made it my mantra.

During his recovery, Steve, a dentist with two thriving practices, decided to expand his interest in business. He searched for an MBA program that would allow him to acquire his degree while he continued recovering. He found one that fit his needs and began the program about a year after the accident.

Within a year, he finished the course work and graduated from the program. He immediately began consulting with dentists in Southern California regarding their dental office overhead control. With a growing clientele and improved health, he began giving lectures around the United States. But, as his success as a consultant grew, I found that I could no longer ignore some of my own health issues. I was advised by my physician to move to a wetter climate. After careful consideration, we decided to move to Salem, Oregon, leaving behind those haunting memories of the accident.

The move to Oregon was an act of faith for our family. We left behind a safety net of family and friends. Yet, we felt inspired to move here. Our children received excellent educations, formed lasting friend-ships, found and married their life partners, and gave us six wonderful grandchildren. We made friendships that bound us to the wonderful community in which we now live. Steve now manages a dental public health program and is doing cutting-edge dental research. I am busy being a grandmother, and continue being creative.

When contemplating the challenges Steve and I have faced in our lives, we have learned that life is not predictable no matter how perfectly we plan. If we question that voice inside that clearly says, go here, take this road, meet this person, we might inadvertently miss something wonderful, something providential. I am reminded of the words in one of Robert Frost's poems: "Two roads diverged in a wood, and I—I took the one less traveled by, and that has made all the difference."

~Joanne Stephenson Duffin

Chapter 9

Find Your Inner Strength

Pursuing Your Dreams

Waiting for Kira

Hope is the companion of power, and the mother of success;
for who so hopes strongly has within him the gift of miracles.
~Samuel Smiles

"I dreamt of the baby again," I told Mike, my husband. "She was beautiful." It was a muggy day, and we were outside on the stone patio of our cozy home in Atlanta. It looked like it might rain. We were enjoying the last drops of our morning tea (and possibly the last of the day's dry weather) when I remembered a detail. "She had your green eyes. Oh Mike, she looked just like you!" Mike looked at me for a moment, uncharacteristically at a loss for words, and then rolled away in his wheelchair. I rolled inside after him.

Mike's accident left him a paraplegic, but he has use of his strong upper body. I was not as lucky when I fell off a horse in my twenties. Most people think of Christopher Reeve when they hear the words quadriplegic, but my injury is known as a C-567 injury. I have limited mobility in my hands and arms and some feelings below my waist. Like Mike, I am able to get around in a wheelchair. A retrofitted steering wheel allows me to drive a van. For the most part, we lead fairly normal lives.

That didn't mean we could easily get pregnant. We would need to go through in vitro fertilization. We would also need a gestational surrogate.... and perhaps, a miracle.

Our lives up to that point were peppered with miracles, so Mike worried that it was a little greedy to ask for yet another one. It was miracle enough we were at this point: married and living together.

When Mike and I met at a wheelchair race in Florida, we had been living on different continents: He lived in England; I lived in South Carolina. Somehow, we persevered beyond our injuries and beyond our long-distance relationship. Years later, here we were, married and not afraid of a challenge. Which was what I told Mike on that warm July day. "Why not try for another miracle?"

Mike did not need convincing. "You are right. Why don't we call that doctor you read about?" he said.

I had read about a doctor who had helped other women with spinal cord injuries. I had studied his picture on the website. Dr. Toledo had salt-and-pepper hair and kind looking blue eyes. Before I could change my mind, I dialed the number and made an appointment.

In person, Dr. Toledo did not disappoint. Where other doctors had been discouraging, he offered us hope. "Shannon, I would not advise you to try and carry the pregnancy. There are wonderful options available for surrogacy should you..." We interrupted him. "Don't worry, Dr. Toledo," we told him. "We have a surrogate in mind."

Mike's sister Julie had offered to carry the baby—a generous offer considering she lived in England. Plans fell into place.

We started the process in high spirits, but over time, our hopes and dreams began to evaporate, one failed IVF after the other. Eventually we ran out of time. Julie returned to England, dejected. We were back in limbo.

Only this time limbo felt more like an abyss. For the first time in my life, I fell into a deep depression, unlike anything I experienced when I was first injured. That had been devastating, but this felt all together more primal: utter desolation.

I had always imagined myself as a mother. Beyond my own worries, I felt awful for Mike. This had been his biggest fear. "Shannon, the only time I cried after my accident was when the doctor told me I would never be a father," he had told me when we met. I talked to God: Lord, he is such a loving man. Why would You deny him the opportunity to be a dad?

For months, I fell asleep praying. I turned over the details like a puzzle to be solved, hitting the same walls and obstacles every time. Our biggest concern at that point was the toll on Julie, who had left her life in England, camped out at our home for months and allowed herself to be subjected to more needles than a pincushion. How could we ask her to do that again?

One night, an idea germinated. The doctor never said I was unable to carry a baby. They only advised against it. What if, instead of Julie, I was the one to carry the embryos?

I prayed. "All you have to conquer is your fear," I heard in my head. That morning, I woke up and started researching. I spent the day on Google. The more I read about the success rate for other women with similar injuries, the more I believed it might be okay.

Dr. Toledo, by this point, had become a trusted friend. He was at a Falcons game when I reached him. "Can I carry our baby?" I yelled over the din, not thinking as to how that might have sounded on the other end. Over the noise of the crowd, I heard him hesitate, only for a second, before he answered. "Of course, but let's give some consideration to the risks—come in and see me."

Having been given a cautionary yellow light by Dr. Toledo, I moved forward with green light determination. "I'm going to carry our baby," I announced to Mike. Used to my occasional flair for the dramatic, Mike looked at me a second before responding. "Are you serious?" I excitedly told him what I had been thinking, the research I had done. We discussed the pros and cons, and in the end, we both decided to try it at least once.

"All you have to do is conquer your fears."

Weeks later, the phone rang. The caller ID indicated it was the clinic. "Shannon?" "Yes?" I answered breathlessly and put the phone on speaker so Mike could hear. "Mike is here too," I said to Dr. Toledo. I could tell by his tone the news was going to be good. His happiness radiated over the phone. "You are going to be parents!" he said. The tears streamed down our faces.

The pregnancy went forth without any complications and the months went by quickly. The delivery room was like a party—my family was there. Mike's family had flown in from England. There was a team of doctors on hand. All around the room, I saw smiling faces. Our child would be welcomed into this world with an overabundance of love.

At 11:30 p.m., Kira Francklin came into this world. I examined my newborn baby from head to toe and all I saw was her uncanny resemblance to her dad. I thought back to that dream, the sleepless nights and that moment when peace had come over, telling me not to be afraid.

God had provided His best miracle yet.

~Shannon Francklin

John

Optimism is the faith that leads to achievement.
~Helen Keller

Gathering my things as I headed out of the office, I said, "I'm off to pick up my brother from the light rail."

My co-worker shot me a sideways glance. "That sucks," she said, then paused. "I thought you said your brother was older than you. He doesn't drive?"

"Nope."

"And you have to pick him up every day?"

"Well, yes, and no. Yes, every day. No, but I don't *have* to. I *get* to."

John, two years older than me, has Down syndrome. Reactions to that vary. Like Great-Uncle Fred who, when John was born, voiced his opinion that John should be institutionalized, as that was the only thing to be done with "kids like that." I didn't even know I had a Great-Uncle Fred until my late teens when Mom mentioned him. Our family hasn't spoken to him since that episode.

In contrast, people who meet John before meeting me always say, "You're John's sister! He talks about you all the time. You are so lucky to have him around! You know, John always calls you 'my beautiful sister, Meghan.' Isn't that the sweetest thing ever?"

Those who know me well will occasionally get up the nerve to ask me the tough question: Was it hard growing up with John in the house?

The short answer is no.

The longer answer is, "Well, there were some differences...." John required a lot of Mom and Dad's attention when we were young, but I never felt neglected. My parents faced some challenges—finding the best programs for John, helping him learn motor skills that come naturally to most children, learning how to communicate with him. But for me, all those things were normal, because John had been there my entire life and that was all I had ever known.

Growing up, I had friends who would tell me about horrible fights and strained relationships with their siblings. In particular, my friend Kathryn's brother screamed that he hated her. That was the first time I realized how different my relationship with John was from the "normal" brother/sister dynamic. When I got home from Kathryn's house that evening, John met me at the door with a smile, a jubilant "Meghan!" and a gigantic hug.

But more than just loving my brother like crazy, John has taught me about dedication. He has an almost unnerving ability to state a goal and achieve it, no matter how unlikely it seems.

When John was in seventh grade, while he and my parents prepared for John's IEP meeting, he said, "I don't want to take all special ed classes anymore." With Mom and Dad's help, John lobbied the teachers and principal. By his senior year in high school, he took mostly normal classes with an aide and only took a small number of special ed classes.

In his freshman year of high school, he saw the homecoming parade and declared he wanted to be Homecoming King. Mom and I glanced at each other, thinking we had to find a way to let him down easy. "John, I don't know if that's going to happen," Mom said. "We'll just have to see."

Three years later, my friend Tess nominated John for Homecoming King. John came home with a card from the student council wishing him good luck. He was beside himself. "I'm going to be Homecoming King!"

Every few days for the next two weeks, the student council had runoffs to narrow the field of contenders. Each time, John brought home another card that read, "You're still in the running!"

Eventually, John was in the top four. At the rally, the nominees were announced one by one.

"Danny Hochstetler!"

Polite applause followed Danny's name, as it did for Todd White and Stephen Wright.

"And John Maste—"

We couldn't hear the last part because the gym erupted into screams, cheers and applause. For a second, I worried—loud noises scared John—but he charged through the doors with his signature smile and his eyes alight. The cheers redoubled as he stepped up to the platform next to the other contenders. The other boys put their arms around John's shoulders, and everyone smiled as the cameras flashed.

John had won.

But John wasn't finished. Next, he said, "I want to go to college!"

John attended the transition program at Sacramento City School District and was wildly successful. He graduated in December 2008. He was the only person slated for graduation that winter, but the program made sure to hold a ceremony just for him. We ran out of chairs half an hour before the ceremony began. My brother's graduation was a standing-room-only event by the time he walked to the makeshift stage.

But that's not all. After Arnold Schwarzenegger was elected to the governorship, John said, "I want to meet the governor... No, I want to work for the governor."

His contacts at the transition program set up John with an internship in the governor's mailroom at the Capitol. John became friends with the governor and Maria Shriver, and he met all sorts of visiting dignitaries. My favorite picture of him at work shows John standing between Governor Schwarzenegger and the president of Mexico.

John asked the governor if his internship could be a real, paid job. A conversation was had, papers were signed, and on his twenty-second birthday John took his oath of office. He has worked as an employee in the gubernatorial mailroom ever since.

Part of John's success comes from his dedication. He sets a goal and goes for it without restraint. He'll tell all his friends about it, gather support, and have at it. I have never seen him fail.

Though I am biased, John is wonderful. Since John is so fantastic, people are excited for him, willing to help him on his way, and go the extra mile.

So, no, it wasn't hard to have John around. In fact, it was inspiring to watch him grow up into the incredible man he has become. And every day, I sling my bag over my shoulder, grab my keys and head for the train, because I get to pick up my brother.

~Meg Masterson

Friends of the Friendless

Never forget that once upon a time, in an unguarded moment,
you recognized yourself as a friend.
~Elizabeth Gilbert, Eat, Pray, Love

In her spare time, my grandmother sews onesies for the babies turned over to her local hospital. She refers to them as the "friendless children." I'm not sure whether she uses this term because she doesn't want to say "orphans" or "abandoned," but every time she talks about her onesies, the phrase is always the same.

She says this, and I wonder if she views me the same way. I had an unusual upbringing. It began with a loving two-parent home where only family was allowed to babysit. By age eleven, it had turned into a very strange circus.

My father was diagnosed with ALS, or Lou Gehrig's disease. There were doctors' appointments, tours of wheelchair vans and lots of lying on the couch by the man who had previously refused to ever take a sick day.

No one really explained anything to me until one day I'd had enough and asked if whatever was going on was going to kill him. He said yes, though in my then-twelve-year-old brain, I figured that meant when he was eighty. Not forty-three.

It was a shock when he passed a few weeks before my fifteenth birthday. My mom and I did our best to forge a new bond. This couldn't have been easy for her, a sudden single mother of a teenaged girl.

We managed to find our synergy, however, and soon accepted that our family was a twosome. It was us against the world for quite a while.

Then came college. I purposely picked a university that was less than an hour's drive from home. My mother took a second job to stay busy, but an empty, dark house is still an empty, dark house, no matter what time you enter it or how tired you are.

I made sure to visit often, but I could tell Mom was struggling. She didn't like to socialize, and while she loved her large family and co-workers, she felt she had too much time on her hands. Especially on the weekends. My mother was always a larger woman, but fifty extra pounds soon became 100, which soon became much more.

She couldn't walk very far anymore. She didn't want to be seen in public. The stares and innocent comments kids can sometimes make hurt her feelings.

She expressed how lonely she was during one of my visits. "I don't have anyone to talk to," she said, bursting into tears. My heart broke for her. She was friendless—not because she didn't have people who loved her—but because she'd gotten herself into such a poor physical and mental state that she was now removed from the functional social world.

I did what I could to include her in my life. In a weird way, she traded in hers for mine. Suddenly, she wanted to know every detail of every day. Questions like "What did you say? Then what did she say? and "What did she order?" filled our conversations. It got old quick. I didn't mind her rooting for my school's football team or taking an interest in my writing, but reliving every banal detail of my day was not the way I wanted to spend my nights.

It got worse when I married. She was thrilled to see me take this life step, but the idea of sharing someone she had had sole possession of for twenty-six years scared her. "Things will never be the same," she said one night as we clinked cosmopolitans at a divey chicken-wing joint, waiting for the premiere of the first *Sex and the City* movie during a rare outing.

There was soon talk of babies, and you could see her excitement in becoming a grandmother. "I could watch them, you know," she'd say, though by this point that was impossible. She could barely make it off the couch. A trip to the bathroom was laborious. She took to using a walker. She was fifty-two.

Apparently it was those talks about the future that made her want to change. During one of our more honest conversations I said I knew she loved food more than she loved me. That was okay, I told her, because it's the truth. She denied it, like any addict does. And though she didn't cry, I could tell I had wounded her. I had meant to.

She enrolled in a weight-loss program, with the ultimate goal being gastric bypass surgery. She lost some weight, and she felt hopeful. I began fantasizing about a second family. Maybe she'd remarry. Maybe I'd have step-siblings. Maybe we'd finally get to do the mother-daughter things that other people got to do.

And then she died.

Despite her size, it was extremely unexpected. Things were looking up. She was going to get better. My mom wasn't the only thing that died that day. The marriage soon unraveled, thoughts of babies disappearing right alongside it.

By twenty-nine, I definitely felt friendless. Like my mom, I had plenty of people in my life who loved me, but at night, in those unguarded, silent moments, it's hard to argue you're not alone in this world.

Ironically, I've combatted my loneliness by diving into a very solitary profession: writing. It was there that I built my community. In being other people's voices, I'm able to find my own. The process of writing is extremely intimate. You get to know a person's thoughts and feelings, and you take a piece of them with you. You keep it tucked away in your brain or perhaps in your heart, until you're able to share it through the written word.

You hope you do them justice. Most of the time you do, and you witness them beam with excitement, pride and accomplishment that their story—however beautiful or tragic—was worth telling to the world. It is a wonderful feeling. One I don't believe will ever get old.

I still want that family one day. To maybe right some wrongs I've held onto for too long. To show another human being absolute, unconditional love. I really hope this happens for me, but until then, I enjoy reaching out to those with a story to tell. Naturally, I am drawn to the underdogs. To the ones who didn't feel like they had a prayer in the world before things turned around, resulting in a redemption story.

As much as I sometimes want to look back on my career and say I made it here myself, I didn't. That childhood was odd, but there were also bedtime stories, sacrifices made for private education and every piece of USC Trojan memorabilia a person could own sitting in a lonely woman's bedroom. Next to a stack of magazines her daughter had appeared in.

I'm not a really emotional person, but the Johnson's Baby commercial with the tagline "You're doing okay, Mom" gets me every time. When I look back on a career I couldn't be more lucky or thankful to have, I realize I'm not a one-man show. I never have been. My redemption story is not just mine, it's also hers. And I think to myself, "You did okay, Mom."

~Nellie Day

Redefining Limitations

Life shrinks or expands in proportion to one's courage.
~Anaïs Nin

I sat in the guidance counselor's office my senior year of high school, bright eyed about the possibilities of college. The counselor sighed and pushed her glasses onto her head. "Are you sure you want to go to college?" she asked. "It will be difficult with your limitations, you know." My limitation, as she called it, was diabetes. I was in three AP classes, a varsity athlete on the track and field team, and nationally ranked in Speech and Debate. But according to her, I was limited.

"Well," I hesitated, unsure of how to respond to her question. Was I sure? Yes, I was absolutely sure that I wanted to go to college. But I started to feel a gnawing monster in my belly, questioning my ability to succeed. Later that night at home, I helped my mom fold laundry in the living room. "What would you think if I just went to community college for a while and figured it out?" I asked her.

She looked at me, confused. My mother had left school to start a family. "What do you mean, figure it out?" I told her about my meeting with the guidance counselor, and watched her face change from confusion to anger. I was glad my mom was by my side for this battle, because I had a feeling it would turn into full-on war.

I talked to the admissions counselor at the school I really wanted to go to. All I was missing was my official high school transcript. I promised to have it in the mail the next day, and took a stamped envelope with my forms to the guidance office. Two weeks later, I received a rejection letter, and I called the admissions counselor in tears. "You promised!" I sobbed into the phone, disconsolate about what I perceived to be my dream school. Soothing me over the phone, she pulled up my file, and told me that they never received my official transcript. I never saw anger in color until that afternoon. I called my high school and demanded answers. I sat for hours in the guidance suite, and brought a ferocious mama bear with me. We couldn't prove anything, and my counselor's simpering smile totally and utterly defeated me.

I was burning. I knew that I could not lie down and accept defeat because then my "limitation" would win. I revamped my college efforts, and eventually accepted a track scholarship to Cabrini College, where I spent four magnificent years growing into a woman that I can be proud of. After the track team was cut for budgetary reasons, I focused on social justice, a specialty of Cabrini. I had started insulin pump therapy my freshman year, which gave me an entirely new outlook on living with diabetes. I was able to throw myself into the service of others.

During January of my senior year, I went on a life-changing mission trip called Rostro de Cristo to a small town called Durán in Ecuador. The week I spent there with my classmates and the wonderful residents of that town created memories that I will never forget. The people, the places, the food — they all hold a special place in my heart.

As I sat on the concrete ground of a schoolyard in Ecuador that week, with a child on each knee, I thought about how lucky I was to have had that guidance counselor in my life. The devastation of what she did to me propelled me to do my best and pursue my passions. As José fingered the tubing coming out of my pocket, I gently explained to him in broken Spanish that it was for my diabetes. He hugged me tightly, taking my breath away, and stood at the gate each day to hug me as we came into the school.

That mission trip lit a fire in me for helping others, and when I got back to the States, I filled out applications for yearlong service opportunities. I graduated in 2012 with two bachelor degrees and my teaching certification, along with high honors and accolades from the honors college. I was accepted by the Mercy Volunteer Corps and went to serve at the Navajo Nation Indian Reservation in rural Arizona. I spent the year after graduation teaching high school U.S. Government and Psychology, and working as a part-time secretary. Now, I am in grad school full-time and working in a high school in North Philadelphia as I study to become a reading specialist.

I still have diabetes, and unless there is a breakthrough, I will always have diabetes. What I don't have are limitations. My ability to serve others and to teach—that's something diabetes cannot take away from me. They are something an out-of-touch counselor cannot take away from me. My biggest "limitation" was not my endocrine system, but my inability to believe in myself. Once I overcame that fear, I realized nothing could stop me from reaching for the stars.

From the streets of Ecuador, to the hogans of the Navajo Nation, to my cluttered classroom in Philadelphia, nothing can limit me. Have insulin pump, will travel.

~Jamie Tadrzynski

Becoming What I Might Have Been

We shall draw from the heart of suffering itself
the means of inspiration and survival.
~Winston Churchill

I was enjoying the summer before entering a master's program in a neighboring town. I was working towards my dream job. I had always wanted to become a licensed psychotherapist. Near the end of August I got some terrible news. "Linda, you have a brain tumor on the underside of your brain."

The neurosurgeon spoke softly, as if attempting to lessen the blow. She held a plastic model of a skull in her hand and poked into the eye sockets and nostrils with a pencil. "Where would we go in? We can't go in here... or here. This is the worst place you could have possibly gotten a tumor. It's growing very quickly. I'm sorry. It's inoperable."

I walked out the doors of her office and through the large medical building, not daring a glance at anyone. I headed towards the elevator. The doors opened and I walked in. I was alone. My body felt numb. I gripped the handrail in the elevator and tried to catch my breath. By the time I met my husband in the parking structure my chest hurt. "It's inoperable!" As I choked out the doctor's words, I fell trembling into his arms, sobs wracking my body. My dream of becoming a therapist and helping others dissolved into my tears.

I had waited until my children were grown, with families of their wn, before starting my own work on a college degree. By then I was ifty-one years old. It had been a dream of mine for almost as long as could remember. But so many things had gotten in my way.

After being kicked out of high school in my junior year, I married my boyfriend. I was running away from a neglectful, alcoholic home. Six months later I was pregnant with our son. My husband abandoned both of us within the year. I struggled as a single mother and seemed bent on a path of self-destruction. Then, when I was eighteen years old, was gang-raped. I lived on the streets for a year after that, attempting o lose my shame in the world of drugs.

A few years later I lost my brother to suicide. My heartbroken ather took his own life three years later. By then I was suffering from serious mental illness myself, but with God's grace and a lot of help eventually recovered. My past prompted me to want to help teens hat found themselves in similar situations.

Through the years I dreamed of going back to school and becoming a psychotherapist. I earned my GED when I was thirty-four years old. I attempted some night classes at a local community college, but working full-time and raising three children on my own made this extremely difficult.

I finally married a wonderful, loving and caring man. I was fortywo years old. We left California to start life over in the beautiful big sky state of Montana. We enjoyed hiking together and fly-fishing for rout in the summer months. Winter found us cross-country skiing or snowshoeing through the vast Montana wilderness. For the first ime I was enjoying my life.

Then, six years into our marriage, a quick fall down some slick wooden stairs in our Victorian cottage put an end to most outdoor activities for me. I had broken my neck! During the lengthy recovery, thought again about my dream of becoming a therapist. I decided it was now or never. With my husband's total support, I went back to school full-time.

Four years later I graduated with a B.A. in Psychology. My three grown children flew to Helena, Montana to proudly watch me receive my diploma. I graduated *maxima cum laude*. As I walked towards the

stage with students less than half my age, my children cheered loudl
from the stands. It was a moment I would never forget. I had gotte
my "do-over." But now it seemed all was for naught. I would neve
have the chance to earn my master's degree.

Several days went by as I grappled with the diagnosis. I cam
to believe God had another plan. I hadn't come this far to go dow
without a fight. I began to do online research to see if someone els
could help me. I was afraid to hope, but within a week I received
call from a neurosurgeon in Los Angeles, California. "I can help you
he began. Those were the words I needed to hear.

I underwent a very risky brain surgery on a sunny fall day i
October 2006. At one point in the middle of surgery, my neurosurgeor
Dr. Shahinian, stopped everything and called my husband Tom to
consultation room right outside the operating theater. "All of the nerve
are wrapped up in the tumor," he told Tom. "It is much larger than
thought. If I take it all, there is a possibility she will not be able to wall
or smile. She may not hear and perhaps she will be blind. If I leav
half of it, she will be back here in five years to do this all again."

My husband conferred with my daughter. Together they made th
hard decision to allow Dr. Shahinian to attempt to remove the entir
tumor in this one operation.

The recovery was horrendous. I woke to a Noah's ark world c
double vision. My optic nerve was damaged in surgery. I completel
lost the hearing in my left ear. I heard what sounded like the roarin
of a waterfall in my head. My balance was terrible, and it seemed as
the floor wanted to come up and punch me in the face.

But I didn't want to live just for the sake of remaining alive.
still wanted to help other people. So after six months of lying in be
I decided to take action. I applied for my master's degree through
fully accredited online university.

It took three years, not only to complete the courses, but also t
regain enough strength to attend out-of-state residencies and work t
complete the 3,000 hours I needed to become a licensed psychotherapis
with the state of Montana. Each step was a challenge. Eventually m
eye righted itself and my balance improved. The roaring in my hea

quieted, and I continued to get stronger. When the going got tough, I held onto the belief that there was a purpose to my life.

It's been seven years since I awoke from brain surgery. I am now a psychotherapist in private practice. I work with teenagers and adults who suffer from many of the things I suffered from myself. And I am writing my memoir, another lifelong dream.

I kept a quote above my desk as I worked my way through both my undergraduate and graduate degrees. A writer named Mary Ann Evans used the pseudonym George Eliot when she wrote her books. Women writers were not well received in the mid-1800s. She said, "It's never too late to become what you might have been." It is my message; not only for me, but also for everybody I meet. It's never too late.

~Linda Lochridge

The Thrill of the Ride

So many people tiptoe through life, so carefully, just to arrive safely, at death.
~Tony Campolo

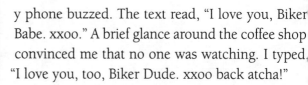

y phone buzzed. The text read, "I love you, Biker Babe. xxoo." A brief glance around the coffee shop convinced me that no one was watching. I typed, "I love you, too, Biker Dude. xxoo back atcha!"

Looking up, I caught my husband's stare across the table and quickly covered my phone. I looked at the floor feeling my face grow warm. Harry spoke first, "You look awfully cute today, Biker Babe."

Meeting his eyes, I returned his grin. "Thanks, Biker Dude."

Life for Harry and me had been difficult. During our forty years together, we had raised two boys and grieved two others. Two severe car crashes, the fault of others, including a drunk, allowed us to survive but took a toll on our bodies. With so many other unpleasant things happening to us, we began to feel that Murphy's Law was written specifically for our lives. Yet we stayed together and remained in love.

Over Christmas 2010, our world transitioned again when Harry was diagnosed with what turned out to be Stage II colorectal cancer. We were told he would need extensive surgery, followed by radiation and chemotherapy.

Once the shock wore off and I went into research mode, we made the decision that the surgery made sense; the other recommendations did not.

The next two years saw Harry trying to come back from the surgery.

Another major and emergent surgery was necessary, two months after the first, to fix a life-threatening blockage caused by adhesions from the first surgery. From there he developed complication after complication. His life had become one of suffering and mine had become one of constant caregiving. It was exhausting for us both.

And then, just when he was starting to feel better, he severely broke his collarbone. The healing was slow and painful and it was just one more bit of proof that Murphy and his law had indeed taken up residence with us.

Finally, Harry started to feel good enough to get restless. He dreamed of earlier days and specifically about motorcycle riding. We'd met in the early 1970s when he was out for a ride on his Yamaha 650 and picked me up hitchhiking. I already had my motorcycle license and it wasn't long before I bought a Honda 350. We enjoyed going on bike trips together and using them for everyday transportation.

When we decided to have kids, we sold the bikes — but with the promise that when the kids were on their own, Harry at least, would get another.

So now seemed the appropriate time for him to get his dream bike. He'd been through a lot; he needed some fun.

Soon after Harry received his Yamaha FJR1300, I scooted onto the back for a ride. I'd forgotten the exhilaration of a motorcycle. When Harry reached around and placed his hand on my knee, I realized I'd also forgotten that electric sensation of falling in love. It was exciting to ride as a passenger, but once a driver, always a driver.

The next summer we decided that my sixtieth birthday present would be a motorcycle. After starting out for a few weeks with a 250, I discovered that my skill set was still sharp. So we bought a beautiful red Honda Shadow Aero 750. Suddenly we found excuses to ride the fifty minutes on challenging, fun roads to a coffee shop in another town. Every day that didn't rain saw us out for at least a two-hour ride. And the endorphins flooded our brains as we experienced the true cliché of motorcycle freedom.

In the same way as hearing a song from one's teen years affords temporary youth, our motorcycles have brought back the enjoyment of

life. Leaving business and problems at home, we don all the appropri
ate safety gear, hop on, give each other a nod, and enjoy the twisties
roads we can find. We always arrive at our destination with big smiles
for the ride and for each other.

My phone buzzed again. "Did I tell you I love you, Biker Babe
:)"

"LOL, yes, Biker Dude. But I'll never tire of hearing and seeing
it. :-*"

~Diane C. Nicholson

Dad and the Grand Canyon

The desert tells a different story every time one ventures on it.
~Robert Edison Fulton, Jr.

"D ad is there anything on your bucket list that you missed? Anything that you wish you could do before you leave us?" I asked sadly as I watched Dad struggle for his next breath.

Dad's eyes brimmed with tears. He whispered, "I've only been to the Grand Canyon six times. My favorite number is seven. It's my favorite spot on earth."

"Well, Dad, how about we ditch this place and enjoy our last road trip together?"

His eyes sparkled, his face took on a new life, even his breathing seem to improve.

"What about your work, Barb? Can you afford it? How am I going to get out of this dark, dingy, stinky hospital?" he asked apprehensively.

"I can't afford not to go Dad. I'd never forgive myself if I didn't at least try to grant your dying wish," I answered.

"Then why are you still standing here? Go find that doctor!" His voice got stronger and more excited by the minute.

I hunted down Dr. Pierce and told him about our plan. Shaking his head, he asked, "Are you prepared to bring your father home in a box?"

"Dad, do you mind coming home in a box?" I laughingly asked.

"Throw me down the canyon and I will be in heaven there," he answered, laughing back.

"I don't advise it," Dr. Pierce stated emphatically. "I will not discharge him. You will have to take him without my permission. Please think this through, I'm begging you. Your father is one sick man."

I packed Dad's few things and we escaped that drab hospital room, ambling out into the cold December air. Dad's colour came back into his cheeks. He said that the fresh air was healing him. think it was just the cold air burning his face, but he insisted that he hadn't felt this good in a long time. I never saw his smile broader or his shoulders squarer. There was a spring in his shuffling steps. Dad was not the weak, tired, sick man we had brought in a week ago with an enlarged heart.

On December 2nd, bright and early at 6 a.m., I packed the car, said a prayer to St. Joseph for a safe and enjoyable trip, and we hit the road. The Grand Canyon was not just Dad's favorite place but mine too!

We drove for two hours and stopped in Kalamazoo, Michigan for breakfast. Dad ordered bacon and eggs. He'd had enough of that soggy toast and watered-down orange juice. "A healthy man eats meat and potatoes," Dad stated.

Besides inhaling his breakfast, Dad also interviewed people at the surrounding tables to see who would make a suitable husband for me. "She's all alone and way too much for an old man like me to handle," Dad said, chuckling.

"Smiling Archie" was Dad's nickname. Always a tease, he outdid himself that morning. His body might have been compromised, but his sense of humour was still as devious as ever.

Once back in the car, we both sang along with our favorite country songs. The day before, Dad had been fighting for his every breath. Today he belted out songs as if he were performing on stage.

Further on our drive, Dad insisted we stop at the Meramec Caverns. Our eyes burned with tears of amazement and we held our breath as we witnessed God's majestic handiwork above and below the ground.

The beauty of the multicoloured stalactites and stalagmites was awe-inspiring.

Dad's water pills and my tiny bladder made it impossible to pass any rest stops. We both got restless and loved to stretch our legs. Dad couldn't wait to strike up a conversation with fellow travelers. "Where you all from? Can't believe the traffic, eh?" Smiling Archie made friends with everyone.

In Oklahoma, Dad insisted that we look for a Western shop. He wanted to buy a suit and a red shirt with tassels to be buried in. Dad loved the colour red. He got his wish.

Northern Texas presented us with large ranches, but New Mexico was our favorite with a multicolored, wondrous surprise at each twist and turn. But the roads were treacherous. We were lucky to be alive when we pulled into the Best Western in Albuquerque. The snow was so thick that it was impossible to drive and the roads ahead were impassable for three days. Dad became fidgety.

He mapped out a new route, and the next morning we headed south to Tucson. He loved the cactus in the desert and needed to say goodbye to them too, especially the saguaros, his favorite.

That night Dad was sore and decided to soak in the bathtub. I ordered in dinner. When dinner arrived I knocked at the bathroom door.

"Dad, the pizza is here," I announced.

"Help, help, potlicker!" Potlicker was his favorite word when he got stressed or annoyed. He sounded desperate.

"Dad, are you okay. Do you need help?" I was suddenly scared.

"I'm stuck, and I can't get out!" He sounded frightened.

I banged open the door and found Dad wedged in, his shoulders stuck under the lip of the tiny bathtub, his knees bent and his feet under the faucet. I tried soaping his shoulders. I tried pulling his arms. I rubbed him and the tub with baby oil to grease him out.

"Gosh darn it, Dad, wiggle yourself out or we'll have to call the firemen."

"If you do, I'll kill you," he snapped.

I panicked and ran to call the front desk. But he finally squirmed himself loose. "I'm out, now put down that blasted phone!"

Once I saw that he was all right, I laughed. I still can't control myself when I think back to Dad's bathtub imprisonment.

The next day, Dad's dream came true. If I could put a face on happiness, it would have been Dad's that day on the south rim of his beloved Grand Canyon. It was an emotional, spiritual experience for both of us. I took a dozen pictures of him glowing with joy and appreciation. Two minutes later, as I snapped pictures, Dad slouched down to the ground. His breathing was labored, his face chalky and he was soaked with perspiration. His pulse was weak and he couldn't speak.

"Oh my God, Dad, can you hear me?" I screamed.

People came running. Someone called 911. We helped Dad to the car and crossed the road to the nearest hotel. Dad refused the ambulance. We stayed at that hotel for the next three days. Enough of his strength finally came back that we could drive home. He insisted on one last look at his heaven.

The drive home was quieter. No boisterous singing, no embarrassing me, not much conversation. But by the third day, Dad picked up again. His silliness returned, his voice was teasing and strong, his whole manner was light and bright. "We are stopping at Gene and Louise's home in Arkansas," he announced.

"We're doing what? Are you kidding me?" I asked.

"You heard me. I always stop there on my way back from the Canyon," Dad declared.

Gene and Louise were his first cousins. Dad and Gene hung around together as children and were great friends. Louise, a talented, beautiful, funny lady, was a joy to know and love. We spent two glorious days with them and their family listening to music, reminiscing and playing cards. Dad was back in all his glory.

On the way home, just before Cincinnati, Dad bellowed: "Pull over! You heard me. If I have to spend one more day in this car with you behind the wheel, I'm going to wish that I was dead!"

He drove the rest of the way home. He had a new lease on life.

We got to enjoy him for an additional nine months.

I still remember Dad's last words to my sister Cathy, my brother Gerry, and myself: "I love you! And you! And you!" He looked at each one of us with pride in his heart, love in his eyes, and contentment and peace in his soul.

With his bucket list complete, Dad went into God's welcoming arms in his new handsome Western suit and his red tasseled shirt.

Every five years, we children make a pilgrimage to the Grand Canyon to honour and visit our adventurous, loving Dad's spirit.

~Barbara Bondy-Pare

Every Day Is Monday

Find a job you like and you add five days to every week.
~H. Jackson Brown

Every day is Monday, eight days a week. That's my motto. As I climbed the ladder to start my day, I was thinking there was not enough time in the day, week, even the month to do all the work that comes my way.

It was the same routine every day. Wake up early, call the boss, get an address, work ten, twelve, sometimes fourteen hours, go home exhausted, fall asleep, get up and do it again. After years of working "eight days a week," I made my phone call one morning to hear, "I'm sorry Bill. I've got nothing going on today. Things seem to be slowing down."

Eight days a week soon became six, then five and three. Before I knew it, the routine call became, "Sorry Bill, I've got nothing for you to do. It's gotten to where I don't have anything to do. I'll call you when some work comes in." After waiting every day for the next week, I couldn't stand it anymore. I picked up the phone and called my boss "Sorry, Bill. I've got nothing."

One day off was great, two days was even pretty nice, but now it had been almost three weeks. I had called every roofer I knew and got the same response. "Sorry Bill, we don't have anything going on."

Panic started to set in. I paced around the house, noticing the stack of bills growing with each day's mail delivery. For the first time in my life I had no idea how I would live. I went out to the back yard. Perfect roofing weather, I muttered to myself.

My eyes stung with tears until I couldn't hold them back. As they spilled down my face, I had a complete emotional meltdown. For the first time, I felt like I needed some divine intervention. I looked at the sunlight glistening through the trees and in a weak voice said, "Jesus, I need some help. I don't know what to do."

At that moment I heard a knock at the front door. I pulled myself together, wiping my face on my shirtsleeve as I went to the door where I found an old friend.

"Hey, how's it going?"

I responded with a weak smile. "I'm okay."

"I want a rematch on that last game of pool we played. Let's go shoot a few rounds."

"I don't know," I hedged. "Money's a little tight."

"Forget about it. I've got a pocket full of quarters."

Reluctantly I agreed. Walking towards the pool hall, I was still distracted by my current predicament. As we walked in I heard somebody call my name. I scanned the room until I saw a familiar face, a carpenter I had worked with years earlier was standing in the corner with his arm raised.

"Hey Bill," he said as I walked over. "I got a job for you." Excitement laced with anxiety raced through my body. "I've already talked to the homeowner and told him you're the best. The job is yours," he said and handed me a card with the contact information. "Just give him a call."

A wave of relief washed over me.

I met with the homeowner the next day and started working right away. This was a huge help, but it didn't get me out of my trouble. As I finished, I was thinking if I could just land three or four more jobs like this one... when I heard the homeowner call me from the ground.

"Hey Bill, my neighbor Tom across the street wants to talk to you about his roof."

I went across the street when I finished cleaning up and put my tools in my truck. I spoke to Tom and agreed to start his roof as soon as I could get the materials delivered. Over the next few days I felt a little better. I was close but not quite out of the hole yet. Pondering how to jump that last hurdle, my thoughts were interrupted by a man walking by.

"Hey, Roofer," he called. "My name's Joe. I live down the street in that white house. Will you stop by when you're done?"

"Absolutely!" I said.

Later that afternoon I shook hands with Joe and we agreed I would start his roof next. As I walked to my truck doing my best to control my joy, wanting to scream out my excitement, Joe called out, "By the way, my neighbors on both sides will be watching you."

"Great!" I said with a genuine smile.

I roofed five houses on that block, one right after the other. When my next bank statement arrived all I could do was sit and stare at it, thinking that I could actually be my own boss.

A few weeks later I again called my old boss. "Sorry Bill," he said, "I don't have anything for you."

"That's okay," I said. "I actually was calling to see if you wanted to do some work for me."

That was during the worst recession since the Great Depression. I started my own business and have been working steadily ever since. The business has grown every year and continues to do so.

Every day is Monday, eight days a week. That's my motto.

~Bill Young

Now That's Therapy!

Success is to be measured not so much by the position that one has reached in life as by the obstacles that one has overcome while trying to succeed.
~Booker T. Washington

The scissors clicked open and shut twice before I trimmed the feather on the fishing fly I was making. Tapping the last material five times "to feel right," I finally completed the fly. I clicked, counted and tapped through thousands of commercially ordered fishing flies in high school. It was my only job aside from lawn mowing and paperboy—solitary pursuits. I not only had obsessive-compulsive disorder, but was also very anxious around people. School was tough enough; more interaction after school in "regular" work was unquestionable.

If you had met me twenty years ago, you'd have said, "Tony Smith will never socialize, never mind be the center of attention for any reason." Maybe it was because I was picked on for my Tourette's or being overweight, but by age fifteen I had diagnosable social phobia. I yearned for camaraderie and wanted to flirt with girls, but I also feared being subjected to intense scrutiny. Lots of people did like me and invited me to get together, but although I recognized this, I still couldn't shake the nervousness and always refused. Despite therapy and anti-anxiety medications, I spent high school as a melancholy loner thinking I was losing my mind.

As I entered ninth grade, where everything involved socializing, I was certainly not partying and I was spineless around the fairer sex. I needed something to occupy myself. When I found *Poul Jorgensen's Book of Fly Tying*, I decided I would get good at fly-tying. While my peers campaigned for class president and fought over girls, I fled to a basement workbench and busied myself bending feathers into fish-catchers, enjoying the company of my inanimate creatures.

On a wintry day in February 1993, happy that I could stay home and tie flies, it dawned on me that I could never use this many! So, I placed an ad in a newspaper. Soon my cigar boxes of flies needed replenishing. I was building a business! As my work refined, I needed better materials and learned of the legendary Hunter's Angling Supplies fly fishing shop a few hours away. One time when my parents drove me up to look for materials, George, an employee, asked to see my work. I mailed up some flies and upon receipt he suggested I tie for them. Magnified by the OCD, I only saw imperfections in my flies, but George's comments boosted my confidence. Soon I branched out, developing an interest in Atlantic salmon flies—storied, complex creations that are easy to get absorbed in because of their elegance.

On Christmas Day 1994, some sought-after salmon fly books awaited me under the festive evergreen. Mouth agape, I looked at the flies of Dave McNeese, Paul Schmookler, John Shewey and others. I had only one thought: "I'll never be that good, but where do I start?" Being so shy, I had no choice but to teach myself how to tie them. After a while, I hit an impasse. There comes a point when people must refine their skills by observing others. Realizing I lived in a hotbed of salmon fly tiers, I attended some shows and met many of the fly-tying celebrities. I mustered some courage to show my work to these stars. I was poised to run out, red with anxiety and shame from the scrutiny I anticipated. Like the first time I asked a girl out, time froze and I held my breath. "Can I have it?" asked Schmookler, making me an offer on a fly I showed him. I left the show with the same feeling one gets after the girl says "yes."

I soon needed work to see me through college, and local fly fishing supplier Phil Castleman needed help. Through him, I connected with a great young tyer in Oregon named Jon Harrang, and we got well acquainted through letters. We eventually thought it would be fun to meet. When I was invited to demonstrate at the Northwest Fly Tyer Expo in Oregon, we had our chance. I felt I knew Jon well enough by then for it to be anxiety-less. The catch was that I needed to demonstrate at the show. "Who cares what you tie, just do something you can't screw up," Jon said, and I shakily accepted.

I was so thrilled to be in Oregon that I forgot how nervous I was... until tying time. I chose the day's end, figuring there would be fewer people to watch me fumble, only to have people crowding the table. Amongst them were multiple Northwest legends such as John Shewey and the late Harry Lemire. (Gulp.) "If I survive this, I can do anything," I thought as I started the fly. Someone asked to keep the fly when I finished, and others asked for my card.

Shortly thereafter, someone called me from the Northwest Atlantic Salmon Fly Guild in Seattle and asked me to come demonstrate, all expenses paid. They saw photos of my 2004 gold medal Irish Open Creation Classic fly and wanted to see it tied in person, and I less shakily agreed to this one.

"You fool! You can't catch anything on that fly in those conditions!" Shewey teased McNeese as they sat in my class. Listening to their banter, it drove home who was present and how far I'd come. Twelve years earlier, feeding the interest I took to in an effort to avoid social situations, I sat in my room staring at their work, fantasizing that someday I'd be that good. Now I was being paid to teach classes, and people I admired felt they could learn from me?

Years of counseling and medications were less useful for my cure than my unbridled passion. My experience taught me that if you work with what is going well despite life's problems, you get better results than just focusing on removing the problems. In psychology, this is known as a solution-focused approach to therapy. Years after my severe anxiety, and as a mental health professional, I was naturally drawn to working with my clients in this manner. I tell my clients that working on their concerns can be like gardening, and relay a quote from the late psychiatrist Milton Erickson that I once heard at a professional seminar: "Sometimes it's easier to cultivate the flower, than to go pulling out all the weeds." It was this mindset that allowed me to fly into success in more than one way. Now *that's* therapy!

~Anthony Smith

Chapter 10

Find Your Inner Strength

Taking Back Your Life

The Ring of Hope

Hope is grief's best music.
~Author Unknown

A rusted metal chair was on the front porch of what would soon be my new home. It looked just as fragile as the splintered wood of the deck on which it sat. It was early on a Sunday morning when I found myself perched on that chair, hours before heading to church. I clutched a cup of coffee that I had brought from the large and beautiful suburban home that I was leaving behind. Everything that had felt comfortable and secure was gone.

Even though the sun was bright that early spring day, my spirit was dark and dull. Hot tears flowed down my cheeks and I wondered how I would find the strength to accomplish the tasks I had to do that morning.

The discovery that our family finances had eroded was shocking. My husband was leaving and I had to find a new home for my teenage daughter and me. In spite of her desperate pleading, we had no choice but to move. We had to pack up almost two decades of belongings and start over. The worn out, garbage-filled townhouse was the only place I could afford. I could not envision it ever becoming a home.

There was crayon on the walls, a hole in the ceiling from a leaky bathtub, and garbage everywhere. This abandoned townhouse was like the mirror image of my broken marriage.

As I sat on the deck that first morning, crying, I was surprised to hear the sound of church bells. They were playing a familiar hymn. I lifted my head. And after a few stanzas, I found myself crying harder and choking out the words "great is Thy faithfulness." When the song ended, somewhere deep in my heart I heard another sound—the whisper of God saying, "Be at peace. I moved into this neighborhood long before you did."

For the first time in many months I felt a flicker of hope. God's reminder that He was near made me feel less alone. The bells rang out His presence and their timing had been perfect. With just enough energy to lift myself from the chair, I put down my coffee cup and weakly smiled at the heavens.

Wearily I opened the front door and began the process of cleaning and reconstructing. The project was enormous. It required a complete demolition and took a small army of deeply caring volunteers to tear down and then rebuild the terribly neglected structure.

In a strange way, the townhouse and I became one. There was tremendous pain in the things torn from my life; what I had believed to be a happy family, a beautiful home, a solid future, dreams and plans, extended family and friendships. But it took a surprisingly short amount of time to remove that which no longer had value, what was destroyed beyond repair, and to clean out the shell before deciding how to rebuild.

Countless hours were poured into the endeavor, and with it, slowly, came the hope that my daughter and I could create a home. For months I painted, laid tile, managed the installation of a hundred details and bore the stress of creating something out of little.

It seemed like a small miracle when the renovation was completed in three short months. When we had settled in, one precious friend, herself cruelly familiar with loss and pain, shared with me that massage had been a therapy for her in managing stress. As a generous housewarming gift, she gave me a certificate for a massage with the man who had helped her so much.

It took me several months to find the courage to make the appointment. It had been a long time since I had been touched in any way by a man; and even though I knew he was a professional, I was anxious.

His practice was in the lower level of a home office building. It was cozy and quiet. He was gentle and kind, but my nerves were still uneasy.

After allowing me a chance to get settled under the warm flannel blanket, he entered the room where I lay face down on the massage table. The lights were low and soft music played. He warmed some oil and began to work on the knots that seemed to have settled permanently in my neck and shoulders.

Sensing my edginess, he asked easy questions and I chattered in response.

"What brought you to my practice?" he asked simply.

I answered that our mutual friend had offered his service as a gift.

"Ah, that is a good friend," he replied.

His response opened the door for me to tell him how difficult life had been, the physical strain I had carried in renovating my townhouse, and the anguish I had experienced over the loss of my marriage, my home, and my dreams.

Then I told him the story of the church bells. The long, firm strokes of his palms on my shoulders paused and then he stepped away from the table. Although I could not see him, I knew he was still in the room and I guessed that he was changing the music, or getting more oil or warming some towels.

But the minutes went by and I heard him softly apologize, his voice cracking. What he said brought us both to tears and will forever remind me that God has a plan and a purpose for everything in our lives.

"My mother," he said haltingly, "was the secretary for many years at the church that rang those bells. When my brother and I were younger we would often climb the big trees on the property while she was at work.

"One day," he went on slowly, "my brother had climbed high, too high. He lost his balance and to steady himself he accidentally touched the nearby electrical wires and was killed instantly." The air was still and silent between us before he finished.

Somehow I knew how he would finish the story and we were

both crying as he said, "My parents donated those bells in honor of his life. It will mean so much to my mother to know how God spoke to you through their song."

Even though I didn't get to see the smile on his mother's face when she learned that her gift had given me so much hope, I have imagined it many times. It is a sweet reminder to me that there are lovely things that can grow from tragedy and that church bells can ring a message of hope through a world of pain.

~Diane Lowe MacLachlan

91

The Ex Ms. Miserable

Other people's opinion of you does not have to become your reality.
~Les Brown

i Ms. Ruble!" my neighbor's son called from the yard as I pulled into my driveway. He said my name as if it was one word: mizzruble.

"Hi John," I replied through the open window. "Hi Richard." My husband was out front too, mowing the grass as he did every Friday whether it needed it or not.

"Where have you been?" Richard scowled, emptying the grass clippings into a lawn bag.

"Matthew's six-week checkup with the pediatrician," I answered. It seemed pointless to remind my husband that we discussed this appointment just last night.

"Oh, yeah. What'd he say?" Richard was already pulling the starter on the mower.

Tears I learned to suppress — "You're way too emotional, Anne" — burned as I blinked them back. "He recommended we take Matthew to see a neurologist. He's concerned about his lack of eye contact and something called abnormal posturing. He gave me a referral."

Richard's eyes blazed. "Jesus Christ! Why in hell are you telling me this now? Can't you see that I'm cutting the grass? Goddammit, Anne. Your timing sucks! And where did you find this quack doctor anyway?" My husband stomped off, his posture as rigid as the parallel lines running across our manicured lawn. I berated myself for not rehearsing the conversation beforehand. After ten years of marriage, I knew better than to approach Richard unprepared or uninvited. If I wanted to avoid his rage, I had to adhere to the unwritten rules that usually protected me: pick my words, plan my defense, prepare to surrender.

Looking back, my bridesmaids should have carried red flags instead of roses when they paraded down the aisle. Richard's narcissistic view that the world simultaneously revolved around him and conspired against him was evident even back in college when we first met. But instead of dwelling on his inability to empathize, I redefined Richard's stoicism as strength, his perfectionism as persistence, and his adherence to regimen as admirable. Wanting "college sweethearts live happily ever" to be our story, I eagerly returned the feelings Richard professed to me. My grandmother's mantra: "Love him for who he is, not who you want him to be," reinforced my determination to love unconditionally.

When Richard finally proposed, I chastised myself for being disappointed with the ring he slipped onto my finger. "I know you really wanted a princess cut," he said. "But the round is a better investment, and really, how important is the ring?" Richard kissed me and added, "Besides, no one will ever love you as much as I do." I ignored my unease that his words rang more like a threat than a promise and accepted his proposal.

Richard's anger, when it was first directed at me, was unexpected and confusing. His senseless and unbridled temper ran contrary to the calm, controlled demeanor of his public self. This volatile side of Richard's personality scared me, but I faced the glare of his anger through rose-colored glasses and went to great lengths to appease him.

When Richard lashed out at me for staining his favorite spatula with spaghetti sauce ("How stupid can you be? Everyone knows to stir tomato sauce with a wooden spoon!"), I purchased new utensils. When he criticized my dream of becoming a writer ("Who do you think you are—the next J.K. Rowling?"), I respected the feedback as a healthy dose of reality. And when he protested ("There's something fishy about these monthly father-daughter dinners with your dad."), I acquiesced and invited Richard along. Not realizing that I was ensnared in an emotionally and verbally abusive relationship, I redoubled my efforts to be more loving, more accepting, more forgiving.

Olivia, our three-year-old daughter, hopped out of the van. "It's okay, Mommy. I didn't see Daddy cutting the grass either." She scampered toward the house with her stuffed bunny clutched to her chest. Once Olivia was safely inside, I pulled the van into the garage and turned off the engine. Deep breaths, I told myself, as I unbuckled Matthew from his car seat and carried him into the house. Placing my son in his swing, I watched as his gaze settled—on nothing. His stare was as empty as I felt.

Yes, John, I thought. I am mizzruble. Miserable Ms. Ruble.

The next four years were consumed by appointments with neu-rologists, nutritionists, optometrists, physical/occupational/speech therapists, and sensory integration training. Despite overwhelming evidence that Matthew was on the autism spectrum, Richard denied that there was anything wrong with our son; I denied my growing fear of my husband. I believed I had to make my marriage work, if only for Matthew and Olivia's sake. I hoped that if I were a better wife, a better mother, a better person, in time things would get better.

And for Matthew, things did improve. Thanks to a devoted team of therapists, our son began to meet developmental milestones. First steps, first words, first bites of real food—I cautiously shared these victories with Richard, who was relieved but also patronizing. "See, Anne? I told you there was nothing wrong." I desperately wanted to believe he was right (in regard to both Matthew and our marriage), but the more Matthew progressed, the more our relationship deteriorated.

It wasn't until Matthew strung together a litany of swear words in precise imitation of his father's tirades, and Olivia again questioned: "Why are Daddies always angry?" that I knew I could no longer stay married "for the sake of the kids."

Emboldened by all the years I had advocated for our son, I told Richard that I wanted a separation. He countered that I didn't have the right to leave him, that I owed it to him to put more effort into our relationship, and that we couldn't afford the financial drain of separate households. "Besides," he chided. "You can't cut the grass or shovel snow." The next day I packed up the kids and moved in with my parents.

I was terrified but determined that my children would not grow up in a household fraught with anger, disrespect and manipulation. Marriage counseling quickly proved ineffective — the demise of our relationship was, according to Richard, all my fault. Realizing divorce was inevitable, I found a therapist who helped me understand that abuse, like autism, has a spectrum. The absence of broken bones and bruises only meant the abuse wasn't physical. Richard's belittling comments and vicious outbursts controlled me as much as an actual slap to my face or punch in the ribs. Contrary to the childhood chant regarding sticks and stones, words can and do hurt.

In the year that it took for my divorce to be finalized, I adopted a new mantra: to love myself for who I am, not who someone else wants me to be. I have regained my self-confidence, my self-respect and my self-reliance. I have stopped scripting my conversations and cowering at the sound of Richard's voice. With the judge's scrawl across my divorce decree I took back my maiden name and ultimately, my life. I am Miserable Ms. Ruble no more.

~S.A. Thibodeaux

92

Silence Is Not Golden

Being deeply loved by someone gives you strength,
while loving someone deeply gives you courage.
~Lao Tzu

y suitcase was packed, in it the remnants of a stolen life. Clothes, shoes, the bare minimum of toiletries, but nothing to indicate a child's sordid life. No photos, no treasured toys, no books with dog-eared pages. And a hurried note from my mother: "I hope you have a happy life."

Twenty-three and terrified of the world, of people who do harm, and even those who don't. Against my parents' objections, I was leaving to marry the man I loved, Ty. Earlier, they had foraged through my room, stealing my memorabilia, and with it, my childhood identity.

"You'll be sorry," they predicted. "After all we've given you, this is how you repay us? Running off with some man you've known for just a month?"

They were not there to say goodbye. Suitcase in hand, I paused at the mirror to glance at the face reflected there. I saw the face of a scared child, eyes clouded by the abuse sustained at the hands of both parents. I saw a face devoid of the spirit of life, with a body wasted by anorexia.

I loaded my suitcase into my Corvair. Then, I went back to retrieve my six parakeets, happily chirping in their cages. A new life was beginning, a new life with breath and hope and love. Somebody loved me really loved me—my Ty, a gentle spirit.

I ran away on a Friday in 1972. We were married the next day in a civil ceremony attended only by our boss and his wife from the radio station where we both worked. My old life was gone—or so I thought—and my new one just beginning. The tears of joy I cried that day belied the perpetual tears of my abuse.

"Don't cry," my husband would often say, not aware of the abuse. "You are Mrs. Willis now and that is all that matters." Life, for him, was simple and recognizable.

It took six years before I told him of the abuse.

With Ty, all things seemed possible. I steered the dark secret like a pirated ship through treacherous waters. As the years passed, communication with my parents ceased. I had finally come to realize that what they had done was not normal. My father, a doctor, continued on as though nothing had happened. I followed his pursuits online first as a doctor at a mental institution, then as a prison doctor. I could not help but feel he was meeting his karma face to face.

"Your father is a jerk," Norma, my co-worker, complained. "My boyfriend said he refused to treat him for a cold." I had mentioned only my father's name to her, but never the abuse. Norma's boyfriend was serving time for armed robbery at the state prison where my father worked as the doctor.

"He has an attitude toward the prisoners," she accused.

Anger made me want to tell her he belonged in prison too. I said nothing, swallowing the bile.

"Pretend nothing happened," was my father's counsel when I asked what I should tell the man I would marry someday.

"Your father doesn't mean it when he calls you names," my mother defended him.

And I was so good at pretending. I had done it all my life. Pretend there was no dark, dank basement, no musky bedroom, no medical office where atrocious acts took place. Pretend there were no belts and switches wielded by my mother on fragile flesh. Pretend that I was an adult when the seeds of a child rattled inside.

The year 1978 began the end of pretense. I gave birth to our daughter Resa. My husband and I were overjoyed. On that day, I gave birth to my "self" too. I told my husband the truth.

"How can a father do such a thing to his daughter?" My husband wrestled with the impact of my words.

Inside, he shared my pain. He listened; he digested my emotions. Though he cared, I still felt alone. I feared it would change his perception of me. Generous in spirit, ever patient, he viewed me still as innocent, one of the qualities he admired in me initially. What he did not comprehend was that my father had stolen not only my virginity, but also my self-esteem. Worse yet, he had corrupted my spirit. How, indeed, can a father, or anyone, do such a thing? Ty's words were aptly spoken. And how could a mother enslave her daughter to her husband? My mother bartered me to keep her marriage intact.

With that admission in 1978, I began my new life, haltingly at first, then with more conviction. I was not the nobody my father had called me. I was somebody. Our daughter grew into a strong woman, and so did I, emerging from my veiled past. Encouraged by Ty, I joined Incest Survivors Anonymous at our local church. I listened to the stories of likewise tortured women and men. I became the shoulder they could cry on, the ears to hear their pain and anguish, all too familiar. I was not alone after all; I was in a brotherhood of many survivors.

At my husband's insistence, I began to write, a dream I'd always had. At first, it was like carving words into stone, shaping feelings of rage and sorrow into healing affirmations. Trying to forget, yet forced to remember for the sake of others.

My husband typed my words. He believed in me, as I did not. Slowly, with impunity, I came to believe too. A seedling took root, blessed by the sun; the memories no longer held me captive. My words liberated me, and many others. Though as a child I was not loved, I have survived to tell my story to the world, and to listen when others speak. Silence is not golden, I have learned, but best when broken.

~Josie Willis

93

Defending Our Children

When you are a mother, you are never really alone in your thoughts.
A mother always has to think twice, once for herself and once for her child.
~Sophia Loren

y husband and I had finally decided to be licensed for foster care. Our children were young at the time, and they were excited to get involved in caring for a little brother or sister. The children we cared for were never much older than three months, almost exclusively female, and African American.

Providing foster care was a fun, rewarding and exhausting ministry. Everyone in the family was involved, pitching in where they could. It truly was an enjoyable experience. There was only one big issue. My father-in-law.

Our first long-term placement was three-month-old Evelyn, who lived with us for two years. She was an even-tempered, fun-loving little girl.

My husband's father was an eighty-year-old immigrant from the "old country." Having suffered a stroke before my husband was born, his body was paralyzed on the left side. My father-in-law didn't like Evelyn because she was African American.

When taking a family picture, he'd make sure she was positioned behind someone. While she sat uncomprehendingly in her high chair, he would point his finger at her and request that she "Go back to Africa."

Mercifully, my children were too young to know what he was saying. My mother-in-law would glare and tell him to stop. But that only worked for a while. It would start all over again at the next visit.

I would leave those weekly dinners with a mix of anger and sadness. This was my child he was talking to. How could he do that? My husband wouldn't address the issue. "That's just him," he'd say. "He doesn't know any better."

After living with us for two years, Evelyn was adopted by her maternal grandmother.

Time passed, and we were ready to accept another long-term placement. I told my husband that I'd have to call his father first. His remarks and attitude would no longer be tolerated. The words were bad enough, but now my children were older, and they would understand his hurtful comments.

If he couldn't change, we would stop visiting. He wasn't going to be a reason to stop fostering, but he'd sure be a reason to stop putting a helpless child in his line of fire. I had to speak up.

I practiced my lines for days. It felt like weeks. The day of the call, I paced around the house waiting for more courage. I muttered to myself, "Come on now! It's just a phone call. What's the worst that can happen? What if he gets so mad, he refuses to speak to me again?"

All of this internal chatter wasn't helping. I was getting short of breath, which happens when I get nervous. Shaking my hands, trying in vain to flip away those nerves, I finally called.

My mother-in-law answered the phone, and we exchanged pleasantries. I asked to speak to my father-in-law. "Oh!" she responded. I never called to talk exclusively to him, so I knew she'd be surprised. Now he was on the phone.

Oh boy. My words came out very slowly at first. My stomach was flipping. "Hi!" I started out brightly. I should get an Academy Award for acting. I was feeling anything but bright.

"Remember how we were foster parents a few years ago?" No response. I plunged ahead. "I know how you treated our daughter last time. You said some mean things, and it really upset me."

It felt like I'd popped the cork from a shaken bottle of champagne.

Finally released from my mind, the words now tumbled over each other in the race to be expressed.

"We are going to be taking another placement soon, and I wanted you to know that I can't accept that kind of attitude toward any child we are caring for."

Continued silence on the other end of the phone. Now for the really scary part. "If you feel that you can't change, we won't be visiting you while we are caring for this child."

And I was done. I felt like I was suspended in midair. Or waiting for the ax to fall. Now what?

Silence.

After a few seconds, which felt like years, he told me he didn't understand what I was talking about. While he did have a thick accent I knew he had heard and understood me. I asked for my mother-in-law and I explained the situation to her. I was a complete sweaty mess at this point.

She told me that she would speak to him as soon as we got off the phone.

Click.

Oh my Lord, call the paramedics. How I hated this. I try to avoid confrontation, and apparently my father-in-law does too. We never spoke of it again. We never had to.

I don't think he had ever been approached this way by any of his immediate family, and the experience probably shocked him. Maybe he was as surprised as my husband that he was capable of changing his behavior.

He accepted our next daughter. Not with open arms, but with tolerance. He would offer her little treats at the dinner table, and praise her block-building skills. It was a transforming moment for me to see him change so radically. Actually, it was probably more transforming for him.

We went on to care for ten more children, and with each one he became more and more at ease. Seeing him finally singing "Happy Birthday" to our foster children, I knew his heart had changed.

This whole episode showed me how important it is to stand up

or what is right, with or without fear. It taught me that sometimes you
ust have to take the lead, bite the bullet, grab the bull by the horns...
ick your favorite cliché.

In spite of my anxiety, I had to do the right thing and speak up.
You know what else I learned? That words can change the world, one
person at a time.

~Ceil Ryan

94

Old News

Love yourself first and everything else falls into line. You really have to love yourself to get anything done in this world.
~Lucille Ball

"Oh, honey, I'm so sorry," my sister said, hugging me. "We're all still in shock."

She was in shock? I was the one whose marriage had just fallen apart. I was in my parents' basement, trying to survive our first family gathering since my not-so-happy announcement.

More hugs. More sympathetic looks. I knew they meant well, but frankly, I was tired of the pity party.

"Can we just play a game or something?" I asked, trying to smile. "I just want to pretend for this one night that everything is okay."

"Oh, of course," my brother said too quickly. My siblings and their spouses hurried to the game closet, everyone rushing to do as I'd asked.

Before we could agree on a game, my mom came downstairs. She put her arm around my shoulders and said, "Aunt Betty is here and she'd like to talk to you."

"Why me?" I asked. "Doesn't she want to see all of her nieces and nephews?"

My mom gave me a look. "You know why she wants to see you." She squeezed my shoulder. "She's been through this herself and she just wants to make sure you're all right."

I sighed and swallowed hard against the sudden lump in my throat. Why can't everyone just treat me like they always do? Neither of the boys has even teased me. How weird is that?" I shrugged and added, "It's not like I'm made of glass or something."

But even as I said the words, I knew they were a lie. The truth was that I could shatter at any moment and everyone in the room knew it.

"We're just trying to be supportive," my mom said.

"I know, and I love you guys for it," I said. "But right now, what would help me most is distraction. I want to just forget for a little while."

My sister-in-law patted my shoulder. "It's okay, Diane. All of this attention is just temporary. Pretty soon, something will happen to someone else and this will be old news."

I knew she wasn't trying to be unkind, but I was crushed. The very idea that my heartbreak would be "old news" was preposterous. My life had completely fallen apart. The man who had promised to love me forever no longer did. My kids would endure a painful divorce and we were about to lose our home. Everything was a mess, and in that moment, I was sure I would never be happy again.

No, my divorce was never going to be old news. Not to me.

Over the next few weeks, I recalled my sister-in-law's words. The pain was still so fresh and it had invaded every aspect of my life. My marriage had failed, and it made me feel like a complete and utter failure. In marriage and in life.

Nope, no old news here. Months after my husband left, my heart-break was still very, very new.

I picked up a book on improving self-esteem. The book was filled with clichés, like "Focus on the positive" and "Tomorrow is a new day." But one piece of advice actually made me laugh out loud. The book said I should start writing down every compliment I was given, no matter what it was or who said it.

I looked in the mirror and laughed as I imagined the compliments people would give me. "Wow, Diane, the bags under your eyes look a little less giant today," and "Gee, Diane, you're looking quite thin lately. The gaunt, hollow look becomes you."

I laughed, but it wasn't funny. My life had fallen apart, and the mirror showed that my body wasn't far behind.

The chance that I would actually receive a compliment seemed slim, but I decided to start tracking them anyway.

Two days later, an elderly woman at the grocery store smiled at me. I smiled back, just to be polite, and the woman exclaimed, "Oh dear, you should do that more often. Your smile lights up your face."

Of course it does, I thought, since I haven't bothered with make-up in months.

And with that self-deprecating thought, I wrote down her compliment.

A few days later, my children and I were eating lunch at a fast food restaurant and my son asked if he could finish my fries for me. handed them over and the man at the next table told my son he was lucky to have such a nice mom.

Just watching my gaunt figure, I thought, but I still wrote down the compliment.

Over the next week, a co-worker told me I was clever, a lady at church liked my potluck casserole, and my daughter told me my hair looked pretty.

I also received a complimentary e-mail from the editor of a magazine I wrote for, as well as a very positive evaluation at work.

I wrote down these compliments and then read over the list. It was an eye-opening experience. If what these people said was true, I was a clever, capable, creative person with a nice smile and pretty hair.

And I made a mean chicken casserole too.

I decided to believe the kind words of others and disregard the unfavorable thoughts I so often had about myself. In short, I needed to stop beating myself up.

It wasn't easy and it didn't happen overnight, but gradually, realized that a failed marriage didn't make me a failure as a person. Other people saw good qualities in me, and I needed to recognize them in myself.

I continued writing down the compliments I received, and I actually started to believe them. And one day, I realized that I wasn't hurting anymore. I'd moved on with my life. I wasn't a failure, and I'd actually started to like who I was again.

My sweet sister-in-law was right. She said that someday my divorce would be old news. It took a while, and it wasn't easy or fun, but my heart healed.

And I learned to love myself in the process.

That's not old news, it's big news.

~Diane Stark

95

To Forgive and Not Forget

When you forgive, you in no way change the past—
but you sure do change the future.
~Bernard Meltzer

P eople say that forgiveness helps the one doing the pardoning more than the one being pardoned. They say that holding a grudge damages the holder, not the person who did the hurting.

I never believed them.

After years of drinking, my newly sober dad decided he wanted to be an alcohol and drug counselor. So this wonderful man, who had skipped more high school classes than he had attended (usually to go fishing), went to college.

I was a tutor and Daddy often called upon me for help. We had an arrangement: for every tutoring session I provided him, he would answer a question about my childhood. Any question. Period.

One day I asked, "When was the first time you knew she hated me?"

I didn't need to say who I was talking about. All my life, my mother had expressed herself quite articulately about why she hated me, about how much she hated me, about how she wished I'd never been born. She called me "fatty" long before I ever had an ounce of extra weight on my body and she ridiculed me in public every chance she got. The family—my parents, my siblings and I—would go shopping. If I said anything within her hearing that rubbed her the wrong way (and nearly everything I said rubbed her the wrong way), my mother would stop in her tracks and say, in front of family and strangers alike, "How did anything so stupid come from my body?"

My dad left home when I was fourteen and things got worse. Once, my mother and I were at the pharmacy. As we stood at the register ringing up our purchases, my mother turned to the cashier and said, "I wish it was legal to abort seventeen-year-olds."

So, my dad knew very well who I was talking about when I asked, "When was the first time you knew she hated me?"

I could tell that my dad didn't want to divulge that information, but this was our deal. He'd gotten his tutoring session; now I was getting my answer.

What Daddy told me chilled me to the bone. I was born at a local Catholic hospital, and the day I was born the nuns gave me to my mother to be fed. My dad stepped out to get a cup of coffee. He came back to bedlam.

"There were screams coming from your mother's room," Daddy explained. "When I ran in, your mother was shaking you, screaming, I hate you! I hate you!'"

Daddy cleared his throat, hoping, I think, I would stop him from going on with the story. "The nuns had to take you away from her. Three days later, they gave you back."

I thought the story was over, but my dad went on.

"The next day I had to go to work," Daddy said. "When I came home, your mother was slamming your crib against the wall over and over, saying, 'I hate you!' as if she couldn't speak different words if she tried." Daddy looked at me, pleading with his eyes, but I didn't know what to say. "Every weeknight was the same. I came home to the same nightmare. On the weekends I was there with you and your mom never even looked at you, but weekdays I always came home to that same horrible scene." Daddy breathed hard. "It was weeks before I told anyone. After that, your granny came every day, from morning till night. We... tried to protect you."

The story stunned me. That my mother hated me was no secret. The extent of her hatred towards my infant self was a huge surprise though. After several minutes of silence, Daddy said, "I'd kill for a pork barbecue sandwich. Are you hungry?"

"Famished," I said.

And that, as they say, was that.

My mother continued to "slam" me as I grew, mostly with words and often with anything she could reach that would inflict pain. Realizing as a teenager that my mother was a drug addict did not assuage my resentment toward her. After all, my siblings were not being pummeled with vitriol and rage. As soon as I was old enough, I walked away from my mother. I stopped answering my telephone. I avoided family gatherings.

The culmination of those years of torture was that I didn't see or speak to my mother for a number of years. It was the healthiest thing I could do for myself.

One night, my brother phoned. Our mother had overdosed on opiates. It was her fourth overdose and by far the most damaging. My mother suffered seventeen seizures her first day in the ICU. Her body survived, but her mind was gone. It was like instant Alzheimer's. The level of her deterioration was alarming and my siblings transferred our mother to a nursing home because she could no longer care for herself.

Three nights later, my phone rang very late. Someone-has-been-killed-in-a-car-crash late. I answered automatically. It was my mother. She was sobbing. "Please come and get me!" she cried. "I need to go home!"

That call unhinged me. My mother had locked me up on false charges more than once when I was a teenager. I spent my sixteenth birthday in jail because she lied to the courts and said I had knocked her out. I had to make up my entire sophomore year of high school on my own time because my mother locked me up for the last two months of the school year. I knew the desperation she felt.

I talked to her. I had pity on her, even though I really tried not to. Somehow I calmed her enough that she could go to sleep.

I didn't sleep at all. I was feeling empathy for a woman who had tortured me, a woman who wished I'd never been born, and it infuriated me. I stood at the bathroom mirror and looked at myself, something I never did because my mother had convinced me early on that I was ugly.

I stood there and I prayed. At first, I had no words, just raw emotion. Memories of taunts and starvation and beatings flooded my brain and left again. Finally I said, "Okay, God. I forgive her."

It was the hardest thing I'd ever done, but I let the past exit my brain so I could be for my mother what I reveled in being for others every day of my life. After that prayer, I talked to my mother every evening for the rest of her life. Her brain damage from the overdose turned her into a funny person who chatted almost exclusively about Elvis Presley and bad nursing home food. Occasionally she'd return to her old self, and I'd politely get off the phone without fighting with her.

My mother died unexpectedly in July 2013. I didn't cry, but sometimes I wake up missing the mother I never had, and I weep. Mostly, though, I'm thankful for finding the strength to forgive. It matters. It has made a difference.

~Marla H. Thurman

My Sobbing, Shaking Strength

Life is very interesting... in the end, some of your greatest pains,
become your greatest strengths.
~Drew Barrymore

never thought I would be someone who woke up one day in an abusive relationship. Of course, in reality it didn't happen all of a sudden. My relationship wasn't perfectly healthy and happy one day, and then abusive the next. The changes happened gradually, so gradually I didn't even notice that things were changing between us. Ever so slowly, he became more and more controlling, more and more volatile and unstable.

Yet if you had asked, I would have told you that we were happy. I thought our relationship was beautiful and filled with love. Sure, we fought sometimes, but doesn't every couple? It was true that he was perhaps a little too dependent. He didn't like when I got together with my friends because he missed me too much when we were apart, even for just a few hours. And yes, he made me feel guilty about going home to visit my family during the summer because he couldn't stand to be apart for days, much less weeks.

But these things, I rationalized, were signs that he loved me. If you had told me I was slipping down a rabbit hole of increasing emotional abuse, I would not have believed you. I defined myself as a strong person, and I didn't think that strong people could get tangled up in abusive relationships.

Inner strength has been part of my identity and my own personal narrative since birth. I was born three months prematurely, weighing a terrifying two pounds, six ounces, and I stayed in the hospital for months as I fought to live. I needed a respirator to help me breathe and feeding tubes to help me eat. My feet were pricked countless times for blood samples, and my heart was monitored closely because of a small hole that eventually healed itself. "Your daughter is a fighter," the surgeon told my parents. Against all odds, I battled my way into the world, and throughout my life I have drawn strength from the story of my birth: my experience of survival.

As I grew into a healthy little girl, my underdeveloped lungs grew strong. In middle school and high school I ran cross-country and track, where my teammates voted me "most inspirational" and team captain. I hiked to the summit of Mt. Whitney, the tallest mountain in the contiguous United States. I traveled to England on my own and backpacked through eight countries in Europe. I was the friend others leaned on; I was independent; I was strong. I didn't think of myself as someone who needed help from others.

And then I woke up one morning and found myself in an abusive relationship, engaged to be married to a man who was steadily becoming more and more frightening. Day by day, I could feel myself growing quieter, smaller, lonelier. I was becoming lost. I knew I should reach out to a friend or family member—I had many people in my life who cared for me deeply and who would drop everything to help me, just as I had helped them through various life disasters and problems.

But I felt ashamed. I thought I was strong, but obviously I was wrong about myself—how else could I have fallen so deeply into such a bad situation? And what made things worse and more complicated was the fact that, despite everything, I still loved this man. I was afraid to be on my own without him.

The red flags, however, kept piling up. When we argued, he threw books against the wall in frustration. One night while driving he angrily slammed the steering wheel and the car nearly veered off the road. When I was offered the career opportunity of my dreams, he ordered me to turn it down because it was halfway across the country. He couldn't bear for us to ever be apart and wasn't willing to make any changes in his own life so he could move there with me.

When he coldly shook his head, refusing to even glance at the letter I'd received congratulating me on this opportunity, my heart was ripped wide open. I had reached the breaking point. This was a red flag I couldn't ignore.

That day, the day I finally left, I would have told you that I looked like a weak person. I certainly felt weak. I was a complete mess. My legs shook. I sobbed. I hadn't been able to eat or sleep. It took all the strength I possessed to look into the eyes of this man I still loved and tell him, "I'm sorry, but I can't do this anymore. This isn't a healthy relationship. I can't marry you."

It was the bravest, most difficult thing I have ever done. And I didn't do it alone. My brother hopped on a plane and stayed with me for a week, driving me to work and bringing me dinner, making sure I ate and drank water and slept. My best friend drove six hours to be with me, and for an entire weekend she held my hand and rubbed my back as I cried. I continually received phone calls and e-mails from friends and relatives, checking up on me and asking if I needed anything. Even acquaintances I hadn't known I could count on were there for me, inviting me out for coffee and lunch, making me feel part of the world again. The kindness and love I felt were overwhelming.

Inner strength, I learned, isn't about putting up a façade. Inner strength isn't refusing help from others. Inner strength isn't relying only on yourself. My true inner strength came when I finally reached out to those around me and confessed that I was in a bad situation and I needed their help to pull myself out. I learned that real inner strength comes from being true to your own authentic self, your desires, your needs.

Now, I still draw strength from the story of my birth, from the photo on my desk of my tiny newborn self, hooked up to an array of tubes and monitors in an incubator in the NICU. But I also have a new story to draw strength from. When I was a sobbing, shaking, heart-wrenched-wide-open mess, all I could see at the time was weakness. But now I can see that the opposite is true: I was actually a study in strength. I think of that day—one of the most difficult days of my life—and I am proud of what I went through. I am proud to be me.

~Dallas Woodburn

A Breath of Hope

Sometimes the most important thing in a whole day is the rest we take between two deep breaths.

~Etty Hillesum

t's easy to get caught up in the hype of back-to-school season. The month before Joshua started kindergarten—even though I worked a part-time job at a non-profit, shuttled my two small boys around town to their various activities, and managed our unmanageable household—I deemed it necessary to spend hours upon hours shopping for the perfect little backpack for Joshua's grand entrance into academia.

I began the quest by visiting all the major local retailers. I stopped at several specialty shops. I tried the sporting goods stores, toy outlets, and even a couple of luggage places. When all of these options failed to produce my ill-defined concept of that perfect backpack, I turned to the Internet—Lands' End, L.L. Bean, Amazon. In the end, I went with a junior-sized, monogrammed, ocean-blue, featherweight variety. It looked adorable on Joshua.

I went through the same process with the lunch box that would go inside the backpack, and then with the Thermos that would go inside the lunch box. And don't even get me started on my journey to satisfy the school supply list—that beast involved five different office supply stores. I was determined that Joshua would have all the correct quantities, requested brands, and specified colors of the various items that were apparently essential to the scholarly well-being of my five-year-old.

I selected the perfect first-day-of-school outfit for Joshua. I even "suggested" that we go ahead and lay out his entire first-week-of-school clothing choices in the cubbies of the new, specialized closet organizer (with Monday-through-Friday compartments) recently purchased for this task. After some consideration, I also went ahead and bought him a pair of Skechers sneakers—even though they cost $45 and he'd probably outgrow them in a month. (All the little boys seemed to be wearing them.) Finally, I took him to get a haircut.

It was all a lot of work. It was also rather stressful to get through that big old to-do list in time for the start of school. But, in the end, my little boy was officially "ready."

Three years later, my younger boy, Jonah, started kindergarten. I had actually relaxed quite a bit by then about the whole back-to-school venture, realizing that if I couldn't find the specified 20-count Crayola box after the first couple of stores, the world wouldn't end if I sent him to school with the 24-count variety. Also, when he told me that he didn't want a haircut, I let the haircut thing pass. To make up for looking like a slacker-mom though, I went ahead and signed up to be a volunteer in the classroom and to chaperone field trips.

Outside of school, of course, I planned to continue my duties as Team Parent for both boys' soccer teams. I was also simultaneously looking for a new job and training for a half-marathon in my spare time.

You get the idea.

Looking back, I don't know why I thought that getting the perfect backpack would make me some sort of super-mom. I don't even know why I thought that being a super-mom was important to begin with, but in my defense, all of that happened before my whole world shifted.

About two weeks after Jonah started kindergarten, I—a non-smoker who was previously considered to be a healthy, fairly fit individual—was diagnosed with a rare form of lung cancer. I had lost my own mother, also a non-smoker, to lung cancer right before I got pregnant with Jonah. As a result, when I was first diagnosed, I feared the worst. I feared that I might not be around to send my boys back to school in the future.

The doctors seemed convinced that the cancer was localized to my lung — a very good thing — and the recommended treatment was surgery. My overall prognosis seemed quite positive, so I underwent major surgery that fall. Half of my left lung was removed.

I didn't see my boys the entire time I was in the hospital — eight days of misery — because kids weren't allowed into the critical care unit. Beyond that though, I didn't want them to see me connected to the chest tubes, the IVs, the morphine epidural, or the various breathing apparatuses. For the first time in my life as a mom, because of the intense levels of post-surgical pain, I also didn't want either of them to enthusiastically hug me. It was the longest I'd ever been apart from them.

I went home to begin my recovery on the day of Joshua's third grade fall concert, his "Black Light Show," so I missed that. It was the first big school event of his life that I didn't attend, and that was very hard for me.

I was in horrible physical pain for months after the surgery — and horribly depressed. Halloween was soon after the Black Light Show, but I wasn't up for trick-or-treating. I also wasn't allowed to drive for the next two months due to heavy pain medications — I missed an awful lot during that time.

My amazing husband stepped up and managed to take care of all of us. And I recovered from my surgery, although it took many months, and most of the school year had passed before I really began to adjust to my new normal. I was exhausted — physically and emotionally.

Last fall, we found ourselves at the beginning of another new school year. Though I've racked my mind, I don't actually recall doing any of the usual back-to-school preparations. That school year passed somewhat uneventfully and it has now been two full years since my diagnosis.

It is back-to-school time once again, and it now means something quite a bit different than years past.

This year, I can truly say that I don't care what my boys wear on their first day of school. I don't care which Star Wars character is on Jonah's thermos. I don't care what color Joshua's lunch box is, and I don't even really care that the school supply list said twenty-four "sharpened" pencils. I doubt I will get around to sharpening them. Call me a rebel — but I'm going to send them in anyway. I suspect that the world will go on spinning despite copious quantities of unsharpened pencils and I realize — for real this time — that none of these details really matter.

So I take a deep breath, because I can — and I simply hope. Because for me, what does matter is hope.

First, I hope for all the usual things moms hope for when kids go back to school. I hope that my boys make lots of new friends this year. I hope that this is the year they both make straight A's. I hope that nobody gets bullied, that my kids do their homework without me nagging them, and that I don't get any calls from the teachers about any playground incidents.

I take an even deeper breath. Hope matters, and so I hope for the thing that matters to me most.

I hope that next year I will still be here as my boys once again go back to school. I hope to send them off with new, though generic-brand, shoes on their growing feet, and with unsharpened pencils tucked away in their not-so-perfect, crumpled-up-paper-filled, slightly-gooey-crumb-bottom-lined backpacks.

~Lisa Pawlak

The Beauty of Aging

Take time today to appreciate beauty — natural beauty, art, people.
Slow down, breathe deeply, smile. It's a beautiful world.
~Jonathan Lockwood Huie

J ason and I talked about getting married, but it was really only talk. I knew we were over when he refused to go home with me on a cold, snowy New Year's Eve in New York City. He wanted to stay at the party to be with his new friends, and I didn't hear from him until after 7 p.m. on New Year's Day. We broke up by 10 o'clock that night.

Jason and I had been together for three and a half years, and we had spent ample time with each other's families while we were dating. My favorite person in his family was his younger sister Dayna. Dayna was twenty-nine, just two years older than me, but she seemed to be living a far better life. She had tons of friends and a great career working for Target in fashion design. When she walked into a room, her smile just lit up the whole place. From the day I met her, I knew Dayna had a spirit uniquely her own. She loved life and was genuinely happy. I admired her.

After Jason and I broke up, though, I stopped talking to his family. It just seemed like the right thing to do. That is until I heard the news: Dayna had been diagnosed with pancreatic cancer at the age of thirty-three.

I couldn't believe it. It was so sad, such a tragedy. She was too young and had her whole future ahead of her, but cancer has no boundaries.

Dayna immediately started an online journal at CaringBridge. com. There, she recorded her journey from the beginning: meeting the many doctors who were trying to save her life, going through her first rounds of chemotherapy and radiation, feeling so sick and tired she wondered how in the world this "medicine" could be working to cure her. But at the end of each journal entry, no matter how difficult the day had been, Dayna would sign off saying, "Smile Today!"

When she received her diagnosis, Dayna had already left New York City for Minneapolis to work at Target's headquarters. It just so happened that I was going to Minneapolis for a convention so I decided to give her a call to see if we could get together. Ever the sweetheart, she invited me over to dinner with her and her fiancé, Tom.

When Dayna picked me up at my hotel, I took one look at her and was flooded with compassion. She was so thin and pale. She no longer had that long mane of blond hair with pink highlights that had made her so funky and stylish in the past. Instead, she was wearing a knitted beanie to keep her head warm. But her smile was still there. So was the sparkle in her eyes. Even though she was tired and cold, her spirit radiated from within. I was so glad to see that cancer hadn't stolen her fire, especially since she had lived with it now for over three years, a near miracle since the cancer had spread to her lungs.

Just a few months ago, while I was reading Dayna's online journal, I was inspired by what she wrote. This was not the first time Dayna's words had touched my heart, but a clear message came with her words. She wrote:

"Thirty-seven, this is heaven. I am so happy to be growing older. When a doctor tells you with a sad face that you have a few months to live, each passing birthday is an event to cherish. I don't take the fact that I am getting older for granted because there are too many that don't get this opportunity."

I'm pretty sure that prior to reading this journal entry, I was bemoaning the fact that I was getting older. It was harder to lose weight, and I was starting to notice some wrinkles.

Aging does have its downfalls, but the fact remains that we are all so blessed, so lucky, so fortunate to even be alive. And we take this fact for granted every single day. There is a great beauty to aging. If we have lived well, we are now stronger, more loving, and more understanding than we were before.

These days, Dayna spends a lot of time sleeping. But still, whenever she writes in her online journal, she mentions three things that she loved about her day. On the 4th of July, she listed chatting and laughing with her younger sister, getting a postcard from some old friends and watching the sun shine through colored glass bottles in her bedroom. It's the simple things that are most wonderful in life, like love and beauty.

Every time I find myself bemoaning the fact that I'm growing older, like when I panic that I'm thirty-five and haven't had children yet, I think about Dayna. She has taught me to appreciate each day for what it's worth, which is everything, and she has reminded me to smile. No matter what our circumstances, we are all so blessed to be alive. Smile today!

~Mandy Iahn

Tragedy Without Villains

Life is an adventure in forgiveness.
~Norman Cousins

Whether it be god or mere mortal, someone has to be blamed when events go awry in the affairs of man. Any ancient Greek would have told you that. Whoever heard of a tragedy without a villain?

During the years after the tragic breakup of my marriage, I listed the candidates for the role of villain and went down the list one by one, crossing off those who were ineligible. One day, surprisingly, none were left.

My marriage existed in a small Southern textile town that dreamed its way through the turbulent 1960s and the disruptive aftermath of the 1970s. Bill and I were part of the quiet generation, the dutiful kids of the 1950s, and we lived on the sidelines of those disorderly times, insulated in our rural setting miles from the mainstream. It would be difficult for me to make a villain of the times.

Bill is Southern, a product of upper middle-class America—servants, white-pillared house, Boy Scouts, football, and West Point, where he became First Captain his last year. His values were set by his Southern upbringing and confirmed by West Point: duty, honor, country. He never questioned them. Was a villain lurking there? Not unless we condemn our culture.

I am English, the daughter of a soldier; a high school dropout, having given up a formal education to ice skate professionally all over

Europe, the United States and Canada. I soaked up experiences like a sponge, forming and reforming my values along the way, unorthodox by some standards, but not villainous.

Bill entered the family lumber business having much knowledge of commanding troops and firing howitzers, but knowing little about selling two-by-fours. He pushed himself to make a name in the community—Jaycees, Rotary, the Methodist Church. He ran for County Commissioner and led the ticket, but the party went down in defeat. Before long, he had taken on all the burden of the family business, sired three sons, and settled his family on a beautiful forty-acre farm.

Meanwhile, I learned to wait—to wait for Bill to come home; to wait for his mood to improve; to wait to be included in the small part of his life he shared with me. I was demeaned by waiting, but I was only doing what my mother had done, and he was only doing what his father had done... and our mothers and fathers before us... and not a villain to be found in the whole lot.

I loathed what I saw as the hypocrisy of the South but learned to live with it. Bill controlled the family finances and made all the important decisions. He ate breakfast uptown, and often lunch, and stayed late at the club after work. I took care of the house and the kids and I was very lonely. He had an affair; I was forgiving. He was domineering; I was submissive. He said he was happy; I was not. He was getting more out of this arrangement than I was and, suddenly, my own survival became more important than the survival of my marriage. I was in a trap and I began to plot an escape, but quickly realized I had nowhere to go. Who wants an aging ice skater? I needed a roof over my head and three meals a day. Like it or not, I was married to the marriage. It's a couple's world and the bills were paid, and if Bill would just disappear everything would be very nice.

So in a way I made him disappear. The boys went off to college and I renewed old friendships and made new friends. I went often with them to dinner, the theater or shopping in a nearby city. Bill and I did go to a couple of conventions—he was required to take a wife—and we met in the middle of the bed most nights. But, away from Bill, I found I was free to voice my own opinions, to be myself. Now I was getting more out of this arrangement than he was. I told myself I was very happy. Bill was not.

One day, in the twenty-second year of our marriage, I was out with friends when Bill came home, quietly packed his bags and left.

The loneliness was appalling. I spent the nights stalking the empty house looking for the villain and waiting for daylight to get out to a job and temporarily ease the misery. When the boys came home on vacation they divided their time between their dad's bachelor pad and the farm. Everywhere in that town I was the wronged wife, the leftover half of a couple. I was cut from the social list and asked out only by the girls" when their husbands were out of town. I drowned in self-pity. By this time, I had found a dozen candidates for the role of villain, and that small Southern town was number one on the list.

And so I ran away. I ran over the Blue Ridge Mountains, across the dusty windswept Plains, and high into the Rocky Mountains and found a refuge where I could lick my wounds in peace. I found a job as a hostess in a ski lodge. In summer, I hiked high alpine meadows knee-deep in wildflowers and, after work in the winter I skied between evergreens flocked with snow. I met ranchers and real estate agents, builders and busboys. Young and old, they were vigorous and vibrant, geared to the outdoors, glorying in the brief summers, uncomplaining of the harsh winters. It was like a tonic to live among them. I began a love affair with all things Western.

From my window, I looked across a wide valley to mountains covered with aspens and evergreens; I grew geraniums on the porch in summer and adopted two cats for company, and slowly began to find my own quiet center. I learned that loneliness is a gift, although it was often hard to see it that way; that it shakes the cobwebs loose and weeds out the dead things of the past like a bracing wind. And I learned, painfully, that Bill and I had never had the talent to achieve a balance in our marriage, and that we are better people without each other.

I missed my old friends and my sons; and when my first grand-daughter arrived, I returned to the South knowing that, as Henry Miller said, our destination is never a place but rather a new way of looking at things. And as I crossed the windy Plains again and looked back over my shoulder at the high peaks along the western horizon, I silently thanked them and their people for sheltering me while my wounds healed.

So who is the villain of this piece? The husband? The wife? Society? On whose head can we pour out the venom of our bitterness and hate for the pain we have suffered? There is no one… and slowly the venom evaporates in the bright clean light of reason, leaving only a residual sadness. I have lived through the tragedy. I have three wonderful sons and the twenty-two years hold some good memories. I don't need a villain to cloud those memories.

~Bridget Fox Huckabee

Out of the Ashes

I know God will not give me anything I can't handle.
I just wish that He didn't trust me so much.
~Mother Teresa

Wiping the corner of the coffee table with the dust cloth, I stood back to admire the sparkling glass. I glanced up at the staircase landing, pleased with the look of my new oak bookcase, freshly filled with neat rows of books and topped with a vibrant spider plant. At the foot of the stairs, a nine-foot dracaena added to the sense of life within our home. I loved decorating, and was forever adding or changing something in this beautiful, 3,000-square-foot house nestled atop a mountainside, where we'd lived for nearly seven years.

Outside, a hazy yellow glow emanated from the trees. The wildfires in San Diego were burning out of control and we had heard that a wall of flame, fifteen miles wide and twenty feet high, was marching in our direction. Evacuation was a looming possibility.

I thought I'd do some cleaning, just in case we had to leave for a few days. It was always nice to come home to a clean house.

The atmosphere had an eeriness that made this fire seem different than the last one we'd had. This Cedar Fire seemed to have a mind of its own, like a big, devouring monster that gobbled anything in its path—whether clear of brush or overrun with it. We had heard stories of people having ten minutes notice to leave behind everything they owned. Some said you couldn't see the flames coming because the smoke was so thick. You had to take it upon yourselves to get out when you sensed imminent danger.

As I dusted and straightened the family room, I looked over all of the things surrounding me. If I knew I would never see any of these things again, which of them would I take along? The decision wasn't easy. Certainly, photos and family videos would be on the list, but with limited space in our cars, what else should go? As my husband Jerry pulled framed family photos off the walls and loaded them into empty laundry baskets, he grumbled to himself, "What a hassle it will be to put these back up again."

I unhurriedly packed two suitcases with clothing and shoes, and set aside "treasure boxes" including numerous artistic creations by our young daughter Selah, and my writings from childhood. Jerry's SUV was filled with business equipment. My compact car would have to hold Selah, our three dogs, the cat in her carrier, Selah's guinea pig and whatever personal items we could squeeze in.

As we finished loading our cars, our neighbors a short way down the road telephoned. "The smoke just got really thick here. We're going to head out." A few minutes later, not wanting to breathe the ever-thickening pollution, I suggested to Jerry that we go too. Leaving a generator running in the garage to keep our food cold, we followed the trail of cars out of town toward the desert, the only direction open to evacuees.

Staying outside of San Diego County, we were unable to get tele vised news reports about our area, so friends phoned with frequent updates on the fire situation. Around noon on Wednesday, my friend Karen called. "I'm watching the news, and right now they're trying to save your house." For over two hours, the news broadcast showed Department of Forestry helicopters battling to save our home from the air, dropping water and spraying fire retardant.

As we anxiously awaited further news, seven-year-old Selah man aged to bring a smile to my face. "Well, Mommy, if our house burns down, maybe next time we could get me less toys so I won't have to clean my room so much." Leave it to our little girl to keep things in perspective!

A short time later, Karen called back. "I'm so sorry. Your roof just went up." As she continued to watch, a huge wall of flame engulfed the front of our house.

The house was gone. The unthinkable had happened. I curled up next to Jerry and sobbed.

Early the next morning, while Jerry and Selah slept, I sat with my Bible on my lap. I opened it randomly and my eyes fell on Isaiah 3: "When you walk through the fire, you will not be burned; the flames will not set you ablaze." It went on: "Forget the former things; do not dwell on the past. See, I am doing a new thing! Now it springs up; do you not perceive it? I am making a way in the wilderness and streams in the wasteland." It seemed that God was speaking words of encouragement to my heart.

Three weeks after our home burned to the ground, I went for the first time to survey the ruins. I looked across the pile of what had been such a vibrant center of life for our family and friends. Huge, twisted hunks of metal were strewn over piles of drywall and unrecognizable rubble. I could see the corroded corner of Selah's brass bed frame poking out of the ashes—once such a place of comfort and security as I'd tucked her in at night. The springs of our living room sofa, a spot where I'd loved to sit and look out the window and watch wildlife as I prayed, now lay exposed to the elements.

I walked around the perimeter of the refuse, feeling numb. Lord, I prayed, before I leave here, please show me something in the ashes that got saved. My eye caught sight of a charred Christmas ornament lying atop the waste. I made my way over to it. Normally, I would have been climbing into the attic in just a few days to haul out the Christmas decorations that would transform our home into a yuletide wonderland. I realized that this must be the spot where the attic had caved in. I scanned the area, and suddenly saw something poking out of the ashes. A definite shape. I reached down, took hold of it, and pulled. Out of the rubble came a completely intact piece of our beautiful Nativity set—a shepherd. Another shape caught my eye, and I pulled out a wise man, then Joseph, an angel, and Baby Jesus and the manger. One after another, the pieces continued to come up all unbroken.

One thing had changed, though. The intense heat of the fire had burned all the color out of this beautiful, hand-painted Nativity set. All of the figures were now pure white. As I stared at the pieces, the significance of this overcame me. God sometimes allows His purifying fire to burn in our lives, but when we walk through His fire, we will not be destroyed. We will only be changed to reflect more of His glory.

As I held the figurine of the baby Jesus and looked around at the devastation that was once our home, I realized something else. When everything in our lives seems to be falling apart, there is one thing that remains intact. The baby, born 2,000 years ago in a humble manger, is still here. He will never leave us. For us and for hundreds of other families in our tiny community who lost everything, He would be there in the midst of our sorrow and need, sustaining us with His ever-present comfort and strength. And He would walk alongside us into the brand new thing that He was going to do in our lives.

~Sandra Sladkey

Independence Day

Freedom is the oxygen of the soul.
~Moshe Dayan

can still hear those defiant words blaring from the radio in my mother's Volkswagen sedan. Sitting alongside my mother as we scurried about the streets of our little town, running our usual errands, she sang along without missing a beat. She raised her left arm—the other firmly on the wheel—as if to accentuate the melody, and sang with the passion of someone who could relate to the woman described in the song, with the passion of someone with newfound freedom and independence.

From the frequent screaming and fighting, the abusive language, and the love/hate drama that had unfolded between my parents before my eyes, I knew that "Independence Day," written by Gretchen Peters, was more than a just a popular song that summer. For my mother, it was the music of courage and self-confidence. For me, at the formative age of fourteen, it was the music that turned my world upside down.

The song's lyrics told of a woman's response to domestic abuse, seen from the point of view of her eight-year-old daughter. On Independence Day, while her daughter attends the local parade, the woman starts a fire in the house, and she and her abusive, alcoholic husband both perish in it.

The song has double meaning in that the woman was finally gaining her freedom from her abusive husband—thus, it was her Independence Day—and the events occurred on the Fourth of July.

Its message suggests that what the woman did was neither right nor wrong. Instead, it was the only way she could ultimately gain her freedom and, at the same time, protect her daughter from the violent home where her little girl had seen bruises on her mother's face far too many times.

"Let freedom ring, let the white dove sing... Let the weak be strong, let the right be wrong."

Those were some of the lyrics that my mother sang with the deepest passion.

My mother left my father that summer and never went back. A teenager at the time, I was initially angry about it all. The last thing I wanted to do was spend time with the woman who didn't seem to understand me and with the woman whose decision forced me to live in another house, to ride another school bus, to memorize another phone number, and, worst of all, to endure the financial limitations of a single-parent home.

As we continued about our errands that afternoon, I glanced over to the driver's seat at the middle-aged woman my selfish teenage self had begun to resent. With her long red hair, petite figure, sculptured face, and deep brown eyes, my mother truly was a picture of beauty. Although she seemed a bit overbearing and protective at times, she was my strength and I admired her. But she was increasingly down on herself. Inside the radiant beauty that most people saw was an increasingly broken, weary, and sad woman.

She tried to be strong for my younger sister and me, but I'd often see her cry and witnessed how the pain of ending that relationship drove her to a state of depression. I tried to be sympathetic, but there was little that I could say or do to help mend her heart.

Just the night before she had cried herself to sleep and, as we lay beside her, whispered, "I love you girls, more than you will ever know."

As I watched her sing that afternoon, I began to understand why that song was so meaningful for her. And I came to realize how much her freedom, her independence, and her ability to do what made her happy, really meant. I began to gain an appreciation for the sacrifice hat my mother made, not only for her own well-being, but for my sister's and mine as well. Though we struggled financially, her courage and strength allowed us to live in a home free of fighting and verbal abuse. Her decision allowed us to stop living in fear.

When the song ended and she parked the car, she smiled as big as she could, and said, "I'll be celebrating my Independence Day on July 31st, not July 4th. Bring the fireworks."

It's been ten years since the day I watched my mother harmoniously sing along to "Independence Day" while en route to the grocery store. I'm no longer the teenager in the front seat, dependent on a ride to my destination. I no longer use my Sony Walkman to block out her high-pitched singing. But there's one thing that hasn't changed since that hot summer day in the passenger seat: the significant impact the song's message has on me.

When I hear the words "Independence Day," I don't always think about the fourth day in July, the red, white, and blue, or America the free. Instead, I salute those brave women who, like my mother, had the strength and the courage to make difficult and painful changes in their lives, changes that now face me as well.

Perhaps it's true that history repeats itself. Not long ago, when I left my alcoholic husband, I knew the same kind of pain my mother experienced nearly a decade earlier. Perhaps I should have paid more attention to the lessons of my mother, the lessons of my upbringing, and the frequent anguish of my childhood. But perhaps I was destined to follow in her footsteps, to make her mistakes, to feel her pain, and to develop her courage, strength, and independence.

I know she never wanted me to, but now I know. Now I understand. And as soon as I was able to roll the stone away, I had my Independence Day.

Coincidentally, I left my husband on July 31, 2010—exactly eight years to the day my mother left my father. "Hard to believe," she said when she reminded me of our shared date. "Only now do you understand why it was so important for me to leave... for me, for you, and for your little sister."

Not long after our phone conversation, I came across that song, which I hadn't heard in years, on one of my late-night drives. Lik Mom always had, I turned up the radio and sang along with passion And for once that day—probably even that week—it didn't feel s bad to be alone.

Let freedom ring.

~Ellarry Prentice

Meet Our Contributors

Barbara Alpert is a wife, mother and grandmother living on the west coast of Florida. She has written books for children and adults as well as her memoir, *Arise My Daughter: A Journey from Darkness to Light*. She is active in her church, serves as a women's small group leader, and is a Blog Mentor, coaching aspiring authors.

Katie Bangert lives with her husband, three children and many family pets. She is a voracious reader and enjoys nothing more than a good book. Katie partners with a foundation to raise awareness for those suffering from facial paralysis. Her passion is to help others find their smile again. E-mail her at Katiebangert@yahoo.com.

Valerie D. Benko writes creative nonfiction from her home in western Pennsylvania. She is a frequent contributor to Chicken Soup for the Soul and has had more than two dozen essays and short stories published in the U.S. and Canada. Visit her online at http://valeriebenko.weebly.com.

Alicia Bertine is a frequent contributor to Chicken Soup for the Soul, a three-time pancreatic cancer survivor, and a model, businesswoman and motivational speaker. She has served as the Pancreatic Cancer Action Network's "Champion of Hope," and inspired viewers on *Lovetown, USA*. Contact Alicia via www.AliciaBertine.com.

Ginger Boda has had stories published in *Chicken Soup for the Bride's*

Soul, *Chicken Soup for the Soul: Teens Talk Middle School* and *Chicken Soup for the Soul: Power Moms*. Ginger lives in Southern California with her husband of thirty-seven years, and they are blessed with three children and nine grandchildren.

Barbara Bondy-Pare has four children from her first loving husband Ronald M. Bondy. Since he passed away from lung cancer, she has married a high school classmate, Eddie Pare. Their twelve adorable grandchildren keep them young, active and entertained. Barbara is all about love, family and hugs.

Debra Ayers Brown is a writer of inspiration and humor with stories in multiple Chicken Soup for the Soul books. She is also co-creator of Your Write Platform, a marketing boutique for authors and business owners. Connect via www.About.Me/DebraAyersBrown or @coastaldeb on Twitter/Instagram/Pinterest. Learn more at www.DebraAyersBrown. com.

Lorraine Cannistra has a Bachelor of Science in English and Master of Science in Rehabilitation Counseling from Emporia State University. She enjoys advocating, cooking, writing and motivational speaking. Her passions are wheelchair ballroom dance and her new service dog Leah. Enjoy her blog at healthonwheels.wordpress.com. E-mail her at lcannistra@yahoo.com.

Louis R. Cardona lives in Chicago, IL. He is currently taking classes in graphic design. He enjoys shooting pool, writing, reading, and baseball. He is artistic and creative. He wrote this story when he was still in high school, and hopes to do more writing in the future.

Liane Kupferberg Carter is a journalist and award-winning essayist whose articles have appeared in *The New York Times*, the *Chicago Tribune*, *Babble*, *Brevity* and *Literary Mama*. She has just completed a memoir.

Melissa Halsey Caudill is a paralegal, writer, runner, actress, and cancer urvivor. She is the proud mother of two great teenagers and is soon o be the proud stepmother to more wonderful kids when she marries heir handsome daddy in November 2014. This is her third story in Chicken Soup for the Soul and she is working on her first novel.

Rose Couse is a Registered Early Childhood Educator in Cambridge, ON, Canada and holds a Bachelor of Arts in Psychology from University f Waterloo. The proud mother of two grown sons, Rose is passionate bout validating and inspiring others through her writing. E-mail her t rose.46@hotmail.com.

ill Davis lives in Port Orange, FL with her husband, Gary. In her spare ime, she enjoys scrapbooking and walking the beach.

o Davis has articles and short stories published in national magazines. he has written a series of children's books, which she credits to raising ive children as a single mother, and is an accomplished poet. She njoys photography, horseback riding, camping and travel.

Nellie Day is a professional freelance writer who resides on the Las egas Strip with a surly Bull Terrier. She received her M.A. degree in roadcast journalism from USC, and her BAS degree in English and ociology from UC Irvine. When she's not writing for national magazines, Day spends her time finishing up her first novel.

oan Dayton has two adult children, two granddaughters and one dorable great-granddaughter, and is becoming established in a new areer as a freelance writer.

rancis DiClemente lives in Syracuse, NY, where he works as a video roducer. He is the author of three poetry chapbooks, and his blog an be found at francisdiclemente.wordpress.com.

oanne Stephenson Duffin is a 2006 graduate of New York Institute of hotography and is an award-winning photographer, as well as a poet, writer, and singer-songwriter, with a background in interior design. She is the mother of four adult children and grandmother of six. She lives with her husband of thirty-eight years in Wilsonville, OR.

Jo Eager is a freelance writer and broadcaster in San Diego, CA. She currently flies in a television news helicopter, reporting breaking news and traffic. Jo also enjoys teaching several fitness classes. She has two kids — both the inspiration of Chicken Soup for the Soul stories.

Nick Fager received his Bachelor of Arts degree from Middlebury College in 2009. He spent his college summers working for *Survivor* and continued after graduating. Now living in New York City, he is pursuing a master's degree in psychology at Columbia University with aims to become a psychotherapist. E-mail him at nickfager@gmail. com.

Lynn Fitzsimmons, DTM, has developed a courageous spirit. She has achieved things others told her she could not. Lynn is an advocate for the disabled and helps individuals find their true purpose in life. A professional speaker/author, Lynn reaches all audiences to inspire and motivate. E-mail her at lynn@stepoutforsuccess.ca.

Carol Fleischman is a freelance writer. Her essays have appeared in *The Buffalo News*, Chicken Soup for the Soul books, a Guideposts book series and *The Simon & Schuster Short Prose Reader* editions 3, 4 and 5. Her first children's book is scheduled for publication by Pelican Publishing in 2015.

Debra Forman is a magazine writer, radio reporter, and motivational speaker. She and her eight-year-old son enjoy movies, music and traveling to family-friendly destinations. Her goal is to use her writing abilities to improve the world, and her current focus is helping the non-profit Autism Cares Foundation in Richboro, PA.

Shannon Francklin lives in Atlanta, GA with her husband Michael nd Kira. She is a full-time mother and enjoys her soccer mom life. hannon and Michael are grateful to God and Dr. Andrew Toledo, her VF doctor, for giving them Kira. Shannon would like to thank her wonderful friend Caroline Updyke for writing this story.

Karen Frazier is a freelance writer and author who has written two of her own books and ghostwritten numerous others. She also designs jewelry, writes cookbooks, and enjoys spending time with her family. She is married and has a college-aged son and a teenaged stepson.

Patricia Ann Gallegos is a freelance writer, encouraging others through her life experiences while inspiring students at Evergreen School District. She is pursuing a journalism degree, and is published in other Chicken Soup for the Soul books. Visit her at www.patriciagalwrites.com, or contact her at pattygallegos@comcast.net.

Kathy Glow is a freelance writer, blogger, and mother of five boys, including one lost to cancer. When not driving all over town in her minivan, wiping "boy stuff" off the walls, or trying to find the bottom of the laundry pile, she writes for various websites and anthologies. She is working on a memoir about her son.

Genevieve Gosselin has a passion for language and words, which led her to work as an English teacher, translator, proofreader, editor and writer. Gen also loves advocating for the acceptance of people with mental illnesses, a group she is part of. She is single but has a wonderful, supportive family.

Haylee Graham is a twenty-one-year-old four-time novelist and owner of a charitable snapback hat company, Snap Gives Back. She now lives in Las Vegas, NV, and is also co-founder of a music-based charity. Haylee wishes to inspire and encourage others one story, snapback, or charity at a time. E-mail her at Snapgivesback@gmail.com.

Kasey Hanson married her childhood sweetheart and has two boys and one little girl. She loved supporting her husband's NFL football career for eleven years and now can be found on the sidelines cheering for her kids while her husband coaches. Kasey loves working with children and pointing people to Jesus Christ.

Rachelle Harp is a speculative fiction author, blogger, and avid coffee drinker. Her YA novel, *The Breakout*, won the 2012 Novel Rocket Launch Pad Contest, and her short stories have appeared in *Havok* magazine. When she's not writing, Rachelle loves spending time with her family, friends, and two cats.

Born and raised in the South, **Cheryl Hart** is the fourth of five siblings and proud mother of two grown children. As a military daughter and wife, she lived all across the South, worked a variety of jobs, and met dozens of interesting people. She now calls Georgia home, travels overseas and writes Southern women's fiction.

Carol Goodman Heizer, M.E.d., resides in Louisville, KY. She is an eight-time published author whose books have sold in the U.S. and overseas. Her work has appeared in several Chicken Soup for the Soul books. Her previous works may be purchased through Amazon.com, CreateSpace, and in bookstores. E-mail her at cgheizer@twc.com.

Wendy Hoard received her Bachelor of Psychology degree from the University of California, Santa Cruz in 2001. For the last ten years her focus has been caring for her two sons on the autism spectrum. Wendy's love of writing gave birth to her blog *Bugaboos Treasures*, where she shares her personal journey with autism and addiction.

Bridget Huckabee is a freelance writer, a native of England and now an American citizen. She has three sons and five grandchildren. She enjoys writing, gardening, needlepoint, watercolor painting and volunteering at her local art gallery.

Mandy Iahn graduated from Princeton Theological Seminary in 2005 before becoming a minister in the United Methodist Church. She enjoys the beach and boating, tennis and golf and spending time with her family. She writes inspirational nonfiction and children's books.

Marsha Jordan created the Hugs and Hope Club for Sick Children. She's no stranger to illness herself; but through it all, she's kept her sense of humor. She shares that—along with hard-earned wisdom—in her new book, *Hugs, Hope and Peanut Butter*. E-mail hugsandhope@gmail.com or visit hugsandhope.org.

Ginger Katz is the author of *Sunny's Story* and CEO/Founder of The Courage to Speak Foundation, a nonprofit founded after her son died of a drug overdose. She presents nationwide to break the silence about drug use and she spearheaded the development of drug education programs for students and parents. Learn more at www.couragetospeak.org.

Zoe Knightly graduated from the University of Richmond and is currently pursuing her Master of Public Health degree at Emory University. Zoe's mission in life is to inspire people. She is a world record holder in an athletic event despite having an autoimmune disease. E-mail her at zoe.knightly@gmail.com.

Suzanne Koven, MD, a primary care internist at Massachusetts General Hospital, writes the monthly column "In Practice" for *The Boston Globe* and contributes the interview series "The Big Idea" at The Rumpus. She also authored *Chicken Soup for the Soul: Say Hello to a Better Body!* Learn more at www.suzannekovenmd.com.

Cathi LaMarche is a novelist, essayist, and poet. Her work has appeared in over two dozen anthologies. In addition to owning Top College Essays, a college essay coaching service, she teaches composition and literature. She resides in Missouri with her husband, two children, and three dogs.

Jacqueline Lauri is a perpetual traveler who feels at ease everywhere but at home. She received her bachelor of science degree from the University of the Philippines and is now taking MBA-level executive programs from eCornell. At the moment, Jacqueline resides in Norway with her husband, son and cat.

Chelsey-Ann Lawrence grew up in Canada, where she completed her B.A. degree in social sciences and human services with high honors She currently lives in Seattle, WA with her husband and works as a behavior therapist. She loves travelling, cooking, baking, time with family and friends, and writing to inspire others with hope.

Sue LeBreton is a health and wellness writer whose articles appear regularly in regional parenting magazines in Canada and the U.S. The unexpected challenges of her parenting journey have included cancer, autism, life-threatening allergies and diabetes. She uses self-care and humor to help her on her parenting journey.

Foxglove Lee specializes in LGBTQ fiction for teens and young adults. Her books include *Tiffany and Tiger's Eye* and *Truth and Other Lies.* Find out more at foxglovelee.blogspot.com and follow her on Twitter @FoxgloveLee.

Betsy Alderman Lewis is a freelance writer with many interests, especially history. Lewis has a B.A. degree in Cultural Studies with concentrations in writing and literature. She enjoys designing quilt and embroidery patterns. You can visit her website at www.betsylewiswrites.com or e-mail her at info@betsylewiswrites.com.

Jaye Lewis is an award-winning writer who lives in the Appalachian Mountains of Virginia. Jaye has PTSD and is blessed to have a service dog, a ten-pound Dachshund named Dixie Mae. Visit them both at www.facebook.com/DixieMaeDoxie.

Linda Lochridge is a psychotherapist. She is also a speaker and writer.

She lives with her husband Tom and her Goldendoodle Emma in the Rocky Mountains of Montana. She is a mother to five, grandmother to ten and great-grandmother to two. Linda loves to paint, quilt and knit. She is currently working on a memoir.

Sydney Logan is the bestselling author of three novels, *Lessons Learned*, *Mountain Charm*, and *Soldier On*. She received her master's degree from Tennessee Tech University and has been teaching for nearly twenty years. Sydney lives in the hills of East Tennessee with her wonderful husband and their very spoiled cat.

Carol Luttjohann earned her Master of Social Work degree at Washington University in St. Louis. She is in the process of starting a nonprofit organization to support caregivers and keep elderly in their own homes. She has written two books about caring for her mother. E-mail her at mymothersdaughter@gmx.com.

Diane Lowe MacLachlan is a graduate of Hope College and a student of life. The grateful mother of three amazing, adult children, a lovely daughter-in-law, and grandmother to her first grandchild, she loves to enter into the stories of family, friends, and strangers and to find joy in everyday things.

Meg Masterson is a journalism student based in Sacramento, CA. She has a deep love of theater and hopes to launch a career as an arts writer. Many thanks to Jan, family, friends, and—most of all—John. E-mail her at m3masterson@gmail.com.

Sara Matson lives in Minnesota, where she is currently enjoying her new mouthful of shiny, white crowns. (However, she continues to avoid eating taffy.) In addition to smiling widely, she spends her time homeschooling her teenaged daughters and writing magazine stories for children. Visit her website at www.saramatson.com.

Megan McCann is a mom to three children and lives in the beautiful

Shenandoah Valley. She received her Bachelor of Arts degree from SUNY College at Purchase. She dedicates this story to her mother who inspired a great love of writing and the desire to help others to know their greatness. Writing is her heart.

Debbie McNaughton is a writer of short stories drawn from everyday life. She is a member of the National League of American Pen Women and Cape Cod Writers Center. Debbie and her daughter moved from Wyoming to Cape Cod in 2002. They collect mermaid memorabilia, listen to loud rock music and dream of owning a red Corvette.

Like most people who tell their story about singing from the day they were born, **Samantha Molinaro's** passion for writing was seeded at birth. The bottom line remains that for Samantha, writing is an escape and mode of expression in which she hopes others can be inspired to laugh, cry, or even write themselves.

Tom Montgomery is a Michigan native who earned his bachelor's degree in journalism at Central Michigan University in 1985. He has been editor of the *Cass City Chronicle* in Cass City, MI for the past twenty-eight years. He and his wife, Deb, have four grown children and nine grandchildren.

Marya Morin is a freelance writer. Her stories and poems have appeared in publications such as *Woman's World* and Hallmark. Marya also penned a weekly humorous column for an online newsletter, and writes custom poetry on request. She lives in the country with her husband. E-mail her at Akushla514@hotmail.com.

When **Gail Molsbee Morris** isn't chasing after God's heart, she chases rare birds across America. She can be reached through her nature blog at godgirlgail.com or tweet @godgirlgail.

Alice Muschany writes about everyday life with a touch of humor. She went so far as to write her own obituary, mostly so she could get in the last word. Her family, especially her grandchildren, make wonderful subjects. Her essays have appeared in numerous anthologies and magazines. E-mail her at aliceandroland@gmail.com.

Andrew Nalian is the author of *50 Deeds for Those in Need*. He believes that if you focus on doing one good deed a day, the world will be rich with something money can't buy — happiness. If you were influenced by Andrew's story, he would love to hear from you at TheDeedDoctor@gmail.com.

Diane C. Nicholson is a writer and professional photographer/photo-artist, specializing in companion animals and special needs children. A long-time vegan, her affinity and respect for animals and patient understanding of children with special needs is reflected in her art. Diane has nine stories published by Chicken Soup for the Soul.

Nick Nixon is a retired advertising executive who now writes humour columns and creates cartoons for various publications. He also does caricatures for cancer patients, family and friends. Plus, Nick writes and illustrates children's books. He records these stories and does voiceovers for commercials and videos.

Kathleen O'Grady is a writer and political strategist living in Ottawa, Canada. She is a Research Associate at the Simone de Beauvoir Institute, Concordia University and the author and editor of numerous books and articles on health policy, women's and cultural issues. She is a mother of two young boys, one with autism.

Nancy Emmick Panko is a retired registered nurse. She belongs to The Light of Carolina Christian Writers group and the Cary senior writing group. She has written several children's stories and a novella, *Guided Missal*. Nancy and her husband live in North Carolina.

Lisa Pawlak is a freelance writer, mother of two boys, and lung carcinoid cancer survivor. Her diverse work can be found in the Chicken Soup for the Soul series, *Coping with Cancer* magazine, *The Christian Science Monitor*, *San Diego Family* magazine and *Carlsbad* magazine.

A journalist in rural Minnesota, **Ellarry Prentice** studied travel and tourism. In addition to her work as a reporter for her hometown newspaper, she is a freelance writer and photographer, and an advocate for mental health and alcoholism awareness. She enjoys reading, volunteering, and traveling with her husband, Greg.

Susan Randall is a hospice nurse in Montgomery County, Maryland and the proud mother of two grown children. Her heartwarming nonfiction stories have been published in a previous Chicken Soup for the Soul book and a magazine called *Spotlight On Recovery*. E-mail her at rnsue19020@aol.com.

Sadia Rodriguez is a working single mother of identical twin daughters. She coordinates and writes for the mothers of multiples blog *How Do You Do It?* at http://hdydi.com. After a childhood in the UK and Bangladesh, she has settled in Texas. She advocates for healthy and wholesome parenting, meeting each child where he is.

Sioux Roslawski is a third grade teacher by day, and a freelance writer by night. On the weekends, she rescues Golden Retrievers. She's a friend to Darice, a wife to Michael, a mother to Virginia and Ian and a grammy to Riley. You can read more from Sioux at siouxspage.blogspot.com.

Tammy Ruggles is a legally blind freelance writer, artist, and retired social worker who lives in Kentucky. She enjoys photography, film, and spending time with family and friends, especially her two grandchildren, who sometimes help her create cover art for her children's stories.

Ceil Ryan is a wife, nurse, mom and nana of three living in the Midwest. After working more than twenty years, she hung up her nurse's cap to start writing and blogging full-time. Ceil enjoys nature walks, campfires and leading small groups. Her passion is sharing personal stories with an emphasis on faith and encouragement.

Theresa Sanders is honored to be a frequent Chicken Soup for the Soul contributor. An award-winning technical writer, she lives with her husband near St. Louis, where she is completing her third novel. Theresa would love to connect with you on Facebook at www.facebook. com/pages/Theresa-Sanders-Author/208490939276032.

Gwyn Schneck is retired from thirty-three years of teaching and counseling high school students. She continues to live healthy and happy as a writer, speaker, wife, mom, and grandmother. She loves to bring life lessons and humor to audiences of parents, students, and women. She can be reached at www.mykidscounselor.com.

Kim Seeley lives with her husband Wayne in Wakefield, VA. She is retired from a career in teaching and library work. When she is not traveling, she is busy entertaining and being entertained by her three-year-old grandson, Evan, and her six-month-old granddaughter, Delaney, who bring her incredible joy.

Debbi Singer is a restaurateur, artist and five-year cancer survivor from Venice Beach, CA.

Since the mid-1980s, **Sandra Sladkey** has directed Milk 'n' Honey Ministries, presenting Bible-based programs to children through puppetry, Gospel illusion, skits, and storytelling. With her daughter leaving for college, Sandra plans to finish writing a children's book she started before the fire. Read more at http://heaven-headed.blogspot.com.

Alaina Smith's true tales appear in anthologies, including four Chicken Soup for the Soul books, six Chocolate for Women books, five Cup of Comfort books, and more. When not working part-time, she pursues her love of great stories by writing, reading, and watching movies with her husband, Frank.

Anthony Smith is a licensed mental health professional in Massachusetts. He currently performs psychological evaluations in the juvenile justice system, maintains a private psychotherapy practice, and is an adjunct psychology professor at Bay Path University. He continues to tie flies with a passion when he is not hiking and backpacking.

Gail Sobotkin is a retired nurse who likes to write inspirational stories, medical and travel articles. Her work has been published in *Delaware Beach Life*, *American Journal of Nursing*, *Delmarva Quarterly* and *Mysterious & Miraculous Books I* and *II*. Her blog can be viewed at happyboomernurse.hubpages.com.

Diane Stark is a wife, mother of five, and freelance writer. She loves to write about the important things in life: her family and her faith. E-mail Diane at DianeStark19@yahoo.com.

Leigh Steinberg is renowned as one the greatest sports agents in history and the first prominent one to impress upon his clients the need to give back to their communities. Currently CEO of Steinberg Sports and Entertainment and an advocate for player safety, Leigh continues to use sports as a platform to invoke positive changes in the world.

Anita Stone is a retired science education teacher, a reading specialist, an author, naturalist and certified Master Gardener. She teaches adult education classes at a homeless shelter, including landscaping, culinary, hospitality, home healthcare, and CPR. Anita is a member of the Triangle Area Freelancers.

Jamie Tadrzynski received her master's degree in May of 2015 as part of the Alliance for Catholic Education at Saint Joseph's University. Prior to grad school, she served as a yearlong volunteer teacher at Saint Michael Indian School on the Navajo Nation in Arizona. Read more at www.joysandsorrowsmingled.blogspot.com.

Lizbeth Tarpy is a freelance writer whose articles have appeared in *The Writer's Journal*, *Reader's Digest* and *The Armchair Detective*.

Rajkumar Thangavelu graduated from Bucknell University with a B.A. degree in Economics and Political Science in 1998. He currently works for the federal government in Washington, D.C. He loves to travel and enjoys volunteering with children. E-mail him at rajkt@hotmail.com.

S.A. Thibodeaux has a B.A. degree in English and minors in Communication and Psychology from the University of Dayton. She does volunteer work and enjoys running, spinning and is drafting her first novel. She recently moved to San Antonio, TX, where she now resides with her new husband and their four children.

Marla H. Thurman lives in Signal Mountain, TN with her dogs Sophie and Jasper. They love reading great books and they love writing even better. E-mail Marla at sizoda1@yahoo.com.

McKenzie Vaught is currently enrolled at Somerset Community College and plans to go to Eastern Kentucky University to complete her degree in psychology. Her mother gets out of prison in September of 2014.

Ann Vitale lives in the Endless Mountains of northeast Pennsylvania where she teaches writing at adult schools, lectures on canine behavior so people can have a better understanding of their human/dog interactions, and enjoys the wildlife on her acres of fields and woods, even when said wildlife munches on her flowers.

Elizabeth Waters has kept a journal for over forty years. She was initially inspired by reading *The Diary of Anne Frank* at the age of twelve. Recently she and her family moved from a big city to a rural area, where she lives with her husband and two young adult sons. She desires to encourage others with her writing.

Rissa Watkins is writer, mother, and leukemia survivor. When not busy keeping her family alive (which is a lot harder than it should be), she can be found hunched over a keyboard working furiously on her next novel. You can see what else she is up to on her website www.RissaWatkins.com.

Genevieve West is a wine-drinking, coffee-chugging writer and relationship consultant. She lives in Portland, OR with her loving husbnad and their three children.

Josie Willis is committed to healing other people through her writing. Her nonfiction and poetry have been published in many venues. Her current project is a book of grief poetry. She lives in South Florida with her four parrot muses: Taco, Paco, Nacho and Coqui. E-mail her at josiewillis2000@yahoo.com.

Sherri Woodbridge hopes to encourage others through her writing and photography with what she has learned on her life's journey. She loves spending time in her garden and with her greatest treasures—her family.

Dallas Woodburn has written fiction and nonfiction for a variety of publications including the *Nashville Review*, the *Los Angeles Times*, and *Louisiana Literature*. Her short story collection was a finalist for the Flannery O'Connor Award for Short Fiction. Connect with her at writeonbooks.org and daybydaymasterpiece.com.

Following a fifteen-year career in nuclear medicine, **Melissa Wootan** is finding her joy by exploring her creative side. She enjoys refurbishing old furniture but is most passionate about writing. Her stories have appeared in the Chicken Soup for the Soul series and *Guideposts*. You may contact her at www.facebook.com/chicvintique.

Bill Young lives in Sherwood, OR, with his dog Jake, where he continues to build his roofing business.

Mary Ellen Ziliak, RN, is coauthor of *MS: Beyond the Red Door* and serves as an MS Ambassador. She offers hope and encouragement to her audience as she shares her amazing life journey with multiple sclerosis. When not on the lecture circuit, she enjoys *Scrabble* and walking the riverfront in her hometown of Newburgh, IN. Learn more at msreddoor.tateauthor.com.

About Amy Newmark

Amy Newmark was a writer, speaker, Wall Street analyst and business executive in the worlds of finance and telecommunications for more than thirty years. Today she is publisher, editor-in-chief and coauthor of the Chicken Soup for the Soul book series. By curating and editing inspirational true stories from ordinary people who have had extraordinary experiences, Amy has kept the twenty-one-year-old Chicken Soup for the Soul brand fresh and relevant, and still part of the social zeitgeist.

Amy graduated *magna cum laude* from Harvard University where she majored in Portuguese and minored in French. She wrote her thesis about popular, spoken-word poetry in Brazil, which involved traveling throughout Brazil and meeting with poets and writers to collect their stories. She is delighted to have come full circle in her writing career — from collecting poetry "from the people" in Brazil as a twenty-year-old to, three decades later, collecting stories and poems "from the people" for Chicken Soup for the Soul.

Amy has a national syndicated newspaper column and is a frequent radio and TV guest, passing along the real-life lessons and useful tips she has picked up from reading and editing thousands of Chicken Soup for the Soul stories.

She and her husband are the proud parents of four grown children and in her limited spare time, Amy enjoys visiting them, hiking, and reading books that she did not have to edit.

About Fran Drescher & Cancer Schmancer

Fran Drescher has a reputation for passion and commitment. She received two Emmy and two Golden Globe nominations for her portrayal as the lovable "Miss Fine" on CBS's hit series *The Nanny*, which she both created and executive produced. An accomplished author, Fran received the prestigious NCCS writer's award for *Cancer Schmancer*, which along with *Enter Whining*, were both New York Times Best Sellers. Fran starred in, created and executive produced the series *Happily Divorced*, and most recently made her Broadway debut as "Madame" in Rodgers + Hammerstein's Tony-award winning *Cinderella*.

A twelve-year uterine cancer survivor, Fran turns lemons into lemonade and pain into purpose through her leadership as a cancer advocate. Her mission is to shift America's focus toward proactive health care and healthy, toxin-free living. She believes that that the best cure for cancer is not getting it in the first place.

As Founder, President & Visionary of the non-profit Cancer Schmancer Movement, she focuses on three prongs to fight the disease: Early Detection, Prevention, and Advocacy.

The organization's early detection Fran Vans provide free mammograms to women without access to health care. Its Detox Your Home prevention campaign educates people of all ages to reduce risk through

Cancer Schmancer Movement

healthy living, and Fran uses her unique voice on Capitol Hill to advocate for a range of health issues.

Fran was instrumental in passing the bi-partisan "Gynecologic Cancer Education and Awareness Act," earning two commendations in the Congressional Record. She is a U.S. State Department Public Diplomacy Envoy for Women's Health, traveling globally to meet with heads of state, cancer patients, local NGOs, and others fighting cancer. *The Washingtonian* named her one of the most effective celebrity lobbyists in D.C.

Fran won the Human Rights Campaign's Ally for Equality Award for her efforts to defend civil liberties. She received the John Wayne Institute Woman of Achievement Award, the Gilda Award, City of Hope Woman of the Year Award, The Albert Einstein Medical School Lifetime Achievement Award, and the 2014 Citizen Artist Award. The Knesset in Israel honored Fran as the first Jewish actress who played an openly Jewish character embraced by not only Israel, but by many Arab nations.

Fran is the author of a children's book, *Being Wendy*, and she was awarded the Ally for Equality Award by the Human Rights Campaign for her efforts to defend civil liberties.

Thank You

We owe huge thanks to all of our contributors. We know that you poured your hearts and souls into the thousands of stories that you shared with us. We appreciate your willingness to open up your lives to other Chicken Soup for the Soul readers and share your own experiences, no matter how personal. As I read and edited these truly awe-inspiring stories, I was excited by the potential of this book to inspire people, and impressed by your unselfish willingness to share your stories. Many of you said this was the first time you were sharing your incredible story, so we thank you for letting our readers be your confidants.

We could only publish a small percentage of the stories that were submitted, but every single one was read and even the ones that do not appear in the book had an influence on us and on the final manuscript. Our editor Susan Heim read every submission and pared the list down to several hundred semi-finalists. After I chose the 101 stories, managing editor Kristiana Pastir put together the initial manuscript and chose most of the wonderful quotations that were inserted at the beginning of each story, which we think add so much richness to the reading experience. Our assistant publisher D'ette Corona worked with all the contributors to make sure they approved our edits, and she and senior editor Barbara LoMonaco performed their normal masterful proofreading job.

We also owe a very special thanks to our creative director and book producer, Brian Taylor at Pneuma Books, for his brilliant vision for our covers and interiors.

~Amy Newmark

Sharing Happiness, Inspiration, and Wellness

Real people sharing real stories, every day, all over the world. In 2007, *USA Today* named *Chicken Soup for the Soul* one of the five most memorable books in the last quarter-century. With over 100 million books sold to date in the U.S. and Canada alone, more than 200 titles in print, and translations into more than forty languages, "chicken soup for the soul" is one of the world's best-known phrases.

Today, twenty-one years after we first began sharing happiness, inspiration and wellness through our books, we continue to delight our readers with new titles, but have also evolved beyond the bookstore, with wholesome and balanced pet food, delicious nutritious comfort food, and a major motion picture in development. Whatever you're doing, wherever you are, Chicken Soup for the Soul is "always there for you(tm)." Thanks for reading!

Share with Us

We all have had Chicken Soup for the Soul moments in our lives. If you would like to share your story or poem with millions of people around the world, go to chickensoup.com and click on "Submit Your Story." You may be able to help another reader, and become a published author at the same time. Some of our past contributors have launched writing and speaking careers from the publication of their stories in our books!

We only accept story submissions via our website. They are no longer accepted via mail or fax.

To contact us regarding other matters, please send us an e-mail through webmaster@chickensoupforthesoul.com, or fax or write us at:

Chicken Soup for the Soul
P.O. Box 700
Cos Cob, CT 06807-0700
Fax: 203-861-7194

One more note from your friends at Chicken Soup for the Soul. Occasionally, we receive an unsolicited book manuscript from one of our readers, and we would like to respectfully inform you that we do not accept unsolicited manuscripts and we must discard the ones that appear.

Changing lives one story at a time™
www.chickensoup.com